Volumes previously published by the University of California Press, Berkeley, Los Angeles, London, for the Center for Chinese Studies of The University of Michigan:

MICHIGAN STUDIES ON CHINA

Alan P. L. Liu
Communications and National Integration in Communist China

Richard Solomon
Mao's Revolution and the Chinese Political Culture

Kang Chao
Capital Formation in Mainland China, 1952–1965

Martin King Whyte
Small Groups and Political Rituals in China

Edward Friedman
Backward Toward Revolution: The Chinese Revolutionary Party

Andrew Nathan
Peking Politics, 1918–1923: Factionalism and the Failure of Constitutionalism

Joseph W. Esherick
Reform and Revolution in China: The 1911 Revolution in Human and Hubei

CHINA'S TRANSITION TO INDUSTRIALISM

Michigan Studies on China
Published for the Center for Chinese Studies
of the University of Michigan

MICHIGAN STUDIES ON CHINA

Alexander Eckstein
China's Economic Development: The Interplay of Scarcity and Ideology

Allen S. Whiting
The Chinese Calculus of Deterrence: India and Indochina

Ernest P. Young
The Presidency of Yuan Shih-k'ai: Liberalism and Dictatorship in Early Republican China

Rhoads Murphey
The Outsiders: The Western Experience in India and China

Donald J. Munro
The Concept of Man in Contemporary China

Daniel H. Bays
China Enters the Twentieth Century: Chang Chih-tung and the Issues of a New Age, 1895–1909

Evelyn Sakakida Rawski
Education and Popular Literacy in Ch'ing China

Thomas G. Rawski
China's Transition to Industrialism: Producer Goods and Economic Development in the Twentieth Century

The research on which these books are based was supported by the Center for Chinese Studies of The University of Michigan.

China's Transition to Industrialism

Producer Goods and Economic Development in the Twentieth Century

THOMAS G. RAWSKI

Ann Arbor *The University of Michigan Press*
Folkestone, England *Dawson*

Published in the United States of America by
The University of Michigan Press and simultaneously
in Rexdale, Canada, by John Wiley & Sons Canada, Limited
Manufactured in the United States of America

Published in 1980 in Great Britain by
Wm. Dawson and Sons, Ltd.
ISBN (U.K.) 0-7129-0989-3

Acknowledgment

Quotations from "The Growth of Producer Industries, 1900–1971," by Thomas G. Rawski, in *China's Modern Economy in Historical Perspective*, edited by Dwight H. Perkins. Included by permission of the publishers, Stanford University Press, © 1975 by the Board of Trustees of the Leland Stanford Junior University.

Library of Congress Cataloging in Publication Data

Rawski, Thomas G 1943–

China's transition to industrialism.

(Michigan studies on China)

Bibliography: p.

Includes index.

1. China—Industries. 2. China—Economic conditions.

I. Title. II. Series.

HC427.8.R38 330.9'51'05 79-18601

ISBN 0-472-08755-X

To Knight Biggerstaff

Preface

This book is an outgrowth of my doctoral dissertation on China's machinery industry. During the lengthy process of revision, I have relied on the acute criticisms of my advisor Dwight Perkins and of Evelyn Rawski, each of whom has patiently read and discussed numerous versions of this study. I am also indebted to Sherman Cochran, Robert Dernberger, Alexander Eckstein, Nicholas Lardy, Donald Keesing, and an anonymous critic for reviewing the entire manuscript, and to the University of Toronto, the Canada Council, the University of Toronto–York University Joint Centre on Modern East Asia, the University of Michigan's Center for Chinese Studies, and the Social Science Research Council for generous financial support. I have drawn extensively on the bibliographic knowledge of librarians at the Harvard-Yenching Institute, the Institute for Developing Economies, the Universities Service Centre, the Library of Congress, and the University of Michigan. Finally, I must express my gratitude to Pei-shin Ni and Rikuzō Kamikawa for their efforts to improve my language skills.

Contents

Tables

Introduction

In 1900, China's economy was overwhelmingly agricultural. Her few dozen mechanically powered factories and mines, some controlled and managed by foreigners, provided only a minute fraction of total product. Today, China is a rising industrial power whose economy displays many features associated with Kuznets's concept of modern economic growth. Industry is now the largest economic sector in terms of output value, although agriculture continues to dominate in employment. Domestic enterprises apply advanced technology to an ever-growing range of activities with only modest dependence on imports of commodities or services. Nuclear weaponry, petroleum exports, and an annual volume of machine tool production surpassed only by the USSR illustrate the extent of twentieth-century economic change.

This book is a study of China's transition to industrialism and, in particular, of the contribution made by domestic producer industries to the emergence of a viable and basically self-sustaining process of overall economic development. The producer industries, including the machinery, metallurgy, chemical, building materials, energy, and mining sectors, are industries whose output consists primarily of intermediate and capital goods. In part, this is a definition of convenience chosen for its correspondence to the post-1949 Chinese statistical practice of separating industry, which includes mining and utilities as well as manufacturing, into producer and consumer sectors, or into somewhat different categories of heavy and light industry.

The concept of producer industries is also analytically useful. In a large economy, which in the long run must inevitably supply the bulk of its requirements for intermediate and capital goods, it is the industrial branches included in the producer sector whose output is essential to the transformation of society's production possibilities. In this sense, development of the producer sector is central to the process of economic growth. For, as one Chinese observer notes, it is this sector that uses "modern technology to equip agriculture, industry, the military and science for achieving the modernization of all these sectors."[1]

One important task of the present study is to describe and analyze the mechanism by which application of modern techniques to individual problems encountered in various phases of production leads to a cumulative and mutually reinforcing process of technical development and economic expansion. The introduction of modern techniques into China's economy began with the efforts of nineteenth-century regional officials to bolster military strength by developing arsenals, factories, and transport facilities. Toward the end of the century, a second group of producer enterprises appeared, largely without official stimulus. These firms emerged from a cycle of backward linkage and import substitution associated with new modes of production and transport introduced from abroad.

The appearance of steamships and railways and the growth of manufacturing, mainly of textiles and foodstuffs, created demands for materials, spare parts, and repair services. Initially, imported commodities and foreign artisans were employed, but as the Chinese familiarized themselves with new products and techniques, simpler tasks were assigned to native underlings, and then to native enterprises that grew up to service the modern sector. As Chinese experience and capital grew, native mechanics increasingly replaced foreigners. This process of import substitution spread from services to commodities, with Chinese firms acquiring significant market shares, first for spares and machine parts and then by the 1930s for a variety of industrial machines and chemicals as well.

The continued significance after the Communist revolution of 1949 of development sequences beginning with imports and leading successively to ancillary or repair work, partial production, full-scale manufacture, and eventually to expansion of domestic production beyond the initial range of imports suggests a model of technical advance that can describe China's producer sector both before and after 1949.

Economists have recognized the contribution of experience to industrial productivity ever since Adam Smith's celebrated disquisition on the manufacture of pins. A simple extension of the concept of learning by doing leads to the hypothesis that repetition of an initial task not only raises productivity, but also creates transferable skills that can facilitate the performance of related but as yet untried operations. The accumulation of experience on the part of individuals and firms makes it possible to develop new activities calling for previously unattainable skill combinations. As entrepreneurs, who may be private businessmen or socialist managers, respond to the declining cost of innovation by introducing new activities into the economy, fresh experience acquired during the process of innovation will stimulate further skill development, which again creates opportunities for innovation, and so on.[2]

In this formulation, technical advance, which includes the introduction of new products, processes, and materials as well as reduction of the resources needed to produce each unit of output, arises from the interplay of economic incentive and technical potential. Technical potential is partially determined by the institutional framework, by the morale and work habits of the labor force, and by the quantity and quality of available equipment, materials, education, and managerial skills. But, as the following chapters will show, the pattern of twentieth-century technical advance in China's producer sector justifies the central position that this simple model assigns to the gradual accumulation of industrial skills in shaping the process of technical development.

Chapter 1 surveys China's producer industries during the years 1900–37. This was a period of significant but limited import substitution, as well as expansion and diversification by the private sector within China proper and, on a larger scale, by Japanese-backed enterprises in Manchuria. The limitations imposed by indivisibilities, marketing problems, and capital scarcity created a significant gap between technical potential and economic achievement during the prewar era.

Exploitation of this untapped potential provided important support for the burst of industrial growth during 1949–57, the period that forms the focus of chapter 2. These were years of rapid expansion in the sheer volume of industry's resources and output, with qualitative concerns systematically relegated to the background. This expansion created further untapped opportunities for technical advance, as did the massive infusion of equipment, training, and advice provided by the Soviet Union and its East European allies during these same years.

The mixed results achieved under the First Five-Year Plan (FFYP) during 1953–57 elicited many suggestions for reforms aimed at improving industry's qualitative performance. New policies were implemented in 1957, but the Great Leap Forward (1958–60), with its overwhelming emphasis on raising output volume, blunted their impact. Together with the sudden withdrawal of Soviet assistance and advisers in July 1960, the failures of the Great Leap plunged China into an economic crisis that compelled industry to modify its former concentration on quantitative expansion.

Chapter 3 focuses on the results achieved since 1960 under policies that have emphasized quality and complementarity rather than sheer growth of industrial output. Both the key role of Shanghai and other prewar industrial centers in meeting the unforseen demands of the 1960s and the subsequent emergence of newer industrial bases as additional sources of innovation support the hypothesis that experience is an important determinant of industrial capabilities.

The post-1960 flowering of innovative capabilities within the producer industries shows that China's economic growth has entered a new phase in which economic gaps are filled and new technologies are furnished increasingly by domestic rather than imported resources. Chapter 4 reviews the process of growth and technological change in the producer industries since 1949, focusing on an analysis of the increasingly self-sustaining nature of Chinese economic expansion.

Chapter 5 investigates the question of how China's producer sector could succeed in shifting its priorities from quantitative toward qualitative considerations while working within a Soviet-style institutional framework that is well known for its bias against quality, innovation, and complementarity—the very features that characterize recent performance in the producer industries. Administrative reforms and managerial morale emerge as key features in understanding the post-1960 reversal in industrial priorities.

The final chapter summarizes the findings of this study, presents some historical and international comparisons, and considers the extent to which China's successful pattern of industrial and technical development may be relevant to the issues now confronting other latecomers to the industrialization process.

People's Republic of China

Chapter 1

The Producer Industries to 1937

At the time of China's republican revolution of 1911, activity in the producer sector was limited to a handful of isolated units: a few mechanized mines and railway repair shops, railmaking facilities at the *Han-yeh-p'ing* ironworks, the *Ch'i-hsin* cement works in the north, and a small number of urban utilities catering largely to nonindustrial users.

As is shown in table 1.1, the ensuing decades witnessed substantial growth of producer output. As a result, the outlines of an integrated producer sector, though far from complete, can be discerned by 1937. New industries appeared and were joined to one another by expanding commodity flows linking enterprises managed by men familiar with

TABLE 1.1
Output of Selected Producer Commodities, 1912–52
(in thousand tons, except as noted)

Item	1912	1923	1933	1936	1943	1949	1952
Iron ore	221	1,243	1,903	2,922	10,170	588	4,287
Pig iron	8	171	471	670	1,794	252	1,928
Steel	3	30	30	414	923	158	1,348
Soda ash	0[a]	0[a]	35[a]	103[a]	57[b]	88	192
Cement	90	349	727	1,243	1,830	660	2,860
Electric power (million kwh)	53	291	2,074	3,075	5,220	4,310	7,260
Coal (million tons)	5	17	22	34	50	32	66

Source: Except as noted, data for 1912–43 are from John K. Chang, *Industrial Development in Pre-Communist China* (Chicago, 1969), pp. 117–23. Data for 1949 and 1952 are from Nai-ruenn Chen, *Chinese Economic Statistics* (Chicago, 1967), p. 186.

[a] Table 1.5. The figure for 1936 indicates capacity rather than output.

[b] Manchuria only. Edwin W. Pauley, *Report on Japanese Assets in Manchuria* (Washington, D.C., 1946), p. 201.

Western technology and attuned to market opportunities. Even more important were the qualitative changes of these years, which not only altered the character of prewar producer activity, but also provided a foundation that proved essential to the continuing development of China's producer sector after 1949.

The present analysis of these developments focuses on three industries: engineering, chemicals, and ferrous metallurgy. The disparate evolution of engineering and chemicals, which flourished in the market economy of republican China, and of iron and steel, which prospered in Manchuria, but only with massive subsidies, underscores the importance of a wide range of factors, including technology, finance, market size, and government policy, in any coherent explanation of either the extent or the limits of prewar industrialization.

Engineering

The model of technical advance described in the introduction is of particular relevance to the mechanical industries. The industrial history of many countries shows that the equipment and skills needed to maintain, repair, and manufacture textile machinery, for example, are readily transferable to the production and operation of a wide range of engineering goods. This is because machinery manufacture consists of a sequence of basic operations—design, heat treatment of metals, machining, assembly, and inspection—that can be applied with minimal variation to produce equipment for any sector of the economy. This unique characteristic leads to the expectation that gradual mastery of these basic activities will push individual firms, and eventually the engineering sector as a whole, toward technological thresholds beyond which existing resources of equipment and skill can turn out a vastly expanded range of machines.[1]

The most detailed picture of evolutionary development in Chinese engineering comes from a history of Shanghai's Ta-lung Machinery Works, established in 1902 by Yen Yü-t'ang, an associate of foreign merchants. Yen sensed the profitability of ship repairing and used his foreign contacts to solicit business. A partner managed the actual work, which consisted mainly of general steamship repairs. The small initial capital of seventy-five hundred liang came from three partners, and the labor force of eleven was recruited from foreign-owned factories and from the Shanghai Dockyard.[2]

Ta-lung's origins are typical of many engineering enterprises. Small machine shops were often established by men with experience in foreign firms and, later, with overseas technical training. T'eng Hu-ch'en, a former apprentice trained to repair German warships at Tsingtao, founded the Hua-feng Machine Works in 1920. Yi Chih-chung, a pioneer in needle- and nail-making, was among many machinery entrepreneurs who had studied abroad.[3]

Formation of new enterprises without recourse to financial intermediaries is another feature common to many firms. The absence of indivisibilities and scale economies in the repair work initially undertaken by engineering firms enabled small groups of friends, relatives, business associates, or classmates to enter the trade with only their personal savings. Company histories show that few private machine shops obtained bank loans in their early years.[4] Although larger firms, including Ta-lung, had developed banking ties by the 1930s, a 1938 survey of Chinese-owned machinery plants in Tientsin reported modern or native bank financing in only two of thirty cases.[5]

Men with factory experience formed a growing pool of skilled labor that new enterprises could tap. As early as 1912, the thirty-five railway factories and arsenals administered by China's communications, army, and navy ministries employed over twenty thousand persons, many in positions requiring some technical skill. At the same time, the Japanese-owned South Manchurian Railway employed eighty-nine hundred non-Japanese.[6] Later, the private sector became a fertile training ground; Ta-lung trained an estimated ten thousand apprentices before 1949, many of whom became workers, managers, and owners of machine shops throughout China. Former textile and steel workers also established their own machinery plants.[7]

Ta-lung's growth, which is summarized in table 1.2, illustrates both the Schumpeterian entrepreneurship of its management and the transferability of technical knowledge and skills among various branches of engineering—features shared with other enterprises whose history is less richly documented. Yen Yü-t'ang bought out his partners around 1906 when Ta-lung's work force had risen to fifty. Faced with growing competition from other shipyards, which threatened Ta-lung's profits, Yen shifted his attention to Shanghai's burgeoning textile industry.[8]

Yen's foreign contacts again proved useful, but it was the skill and experience of his workers, readily shifted from marine to factory repairs,

TABLE 1.2
Ta-lung Machinery Works, 1902–71

Year	Gross Output (in million yuan)	Labor Force	Machine Tools	Major Products or Tasks
1902	—	11	10	Ship repair
1905–6	—	50	—	Ship repair; textile machine repair
1913	—	100+	40	Textile machine repair and parts
1920	—	300+	100+	Textile machine repair and parts
1926	—	700+	200+	Spindles; engines; furnaces; machine tools
1933	3[a]	1,300	500+	Spinning equipment
1938	—	30	—	Rebuilding
1940	—	1,193	—	Spindles; munitions
1949–53	6[b]	—	—	Textile machinery; machine tools; engines; mining equipment
1955	10	—	—	Petroleum equipment parts
1956	26	2,950	—	Petroleum equipment parts
1958	53–73	3,420	—	Petroleum equipment parts; metallurgical equipment; lathes; chemical fertilizer equipment
1971[c]	23 × level of 1949	4,300	—	Petroleum equipment; compressors for fertilizer plants and for industrial diamond manufacture

Source: For 1902–58, *Ta-lung*, pp. 3–4, 8–9, 17, 23, 46, 64, 119, 121.

[a] Peak prewar output equivalent in terms of post-1949 currency.

[b] Average annual output.

[c] Information for 1971 from U.S. Consulate General, Hong Kong, *Survey of China Mainland Press* (hereafter SCMP) 5289(1973):124; U.S. Joint Publications Research Service (hereafter JPRS) 29685(1965):12–31; Hsiang Wen, "Changes at Ta-lung Show the Value of Old Plants," *Chi-hsieh kung-yeh* (hereafter CHKY) 20(1964):19; and British Broadcasting Corporation, *Summary of World Broadcasts: Pt. 3, The Far East, Weekly Economic Report* (hereafter BBC) W759(1974):A5.

that brought continued success. Mill owners were prepared to offer high prices, but only for swift and competent service that minimized idle time. When an English firm failed to duplicate a broken steam pipe, Ta-lung completed the job, thereby winning the custom of Naigaiwata, a Japanese firm with over a quarter million spindles in the Shanghai area, and of other Japanese mills as well.[9]

Ta-lung's repair work, which included replacement of broken parts, engine maintenance, installation of bearings to increase machine speed, and adjustment of defective imported equipment, gradually created the skills needed for manufacturing. After 1911, the business expanded to include regular production of spare parts for textile machinery. No special materials or techniques were needed; aside from the spindle itself, cotton textile machinery of the day demanded neither close tolerances, high speeds, nor extreme pressures.[10] Once again, the absence of rigid technical requirements and easy transfer of skills facilitated the firm's growth. Similar transitions occurred elsewhere; Yang Ta-chin notes sixteen producers of equipment for textile workshops and factories were established before 1914, most of them in Shanghai.[11]

The isolation of China's textile industry from foreign suppliers and competitors during World War I provided an opportunity to which neither Ta-lung nor its rivals could respond. Despite a combination of soaring textile profits with restricted supplies, and rising prices of foreign equipment, no domestic producer could meet the demand for textile machinery. China's spindle stock stagnated until the postwar resumption of normal foreign trade flows, which brought an immediate spurt of spindle imports to satisfy the pent-up demand for equipment.[12] At this time, manufacture of textile machinery was simply beyond the skill frontiers of domestic engineering concerns.

This began to change during the 1920s, when growing technical and financial strength enabled Ta-lung and other firms to begin producing textile equipment. At Ta-lung, trial manufacture of components, including looms, picking machines, and bundling and hydraulic presses, was followed by a series of organizational and technical improvements incorporated into a new plant opened in 1926. A new management team led by Yen Ch'ung-ling, a son of Yen Yü-t'ang who had received technical training in Germany, split the workers into specialized groups, formed a design department, and hired a Japanese engineer to improve the plant's casting methods. As a result, modified versions of British spinning machinery were successfully produced for the first time.[13]

The problem of marketing now came to the fore. To avoid a head-on clash with formidable British interests, Yen Yü-t'ang created his own sheltered market by purchasing a bankrupt textile plant in 1927 and stocking it with Ta-lung machines.[14] Yen eventually controlled seven mills, all equipped with Ta-lung machinery and managed by his sons, former Ta-lung apprentices or close friends of the Yen family. The profitability of this combine provided excellent advertising for Ta-lung's products within Shanghai industrial circles.

The outbreak of war with Japan cut short Yen's campaign to penetrate the domestic market for textile equipment. Ta-lung's

Communist historians argue that imperialist restrictions on China's trade policies and the irrational preference of both foreign and Chinese managers for imported machinery condemned Ta-lung to a secondary role as supplier to captive firms controlled by the Yen family. This pessimism was certainly not shared by Yen Ch'ung-ling, who anticipated that the low cost and improved quality of his products would open markets in Southeast Asia as well as in China, and accordingly ordered price lists printed in English as well as in Chinese.[15]

The condition of Ta-lung's operations appears to vindicate Yen's optimism. In 1937, Ta-lung was no longer a handicraft enterprise. Its plant was equipped with over five hundred machine tools and staffed by an experienced work force of thirteen hundred men. Trained engineers directed the production process and introduced a stream of innovations in metallurgy, design, and measurement that lowered costs and raised quality. Business decisions rested in the hands of men with a knack for decisive entry into profitable fields and quick recognition of mistakes. With its strong financial base and technically skilled management, Ta-lung could begin to challenge some of its foreign competitors in the textile machinery industry.

Ta-lung's wide range of products, which included machine tools, stoves, engines, and agricultural equipment as well as textile machinery, its subsequent recovery from wartime damage, and its production of large quantities of cotton spindles as well as munitions during the Pacific war all indicate that by 1937 the Ta-lung Machine Works had crossed the technological threshold dividing handicraft and repair activities from modern engineering operations.[16]

Ta-lung's emergence as a manufacturer of machinery was not an isolated event. A nationwide survey from 1932–33 showed that engineering firms accounted for about 4 percent of factory sales and 6 percent of factory employment in China proper, with foreign-owned enterprises accounting for less than one-quarter of the total.[17] Most of this output was the result of a rapid growth spurt which continued until 1937. K. C. Yeh finds that employment in China proper in the manufacture of machinery and parts rose by 141 percent between 1931 and 1936.[18]

A succession of factory surveys offers a more detailed picture for Shanghai, China's foremost industrial metropolis. In 1928, investigators reported 64 machine shops with captial in excess of 5,000 yuan and 11 electrical machine shops with assets of over 3,000 yuan. These plants employed an average of 58 workers and showed assets of 494 yuan per worker. The number of metal-processing and machinery enterprises using mechanical power and employing over 30 persons rose from 82 to 173 between 1931 and 1933 alone, while output, capital, and employment for all firms in these sectors rose by approximately 300 percent, 100 percent, and 60 percent respectively during the same short period. By 1933 there were 306 Shanghai machinery plants registered under China's factory law; they employed an average of 65 workers and showed assets of 833 yuan per employee.[19]

Less detailed descriptions indicate considerable expansion of machine shops in Wusih, Hangchow, Chinan, Chungking, and other secondary industrial centers. Engineering developments in Chekiang, for example, followed a familiar pattern: after modern factories were established with machinery procured from Shanghai, local people started repair shops that gradually turned to machine manufacture. By 1933, the larger local plants had already begun shipping their products to Shanghai, Hong Kong, and Szechwan.[20]

Expansion in both the volume and variety of output enabled Chinese machinery to begin displacing imports in a growing range of product lines.[21] In textiles, the largest sector of industry, Chinese equipment was noted in nearly all branches of the cotton, wool, and silk trades. One incomplete survey lists ninety-nine manufacturers of spinning machinery, looms, stocking frames, bowing machines, equipment for reeling and weaving silk, cotton gins, and dyeing equipment.[22]

Domestic machines were increasingly prominent in other expanding consumer industries. A 1935 survey of the match industry, in which Chinese producers had captured the domestic market during World War I and fought off later dumping attacks by Japanese and Swedish rivals, reported that "plants established during the past seven or eight years use only Chinese machines."[23] Nearly one-third of the cigarette-making machines in sixty Kiangsu factories were Chinese.[24] Domestic firms supplied a variety of equipment to rice, oil, and flour mills, to canneries and printers, and to producers of ink, leather, glass, candles, and soap.[25]

Engineering firms also contributed to the growth of fixed capital within the producer sector. Larger plants regularly augmented their equipment with machines built in their own shops.[26] Tientsin firms pioneered in commercial manufacture of machine tools, turning out a variety of lathes, milling machines, shapers, and grinders. Te-li-hsing was the largest producer, employing six hundred workers in two shifts and selling up to twenty machine tools each month to small shops in North China and Manchuria. San-i-ch'eng and I-chü-cheng were smaller ironworks that also produced lathes for sale locally and in Manchuria.[27] Chemical plants, cement works, smelters, mines, and railways also purchased a variety of equipment from local producers.[28]

Chinese products rarely matched the capacity, precision, and durability of foreign equipment. When they did, they quickly swept imports from the market, as in 1933–35 when Ta-lung sold ten thousand stoves in North China at less than one-third of the price formerly charged for similar German products.[29]

In general, domestic equipment sold well because its low price outweighed its poor quality. Tientsin machine tools cost only 25 to 40 percent as much as competing Japanese models. Imitations of foreign looms, hosiery machines, welting machines, electric and gasoline motors, and cigarette machines all sold for a fraction of the price commanded by the imported originals.[30] But with high borrowing costs and political instability, chronically underfinanced Chinese businesses often preferred low-cost domestic machines despite their overall inferiority.[31]

The rapid progress of import substitution in China's machinery markets during the 1930s was the outcome of a gradual process of skill development that originated with the introduction of foreign technical knowledge and capital equipment in the latter half of the nineteenth century. The expansion of machine-making capacity owed much to the nature of engineering technology. Table 1.3 shows that Shanghai's engineering firms managed to limit their capital needs to levels that were low even by the standards of other Shanghai industries. This reflects the technical feasibility of pushing forward from repair work into manufacturing without encountering sharply increased capital requirements. The transferability of skills among different branches of engineering was equally valuable to fledgling producers, whose ability to diversify their output even at early stages of development helped them survive under volatile market conditions.

Vigorous entrepreneurship was another essential feature of

TABLE 1.3
Shanghai Factory Data for 1933

Sector	Number of Firms	Average Capital (in yuan)	Average Employment	Average Output Value (in yuan)	Capital per Worker (in yuan)	Output per Worker (in yuan)
Engineering[a]	972	15,946	22	53,516	727	2,441
Acid and soda	4	275,000	50	403,438	5,528	8,109
Cement	1	1,638,600	220	2,283,758	7,448	10,381
Cotton yarn and cloth	248	232,787	296	654,340	787	2,213
Silk and silk cloth	368	27,210	125	131,242	218	1,052
Flour milling	15	405,991	168	4,944,809	2,420	29,480
Rice milling	49	19,444	12	210,566	1,557	16,859
Sugar milling	8	47,000	26	808,821	1,825	31,410
All firms	3,485	54,769	71	208,817	776	2,959

Source: Liu Ta-chün, *Chung-kuo kung-yeh*, 3:6–11. These data include all establishments using mechanical power.

Note: Figures may not check due to rounding.

[a] Includes forging, smelting, manufacture and repair of machinery, metal products, and transport equipment, electrical machinery and parts, shipbuilding, and railway shops.

engineering advances. Although producers of sophisticated machines were few in number, the republican decades showed that many entrepreneurs willingly followed the example of Ta-lung and other leaders in braving the hazards of domestic uncertainty and unrestricted foreign competition. Just as Yen Yü-t'ang's firm had initially occupied a nexus between foreign enterprise and the domestic economy and had gained technical and financial strength by associating with foreign firms, later entrepreneurs often benefited from links with Chinese industrial leaders, beginning their careers as employees, subcontractors, or customers of older firms.

By the end of the Nanking decade, China's few dozen major engineering concerns were backed by hundreds of obscure craft and repair shops whose function as customers and suppliers, as training grounds for mechanics and future entrepreneurs, and as a reservoir of potential expansion should not escape our attention. At the same time the expansion of ironworks and machine shops in areas far removed from the coastal centers of industry meant the start of new and independent development sequences that would parallel the earlier response of Shanghai and other treaty ports to the introduction of Western machinery and transport equipment.[32]

Despite its modest size and limited range of products, China's prewar engineering sector had already embarked upon a process of skill formation and technical development whose momentum, as will become clear in subsequent chapters, has continued to the present. For the moment, the long-run significance of this initial stage of output growth and import substitution may be anticipated by referring to similar stages in the industrialization of other nations.

Historians have traced the origins of modern machinery manufacture in both the United States and Japan to initially inept efforts to copy and compete with foreign equipment. As in China, American and Japanese machinery output was long dominated by inferior goods whose main selling point was their low price, a feature that appealed to customers who were often perilously near insolvency. Despite these weaknesses, we find that in both America and Japan the repair and manufacture of textile machinery formed an early and vital link in the emergence of engineering skills that were later transferred to the manufacture of many other types of machines. Skills developed to meet the needs of the textile industry were gradually applied to the manufacture of transport equipment, armaments, engines, electrical machinery, and, above all, machine tools, through which the influence of engineering skills eventually penetrated into all sectors of the national economy.[33] The recent history of China's engineering industry supports the present contention that the modest prewar achievements of Ta-lung and other machinery producers represent an early stage of a parallel development process in China.

Basic Chemicals

In contrast to engineering, in which it was the gradual accumulation of technical skills that determined the timing and pace of import substitution, the growth of chemical output in republican China closely followed the expansion of domestic demand. The requisite technical skills were supplied with little difficulty by China's small cadre of foreign-trained chemists and chemical engineers.

Prior to World War I, commercial output of chemicals was limited to a single British firm, Major Brothers, which manufactured and sold small quantities of acids before failing in 1922. Although government arsenals also produced acids for their own use, annual output from both sources amounted to only a few hundred tons.[34]

Following World War I, an output spurt in consumer manufacturing steadily raised China's chemical requirements. Factory cloth production, which jumped from 158 to 831 million square yards between 1919 and 1931 and rose by an additional 54 percent during 1931–36, absorbed chemicals for dyeing and bleaching.[35] Plummeting match imports signaled an expansion of domestic output and with it, growing derived demands for acid and soda products. Increasing quantities of basic chemicals were also needed to support the expanding manufacture of leather, paper, metal products, cosmetics, glass, and munitions.[36]

Growing imports of chemicals that could be profitably manufactured in small plants attracted the attention of technically educated Chinese with important political and financial connections. The success of pioneer ventures in the late 1920s sparked a vigorous surge of import substitution via backward linkage, making chemicals perhaps the most dynamic sector of Chinese industry in the years preceding 1937.

China's first important chemical works, the Yung-li Chemical Company (also known as the Pacific Alkali Works), was founded during World War I by Fan Hsü-tung, a Kyoto University graduate who had built a lucrative salt business in Tientsin. A new plant was completed at Tangku in 1922, but a year of trials exhausted the firm's initial capital without eliminating technical obstacles to soda manufacture. Undeterred, Fan formed a chemical research institute and, with additional funds from his partners and his salt enterprise, persevered until pure soda was obtained. Commercial production began in 1924, and brisk sales in both China and Japan pushed output up to forty-five thousand tons in 1935.[37]

Fan's success inspired a wave of imitation, the results of which can be seen in table 1.4. New firms, which by 1936 had spread into nine provinces, quickly established themselves as China's major source of soda products. Incomplete data in table 1.5 show that imports peaked in 1930 and that domestic production overtook imports no later than 1932.

Growing industrial demand for acids led to a similar pattern of rising imports followed by expansion of domestic output. Imports of

TABLE 1.4
Chinese Soda Plants, ca. 1936

Plant Name	Location	Founded in	Output or Capacity (in tons)	Labor Force	Capital (in thousand yuan)
Yung-li Chemicals	Tangku	1916	45,000	1,050	5,500
Po-hai Chemicals	Tangku	1926	6,800	—	600
Hsing-hua Salt Works	Hanku (Hopei)	1929	1,276	49	100
Lao-t'ien-li	Tientsin	1925	256–329	44	15
Ho-chi Chemicals	Kaoyang (Hopei)	1932	2,917	82	200
N. W. Industries Electrochemical	T'aiyuan	1935	(600)	—	400
T'ung-sheng Chemicals	T'aiyuan	1934	363	20	23
Tao-yi Salt Works	Chinan	1934	—	20	10
K'ai-yuan Soda	Shanghai	1930	30,000	20	40
Heng-li Candle, Soap and Soda	Shanghai	—		22	10
Tai-kang Soda	Shanghai	—		3	5
Li-ta	Shanghai	—		56	10
Yung-ta Soda	Shanghai	—	6,000	2	5
Shun-ta Soda	Shanghai	—		3	3
Yung-tai Soda	Shanghai	—		3	3
Lung-mao Soda	Shanghai	—		3	3
Yung-mao-hsing	Shanghai	—		3	3
T'ung-mao Soap	Nanking	—	—	16	5
Shen-yü Salt	Hangchow	1934	604	—	3
Kwangtung Provincial Plant	Kwangtung	1935	(2,116)	200	1,000
T'ien-yuan Electrochemical	Shanghai	1928	1,511	120	600
Ta-ch'ing Soda	Tientsin	1936	1,209	—	25
Wei-hsin Chemical	Tsingtao	1936	2,418	—	500
Chao-hsin Chemical	Shanghai	1931	1,511	—	200
T'ung-yi Soda	P'engshan (Szechwan)	—	423	—	—
Chia-yü Soda	Tungshan (Szechwan)	—	363	—	—

Sources: SSCK, pp. 4, 11, 14, 30–39, 50–58, 66–68, 82–83, 151; Ch'en Chen, *Chung-kuo kung-yeh*, collection IV, 1:504; Liu, *Chung-kuo kung-yeh*, 2:631; Ministry of Industry, *China Industrial Handbooks: Kiangsu*, p. 657.

Note: Figures in parentheses denote unfinished or idle capacity..

three major acids rose swiftly to a peak of 11,106 tons in 1928 and then declined steadily to only 3,361 tons in 1936 as Chinese production advanced in the wake of a flurry of entrepreneurial activity. Table 1.6 lists known commercial acid manufacturers and shows that by 1936 domestic capacity had overtaken annual imports of sulphuric, hydrochloric, and nitric acids. In the case of sulphuric acid, incomplete data show that domestic output surpassed imports as early as 1932.[38]

TABLE 1.5
Output, Import, and Export of Soda Products, 1904–36
(in tons)

Year	Output of Major Producers					Imports[d]	Exports
	Yung-li[b]	Hsing-hua[b]	K'ai-yuan	Po-hai[b]	Total		
1904–13[a]	--	--	--	--	0	17,057	0
1914–23[a]	--	--	--	--	0	36,618	0
1924	3,300	--	--	--	3,300	63,467	0
1925	1,800	--	--	--	1,800	72,434	0
1926	4,500	--	--	—	4,500	76,152	71[e]
1927	14,000	--	--	—	14,000	79,585	5,716[e]
1928	15,000	--	--	—	15,000	84,507	—
1929	18,000	—	--	—	18,000	86,117	—
1930	18,000	—	25,714[b]	—	43,714	92,979	—
1931	23,000	1,208	30,784[b]	—	54,992	73,847	7,568[c]
1932	32,000	1,208	30,000[f]	—	63,208	50,654	3,640[c]
1933	34,000	1,141	—	—	35,141	52,857	7,054[c]
1934	37,000	1,208	—	6,801	45,009	60,659	4,765[c]
1935	45,000	1,175	—	—	46,175	59,974	2,013[c]
1936	(45,000)	1,276	(30,000)	(6,801)	(103,367)[g]	63,675	—

Note: Figures in parentheses denote capacity rather than output; -- indicates date prior to firm's inception.

[a] Annual averages.

[b] SSCK, pp. 15–16, 39, 51, 66.

[c] Ibid., p. 100, including exports to Manchuria.

[d] China, Maritime Customs, *The Trade of China*, various issues.

[e] China, Maritime Customs, *Annual Trade Report and Returns: Tientsin*, 1926 edition, p. 96; 1927 edition, p. 97.

[f] Liu, *Chung-kuo kung-yeh*, 2:631.

[g] Includes all firms shown in table 1.4 for which output or capacity data were found.

A comparison of chemicals and engineering reveals both similarities and differences in the early history of these two industries. In both cases the lure of importers' profits was an important stimulus to entrepreneurship. A compendium of business histories issued in 1935 contains descriptions of several engineering and chemical works that mention the prior existence and profitability of imports, often in the first sentence of brief capsule accounts.[39]

Extensive links between new and old firms were also common in both sectors. Fan's use of earnings from salt refining to establish a salt-consuming soda plant parallels the efforts of Shanghai textile machinery manufacturers to establish sheltered markets by purchasing textile mills. Exploitation of backward linkage was more prevalent, with new

TABLE 1.6
Commercial Acid Manufacturers, ca. 1936

Plant	Location	Founded in	Output, Capacity, or Imports (in tons)			Labor Force	Capital (in thousand yuan)
			Sulphuric	Hydrochloric	Nitric		
Li-chung Acids	Tientsin	1933	907	--	--	49	200
Te-li-san Acid	T'angshan	1931	(484)	--	--	20	50
K'ai-ch'eng Acid	Shanghai	1931	4,474	--	--	96[a]	750
Major Brothers	Shanghai	1901[b]	2,721	151	181	23[a]	—
Northwest Industrial Corp.	T'aiyuan	1934	73	--	68	409	55
Liang-kuang Acid	Yochou	1927	(2,612)	--	--	150	560
Chi-ch'eng-san Acid	Sian	1934	121	--	36	41	50
Yung-li Chemical Industries	Nanking	1936	—	--	—	—	5,500
T'ien-yuan Electrochemical	Shanghai	1928	--	1,500	--	120	600
Po-hai Chemicals	Tangku	1926	--	1,209	--	—	600
Kwangtung Provincial Plant	Kwangtung	1935	--	(1,814)	--	200	1,000
T'ien-li Nitrogen Works	Shanghai	1934	--	--	1,947	—	1,000
Capacity							
Active plants			8,296	2,860	2,232		
All plants			11,392	4,674	2,232		
1936 Imports			350	1,475	206		

Sources: Except as noted, SSCK, pp. 123, 125, 131–32, 137, 144–56. Import data are from China, Maritime Customs, *The Trade of China, 1936*, 2:373–74.

Note: Figures in parentheses denote unfinished or idle capacity.

[a] Ministry of Industry, *China Industrial Handbooks: Kiangsu*, p. 657.

[b] This plant closed in 1922 and was later reorganized.

suppliers being formed by associates of established plants or by the older firms themselves, as when Wu Yün-ch'u, a successful Shanghai manufacturer of "gourmet powder," formed the T'ien-yuan Electrochemical Works to free himself from dependence on unsatisfactory Japanese hydrochloric acid.[40]

Although new chemical plants required more funds than small machine shops, scale economies in chemicals appear to have been less important than they were in some consumer industries, notably textiles and flour milling.[41] Fan Hsü-tung's insistence on building a large plant led to initial difficulties at Yung-li that were not repeated elsewhere; new soda and acid plants were small in scale and often began commercial operation within their first year of existence. Small scale also enabled some new producers to rely in part on locally fabricated machinery. One successful firm was founded by a former distillery engineer who built his own equipment and installed it in an abandoned silk factory.[42]

Technical training, finance, and government assistance were areas in which chemical enterprises differed from their engineering counterparts. Formal technical training was more prominent in chemicals than in machinery. The roster of early chemical entrepreneurs bristles with alumni of world-renowned institutions: Yung-li's founders included graduates of Tokyo and Kyoto universities, and the Po-hai group boasted chemistry graduates from Tokyo and Berlin; Hsüeh Chi-ming, founder of the Kiangnan Acetic Acid Works, held a doctorate.[43]

In contrast to the self-financed machinery sector, larger chemical firms typically obtained external support from the start. Fan Hsü-tung's associates included two bankers, and Yung-li received loans from the Kincheng and Shanghai banks as early as 1917. The T'ien-yuan Electrochemical Works, formed with a "colossal" capital by Wu Yün-ch'u, a "power in the Shanghai business world," probably enjoyed similar good fortune, as did the China Machine Cosmetics Co., a manufacturer of carbon black that dealt with three banks.[44]

Chemical production attracted the interest of men with strong ties to regional and national governments. Politicians including former provincial governors were especially close to the Li-chung Acid Works, established in 1933 by men whom Japanese observers described as "high-level officials" and "warlord adherents." The obvious military importance of chemical manufacture led to direct government sponsorship of new enterprises in Kwangtung, Kwangsi, and Shansi provinces.[45]

Strong political and financial backing helped domestic producers obtain government aid in carving out markets for their products. In 1933 alone, tariffs on nitric and hydrochloric acids and sulphide black rose by 54, 50, and 328 percent. Yung-li's exports of soda ash paid no duties, and hydrochloric acid producers received partial rebates on salt taxes. Japanese dumping of hydrochloric acid was met with railway freight rebates for domestic products as well as tariff hikes.[46]

Even with official support, China's new chemical firms faced stiff competition from imports. As late as 1936, the cost disadvantage of high duties and discriminatory freight charges did not prevent Japanese soda products from underselling Yung-li's Red Triangle brand in T'aiyuan, Shanghai, Harbin, Kwangtung, and even in Yung-li's home market of Tientsin.[47] Continuing competition enabled customers to insist on stable quality as well as low price, and failure to maintain standards drove several Chinese firms from the marketplace.[48]

Continued imports and instances of weakness among Chinese firms cannot obscure the major shift toward domestic suppliers during the final prewar decade. Rising output and sales led to a multiplication of commercial links between the chemical sector and other industries, and within the chemical industry itself. Product flow tables reveal a wide geographic and sectoral dispersion of sales. The K'ai-ch'eng Acid Works, for example, sold its products to manufacturers of munitions, dyes, machinery, celluloid, beverages, and rock salt, and Yung-li's products sold widely throughout the chemical sector.[49]

By 1937, these firms had laid the foundations for building an integrated chemical industry. Although the level of production was low and links with nonindustrial sectors of the economy, notably agriculture, scarcely existed,[50] the expansion of China's basic chemical sector during the last prewar decade created a base from which development could continue after 1949.

Ferrous Metallurgy

If China's engineering and chemical sectors had built a foundation for future expansion and technical transformation prior to 1937, no such favorable conclusion can be suggested for ferrous metallurgy. With the exception of Japanese installations at Anshan and Pench'i, the history of China's iron and steel industry between 1900 and 1945 is one of stagnant output, foreign takeover, and idle capacity.

Why this dismal contrast with progress elsewhere? Available data indicate no failure of demand; China's apparent consumption of iron and steel products nearly doubled between 1910–14 and 1930–34, but production of iron and steel outside Manchuria showed no increase whatsoever.[51] Although the promoters of China's iron and steel industry committed egregious blunders, the Japanese hardly did better at Anshan, learning that local ores required as yet undiscovered enrichment processes only after the blast furnaces were installed.[52]

Instances in which Chinese firms survived only at the cost of growing indebtedness to foreigners cannot be blamed solely on the unequal treaty system, which only created the possibility of foreign takeover. Scarcity of capital from domestic sources opened the door to foreign control of China's nascent metallurgy sector and acted as the chief constraint to the growth of iron and steel before 1937.

Ferrous metallurgy requires large capital facilities and a high rate of output from the start. Gradual buildup of capacity through accumulation of experience and profits cannot transform small workshops into modern enterprises. Prior to World War II, there was no alternative to dependence on imported technology and equipment to build China's iron and steel industry. Investment in ferrous metallurgy thus called for large initial outlays on mines, ore and fuel preparation plants, and ancillary services, along with construction of the main smelting apparatus.

Once the physical plant is installed, start-up costs are likely to be high. Product quality may be decisively altered by small impurities: rails produced by the Han-yeh-p'ing ironworks developed cracks because they contained excessive phosphorus.[53] Cost and quality also depend on appropriate selection and blending of raw materials. The selection process "cannot be carried out . . . on the basis of a priori chemical analysis," but "requires patient and careful full-scale experimentation which means years of painstaking effort to determine the best combinations."[54]

Since initial production costs are typically high and quality low, new plants will find survival difficult without large capital reserves, subsidies, or some form of protection. In China, these difficulties were compounded by the scarcity of raw materials rich enough to bypass expensive preliminary treatment and by the long depression of iron prices following World War I, an unfortunate coincidence that hastened the downfall of several ironworks.[55]

The history of the Japanese-owned ironworks at Anshan illustrates the size of capital and start-up costs in iron and steel. Construction began in 1917 and included two blast furnaces intended to produce 150,000 tons of pig iron annually, coal-washing and coking plants, and a power plant and waterworks. Production began in 1919, when year-end capital, presumably reflecting the cost of construction and equipment, was 38 million yen. Output rose only slowly, and by the time the first 150,000 tons had been produced, total outlay had surpassed 100 million yen. Because of low iron prices and unexpected beneficiation problems, no profits were recorded until 1928. Between 1919 and 1933, annual returns were negative in twelve of fifteen years, with cumulative net losses of 28.5 million yen, or three-fourths of the initial investment.[56] Anshan continued to operate only because of ongoing subsidy from the parent South Manchurian Railway Company.

Chinese businesses could not amass the resources needed to build such large plants and carry them through initial technical and marketing difficulties. Profit flows from existing enterprises were inadequate: annual losses of 2 to 3 million yen were not uncommon in Anshan's history, but Chinese enterprises rarely generated profits of this magnitude, not to mention initial investments needed in metallurgy. After writing off 15 million yen on account of continued losses, Anshan's capital was still valued at 29 million yen in 1932, a figure matched by only a few Chinese firms.[57]

Organized financial markets offered only limited aid to prewar producer industries. Despite rapid growth of modern banking after World War I, financial intermediaries did not exert a major influence on the growth of modern industry until the 1930s.[58] Even then, exceptional yields on government securities drew funds away from industrial finance.[59] The loans that were advanced to industry went almost exclusively to textile and flour mills.[60] Finally, plans for state participation in iron and steel were nullified by World War II.

Under these conditions Chinese iron and steel producers found survival difficult. Some, including the Hanyang and Tayeh ironworks, borrowed heavily from foreigners and subsequently failed to meet their debt obligations. Others, such as the Ho-hsing plant in Shanghai, were driven out of business by foreign competitors. The blast furnace at Shih-ching-shan, hailed by contemporaries as the finest in East Asia, consumed its promoters' entire capital in construction and produced nothing until captured by the invading Japanese. By 1929, Anshan and Pench'i were the only modern ironworks still in operation.[61]

Manchuria's Producer Industries to 1937

Japan exerted semicolonial control over key sectors of Manchuria's economy following the creation of the South Manchurian Railway in 1906. Until the 1930s, however, Japan valued Manchuria as a market for her own producer industries, and her sponsorship of producer industry was limited to a few large enterprises. These units, which were technologically superior to any Chinese factories, formed an integrated and self-contained network whose ultimate task was to deliver raw and semi-finished materials to Japan.

Under Japan's policy of neglecting or even discouraging links between major enterprises and small local factories, the ironworks at Anshan and Pench'i, the Fushun colliery, and other modern industrial complexes affected the local economy primarily through their impact on the skills and purchasing power of the native labor force. And even here, a conscious effort to assign Japanese workers to positions requiring technical skill or managerial responsibility limited the spread effects of Manchurian industrialization.

The policy of support for a few large enterprises, coupled with indifference or even opposition to industrial growth in the private sector, created a pattern of producer development opposite to China's: while the giants prospered, evolutionary growth of smaller units was stifled.[62] As private manufacture of machinery and chemicals blossomed during the late 1920s in nearby Tientsin and other Chinese cities, Manchuria's producer sector suffered a sharp depression. The value of cast iron output, which had surpassed 230,000 yen in both 1925 and 1926, averaged less than 100,000 yen in the subsequent three years. Production of cement, lime, bricks, and dyes also declined after 1926.[63]

Following the creation of Manchukuo in 1932, Japanese thinking began to favor more extensive development of local industry. Even so, the producer sector retained its top-heavy structure throughout World War II, and evolutionary growth in Manchuria's private sector never attained the dimensions of Chinese performance in engineering and chemicals. A similar pattern of impressive but isolated progress among a few large firms is evident in engineering, chemicals, and metallurgy.

Manchurian engineering stagnated during the 1920s; in Japanese-administered areas, employment in machine manufacture did not grow between 1922 and 1928. In 1931, manufacture and repair of machinery, tools, and transport equipment amounted to 42.7 million yen, of which 90 percent came from eight large factories: two arsenals, one shipyard, four railway works, and three machine shops attached to other large enterprises at Anshan and Fushun.[64] The remainder, including Japanese as well as indigenous firms, produced only a fraction of Shanghai's private engineering output.

The investment spurt that followed the creation of Manchukuo raised machinery imports without stimulating local production.[65] Despite the ability of a few large plants to produce locomotives and sophisticated mining and metallurgical equipment, there was no sign of the widespread import substitution that took place in China. The appearance of Chinese machinery in Manchurian markets underlines the dynamism of engineering in China as opposed to Manchuria.[66]

Anshan's ironworks and the Fushun colliery accounted for 94 percent of Manchuria's 1931 production of industrial chemicals. By-products at the ironworks included seven thousand tons of sulphuric acid annually, nearly as much as China's total productive capacity. The South Manchurian Railway's laboratories discovered methods of extracting sulphuric acid, crude oil, paraffin, ammonia, and other by-products from the oil shale covering Fushun's huge coal deposits. But despite a wealth of raw materials and a ready market in Japan, industrial soda production, which flourished in neighboring Hopei province, did not begin before 1936.[67]

Metallurgy in Manchuria was confined to three modern plants at Anshan, Pench'i, and Dairen; other metal refining and metal product manufacture was "quite insignificant." Anshan, the dominant enterprise, was China's most impressive industrial facility, having developed techniques "twenty to thirty years ahead of its time."[68] With most of its output shipped to Japan, however, Anshan, like other modern producers, had little direct interaction with sectors of Manchuria's economy outside the small circle of Japanese-sponsored producer factories.[69]

Conclusion

The development of a dynamic process of output expansion and import substitution in certain producer industries has been the major theme of this chapter. The gradual filling of previously empty input-output interstices provided China in 1937 with the outline of a modern producer sector. Domestic machinery plants offered a growing range of equipment to all sectors of manufacturing. A new chemical industry furnished a domestic base for further expansion of many industries. Manchuria's few large and modern enterprises, although oriented toward Japan, represented a potential source of future industrial strength for China.

During the 1930s, the effects of producer expansion began to spread outside the factory sector and beyond China's coastal industrial areas, creating new demands for transport, machinery, and mechanical skills that would eventually touch agricultural production. Producers of machinery and chemicals tried, although with little initial success, to establish direct links between industry and agriculture.[70]

The extent and timing of these advances varied among different sectors. Engineering growth began at an early stage, but manufacture of basic chemicals had to await the existence of sufficient demand from consuming industries. In the absence of government intervention, technical and financial indivisibilities prevented the growth of ferrous metallurgy in republican China, as plans for state action were stymied by the deteriorating international situation.[71]

Manchuria's experience shows that state participation can overcome many delays and obstacles encountered in a market system. Official investments and formal or informal trade barriers eliminate capital scarcity, shield nascent enterprises from the threat (and goad) of external competition, and can even circumvent the demand problem by simultaneously creating supplier and customer firms, with government standing ready to absorb the initial losses of both.

At the same time, the Japanese policies responsible for the expansion of mining and manufacturing at Anshan, Fushun, and a handful of other large enterprises retarded the growth of small-scale producer enterprises. With few opportunities to interact with industrial leaders as either suppliers or customers, private businesses had little chance of achieving the type of evolutionary progress that occurred in Shanghai and other Chinese cities. The small size of Manchuria's consumer industries—the number of cotton spindles in 1931 was less than Shanghai's total for 1896—also restricted the derived demand for machine parts, chemicals, and other commodities and services that might have come from local suppliers.

In explaining such a wealth of regional and sectoral diversity, broad analyses cast in terms of imperialism, entrepreneurship, or other general concepts must inevitably fail to encompass the totality of China's complex prewar industrial experience, in which technology, finance, demand, foreign competition, and government policy all exerted strong influence on the fate of individual sectors at various times.

Although the external orientation of Manchuria's industrial giants attenuated their potential linkage effect on the domestic economy of China's northeastern region, the overall course of China's prewar industrial history demonstrates the positive impact of foreign trade on industrial progress. The origins of machinery and chemical manufacture in the private sector illustrate the power of Hirschman's contention that "imports . . . provide the safest, most incontrovertible proof that the market is there."[72] Product after product was manufactured domestically only after imports alerted Chinese businessmen to the size and profitability of the local market.

In a market economy, it is only after private business responds to new opportunities that tariff or other protection can spur the pace of industrialization. Though there were no high tariffs during World War I, the war itself curbed foreign supplies of textile machinery, soda, and other producer items without eliciting a prompt response from domestic firms whose technical capacity was still too small to permit them to manufacture scarce and expensive producer goods. This episode shows how premature efforts to shelter domestic industries from foreign rivals may raise costs and reduce domestic investment without stimulating domestic production of the protected commodities. The aggressive response of Chinese chemical producers to higher tariffs after 1930 and of textile machinery producers to wartime isolation after 1937 demonstrates the extent of advance in these sectors during the previous two decades. It does not imply that earlier introduction of trade controls might have hastened industrial advance.

As is evident from the stagnation of China's ferrous metallurgy industry, the presence of adequate demand and energetic entrepreneurs cannot guarantee that new industries will prosper. But, despite this failure, the evolutionary growth of producer manufactures in republican China, combined with Manchuria's state-sponsored projects, launched China onto a path of industrial advance that retained considerable unexploited potential when the process was disrupted by war. The momentum of prewar industrial expansion continued to make itself felt during the 1950s and 1960s, decades that are the focal point of the following chapters.

Chapter 2

Producer Industries, 1949–57

The first decade after 1949 was one of rapid output growth, massive investment, and marked expansion of the potential for qualitative change in China's producer sector. In reviewing these years, both Chinese and foreign observers have stressed the contribution of Soviet technology, advice, and managerial systems to industrial progress. Soviet influence was most prominent in investment. During the First Five-Year Plan (FFYP) period (1953–57), over 40 percent of industrial investment was lavished on a group of under two hundred projects planned in conjunction with Soviet technicians, modeled after Soviet designs, and stocked with machinery imported from the USSR and Eastern Europe.[1]

Despite its importance at the policy-making level in Peking, Soviet influence in the production sphere was hardly overwhelming. Only 30 percent of 1953–57 industrial output came from new or reconstructed plants; inherited factories and mines provided over two-thirds of current output.[2] The strain of simultaneous expansion of output and investment on nascent planning organs delayed the absorption of many products and enterprises into the Soviet-inspired planning system until well into the FFYP period. At the microeconomic level, Soviet systems of organization and administration also took root gradually. As late as 1957, national plans and new management patterns exercised only limited control over a wide range of activity in the producer industries.

Peking's concern first with implementing and later with modifying Soviet techniques of production and management was not the only force shaping China's industries during the 1950s. The patchwork nature of central control left considerable scope for independent initiative at the enterprise level. Not surprisingly, the fullest exploitation of opportunities for unplanned development occurred in the same sectors and regions that had prospered in the laissez-faire economy of the republican years.

Despite a widespread focus on quantity alone, the spread of technical ability and the accumulation of experience by planners, managers, and workers led to improved quality and variety as the volume of producer output rose. More important, the 1950s saw the emergence of institutions and skills that helped produce innovative responses to the hardships of the following decade.

These topics, the penetration of new planning and managerial systems, and the growth of output and of a large but untapped potential for qualitative change, provide the focus for our review of China's producer industries from liberation to the close of the FFYP.

The Gradual Spread of State Control

As the victorious Red armies swept southward in 1949, China's new leaders sought to reorganize industry under a system of state ownership, central planning, and capable and responsive factory leadership. Expropriation of enterprises formerly adminstered by the Nanking government's National Resources Administration placed leading producer enterprises, including Japanese-built plants, in government hands from the start.

The problems of planning and management were more formidable. Paucity of experienced personnel and reliable information meant that only gradual progress could be expected.[3] At the factory level, restoration of production depended on the presence of experienced Chinese leaders and of Japanese or Soviet technicians, on the availability of Japanese or Kuomintang (KMT) designs and blueprints, and on the vigor of individual administrators.[4]

Unavoidable initial confusion was heightened by the speed with which the new regime sought to implement its ambitious industrialization plans. Instead of postponing technical reform and new construction until normal operations were restored at plants that had escaped wartime damage, the Chinese immediately began to add thousands of workers in anticipation of major new construction. The competing demands of rebuilding, innovation, and expansion piled new strains on an already overextended corps of skilled and experienced industrial personnel.

Faced with the impossibility of asserting close control over an industrial system that soon included ten thousand state enterprises, several million employees, and thousands of construction projects, Peking initially concentrated its efforts on key commodities, enterprises, and regions. As one area, product, or unit developed adequate managerial competence, economic administrators directed their energies elsewhere. The slow extension of central control delayed the preparation of China's FFYP until the summer of 1955, over two years after the formal starting date of January 1953.

Growing control was most evident in ferrous metallurgy, an industry in which rationalization was facilitated by the small number of firms and products and by a technology that permits unskilled workers to perform a variety of duties under the direction of a few trained leaders. The Chinese capitalized on the latter feature by instituting forms of teamwork that reduced the importance of individual skills. Japanese personnel prepared detailed manuals to allow ordinary shop hands to work without close supervision. Imaginative application of heat-sensitive paper enabled even the least trained workers to operate delicate machinery: the danger of overheating was eliminated by instructing the operator to switch off his equipment when the paper changed color.[5]

Initial efforts focused on Anshan and Pench'i, China's largest steel centers. Improved technical and economic results showed that even raw village recruits could be quickly integrated into modern factory operations. At Anshan, which suffered from American bombing and Soviet looting near the end of World War II and changed hands eight times during the subsequent civil strife between Communist and Kuomintang forces, pig iron output surpassed the 1937 level as early as 1950. By 1952, output of major products had surpassed wartime peak figures, while labor productivity had risen to three times the 1949 level.[6] As managerial competence grew, the gap between Anshan's planned and realized output diminished from 45 percent in 1949 to only 12 percent in 1952.[7] Pench'i, which suffered only minor wartime damage, quickly regained its leading position as manufacturer of high-quality steel and subsequently led all firms in raising blast furnace utilization rates and other technical indicators.[8]

With production and construction advancing at key plants, conditions at smaller firms came under intense scrutiny. Beginning in 1952, detailed newspaper accounts pinpointed mismanagement at factories in Chungking, Talien, Tayeh, T'angshan, and elsewhere, citing general disorganization, failure to investigate sources of substandard materials, absence of monthly shop plans, neglect of new equipment, and other elementary problems already eliminated at Anshan and Pench'i. The impact of the ensuing reforms is evident after 1953 in the increase of labor productivity at all firms relative to Anshan's performance, indicating higher percentage growth in productivity at the smaller enterprises.[9]

Establishing a system of planning proved to be much more difficult in the machinery industry. In comparison with steel, machinery is characterized by numerous producers, a complex and shifting output mix, and a technology calling for a series of technically exacting operations by a large number of individuals or groups. The need for separate operations of design, casting, forging, machining, assembly, and inspection for thousands of parts, as well as maintenance and repair of existing machine tools, called for a degree of skill and information that strained the managerial capacity of both plant and central authorities.

As in the steel industry, economic planning began with key products, regions, and enterprises. Again, outstanding progress was reported in the Northeast, where even private enterprises were absorbed into the plan framework as early as 1953. The national picture was less encouraging. A 1954 editorial noted that enterprises outside the control of the First Ministry of Machine-building (FMMB), the authority responsible for major producers of civilian machinery, lacked unified direction; eliminating their tendency toward "blind development" would take "a long time." For the present, the ministry was hard pressed to compile output plans that could satisfy national demand for major products; minor items and products of small enterprises could not be controlled and would be brought into the state plan later on.[10]

Even within this restricted scope of operation, the FFMB experienced difficulty in preparing prompt, comprehensive, and consistent annual plans for its ninety-one firms. The 1954 directive issued in early April listed improved balance between supply and demand as the first priority, outranking output growth. In organization, the task was to "encourage the spread of planning" and to "move toward planning by rationally organizing the machinery industry." It was also suggested that future orders for imported equipment be handled centrally.[11]

In the following year, targets were not settled until August, and 1956 saw repeated changes in output plans. Delays and shifts in output quotas disrupted the allocation of raw materials, a task handled by separate organizations that were not involved in production planning. In 1957, when plans were again delayed, the FFMB was singled out for criticism and urged to "balance its supply in a well coordinated and unified way and work out an overall plan of production."[12]

Chronic tardiness, changing targets, and complaints that plans were based on unreliable estimates all stemmed from the inability of enterprise directors, who were preoccupied with the everyday demands of production, construction, labor training, and technical reform, to establish and maintain systems for compiling and transmitting the information essential for smooth functioning of the planning system. A typical report concerns the Shanghai Electric Motor Plant, at which employment rose from 173 to 4,000 and output increased by 6300 percent between 1949 and 1957. Even though this was an older plant in which 60 percent of the 1952 labor force had over five years' experience, visitors found that there was no master account of inventories and no control over tools. Small production groups kept no records and did not understand the contribution of their work to the plant's overall tasks. As a result, management found itself unable to locate, let alone remedy, technical problems.[13] Other plants experienced similar difficulties.

Peking made determined efforts to improve the planning system in 1957, a year of limited output growth. Industrial ministries rushed to complete 1958 plans on schedule.[14] FMMB directives and work teams emphasized the need for basic documentation to systematize manufacturing operations and economic reporting, while factory directors exchanged frank views on conflicting priorities between enterprises and central officials.[15]

Although the onset of the Great Leap blunted these reforms, their impact is revealed in the wealth of comparative data accumulated and published for the first time during 1957 and 1958. With standardized and detailed interenterprise comparisons of inventories, fixed and circulating capital, waste rates, and costs, planning agencies in Peking could now exercise the type of detailed control over major machinery producers that they had applied to key steel plants over five years earlier.

In other industries, the rate of progress in imposing a hierarchy of economic control stretching from Peking to factory workshops fell between the extremes found in the steel and machinery sectors. Investment controls, hampered by the uniqueness of each individual construction project, consistently lagged behind industrial administration, with reports of weak budgeting, disorganization, and cost overruns persisting as late as 1957. The history of the expansion project Shenyang #1 Machine Tool Plant, where actual costs amounted to five times the original estimate, illustrates the flaccidity of project preparation even at key enterprises.[16]

Despite continuing problems in controlling and coordinating activity in machinery, construction, and other heterogeneous sectors, there can be no doubt that by 1957 China possessed an operative system of industrial planning that was already capable of translating centrally determined policy into effective action at the microeconomic level. This planning system, which is discussed in more detail in chapter 5, has remained essentially intact to the present and has proven itself to be a formidable vehicle for promoting economic change.

Sources and Patterns of Output Growth

The years between 1949 and 1957 saw rapid growth of output in China's producer sector. The gross value of output (in 1952 prices) jumped from 3.1 billion yuan in 1949 to 10.7 billion yuan in 1952 and 34.3 billion yuan in 1957, surpassing the FFYP output target by 41 percent. The largest contribution to output growth came from the steel, machinery, and chemical sectors (see table 4.6). Since employment and fixed capital increased by only 59 percent and 35 percent during 1952–57, it is evident that most of this output growth is attributable to higher factor productivity, a broad category that includes fuller use of capacity, labor training, organizational improvements, and other forms of disembodied technical change.[17]

Only a small portion of this expansion represented a recovery of prewar output levels. By 1952, physical output of most major products had surpassed the wartime peaks (see table 1.1); Liu and Yeh's estimates of gross value added by mining, utilities, and producer factories show an increase of approximately 200 percent between 1933 and 1952, of which less than half occurred before 1949.[18]

Producer goods capacity continued to grow after the outbreak of war in 1937. The most significant expansion occurred in the Northeast, where Japanese investment led to an estimated doubling of overall industrial output between 1936 and 1941, with growth continuing in most sectors until 1943 or 1944. Despite wartime destruction, substantial post–1936 additions to Manchuria's industrial capacity survived until 1949, including many plants built late in the war that produced little or no output before 1945. The enlarged stock of fixed assets enabled regional industrial output to surpass the 1943 peak level as early as 1951.[19]

Cessation of warfare and resumption of transport services stimulated industrial expansion in North and Central China as well as Manchuria. Available information suggests little change in the industrial capacity of Shanghai and other major cities between 1936 and 1949. Shanghai's factories suffered heavily under the Japanese invasion of 1937 and the subsequent flight of workers and equipment to the interior, but these losses were replaced, and output was quickly restored to the prewar level. Similar developments occurred in North China, where estimated output growth of 83 percent between 1938 and 1944 probably represents little more than a return to previous levels of industrial activity.[20]

Strenuous wartime efforts to expand producer output in the industrially backward provinces of Free China had little national impact. Many fledgling enterprises were abandoned after V-J Day; in Chungking's metal processing industry, which had grown from 51 to 349 firms between 1933 and 1945, only 135 enterprises were still operating in 1948.[21]

Under these conditions, the restoration of domestic peace, monetary stability, and unfettered access to markets alone sufficed to ignite an industrial spurt of substantial proportions. Morale was high as workers pitched in to help China industrialize. Concrete government policies added to industry's forward momentum by sweeping away restraints previously imposed by the market. The ironworks of North China, for example, idled during the 1930s by scarce working capital and low prices, were quickly returned to production.[22] Officials urged producers to maximize output and provided state funds to finance expansion of inventories and employment. Industrial enterprises could afford to neglect problems of quality and assortment, for substandard products could be forced onto unwilling factories, state commercial organs, and even the army.[23] Ready availability of bank loans and assured sales at cost-plus prices allowed output per unit of labor or fixed capital to exceed levels achieved in the market economy of the 1930s.

Soviet technicians made important contributions to raising output at existing facilities. The iron and steel sector was the chief beneficiary, receiving an advanced and integrated technological system that enabled output and productivity to outstrip wartime Japanese achievements and in some cases to approach Soviet standards.[24] Elsewhere Soviet personnel acted as troubleshooters, and their suggestions often eliminated technical bottlenecks and allowed large jumps in output. The Soviet fast-cutting method and other advanced techniques, for example, permitted a 120 percent increase in machine tool productivity between 1953 and 1956.[25]

Steady growth in the quality of industrial labor was a final source of expanded output. The new regime's determination to press ahead with expanded production and construction from the beginning meant that factory rosters were swollen with unskilled recruits at a time when the ranks of technical and supervisory personnel, already depleted by the flight of Japanese and Kuomintang sympathizers, were further thinned by transfers from production management to planning and construction tasks. Employment in factories and mines, estimated at less than two million in 1933, exceeded three million in 1952. In metal processing alone, the 1952 work force was substantially higher than estimated total industrial employment in 1948.[26] The ignorance of these newcomers, which extended to areas that citizens of advanced industrial nations regard as common sense rather than industrial technology, led to a degree of confusion that is difficult to comprehend.

New workers failed to grasp the importance of protecting machinery against the elements. Numerous plants failed to lubricate their equipment properly.[27] Workers at the Nanking Machine Tool Plant began using imported equipment without checking its lubrication or translating the instructions. One machine burned out after running for two months without oil; another was damaged when workers fouled its moving parts with metal filings. Of twenty-eight new machine tools installed at this plant between 1952 and 1953, fourteen were not level and twenty-two were damaged within six months. Similar incidents occurred at other plants, including Anshan, where repairmen cut the power supply to the blast furnaces without notifying production crews.[28]

This process of "learning by spoiling" was shared by experienced workers, many of whom had learned their skills by rote and found it difficult to adjust to new assignments. Some veteran workers resisted new Soviet techniques, while others opposed new inspection standards, preferring to measure their work by eye.[29]

The short-run cost of diluting the industrial work force was high. At times the results were disastrous, as when the Tz'u-shan (Hopei) Iron Mine experienced an 80 percent decline in labor productivity, soaring expenses, and a rash of accidents after adding several thousand untrained miners.[30] Peking's response to such difficulties was to organize a massive program of industrial education. Drawing on traditional and revolutionary Chinese teaching methods as well as on Soviet models, industrial ministries and enterprises created a whole spectrum of training facilities ranging from technical universities and engineering colleges to crash courses in literacy and elementary technology for common laborers.

Progress was impressive, especially at the lowest level, where thousands of steelworkers, shipwrights, and miners learned to read in night schools. The share of illiterates among Shenyang's industrial workers dropped from 65 to 27 percent between 1948 and 1953. In Peking, Tientsin, and Shanghai, the literacy rate among workers rose from 25 to 50 percent between 1950 and 1956. Higher level personnel were directed toward appropriately difficult subjects: Russian language classes for engineers, and drafting, blueprint analysis, and Russian alphabet lessons for machinists.[31]

As new and old workers accumulated knowledge and experience, the reduced frequency of elementary blunders alone must have considerably increased productivity. The fruits of elementary training were reinforced by increases in both the number and ability of lower echelon technical and managerial personnel. Gradual improvements in the administration of economic planning also contributed to normalizing industrial routines, as did the declining growth rate of industrial employment.[32] Despite continuing reports implying low technical levels—only one-third of Anshan's basic production leaders had attained primary school education levels in 1954—there can be little doubt that the growing technical capacity of the work force was a major source of industrial output growth during the FFYP period.[33]

If the growth of producer output to 1957 can be understood in terms of augmented factor supplies, fuller utilization of capacity, Soviet technical assistance and improved skills, the sectoral pattern of output expansion requires more detailed analysis. As can be seen from table 2.1, the FFYP provided a broadly accurate forecast of the level and structure of 1957 industrial output. Targets for 1957 were generally surpassed, with output of coal, steel, cement, and power clustering around the 20 percent margin by which total industrial output exceeded its quota for the terminal year. Planners correctly projected industrial investment for 1953–57, with actual expenditures exceeding the target of 24.850 billion yuan by less than 1 percent.[34]

Since the Five-Year Plan was not completed until mid-1955, the overall accuracy of its 1957 projections is not remarkable. What is surprising is the massive deviation shown by chemical and machinery output, which not only grew much faster than production in other sectors, but surpassed planned 1957 output targets by 89 and 78 percent respectively.

Production of machinery in 1956 surpassed the 1957 target, set only months earlier, by two-thirds. Although the 1956 total included quantities of useless items, especially in farm equipment, the still larger 1957 output, now nearly 80 percent above the target, was produced with much greater attention to customer requirements. Even so, widespread reports of idle capacity and excessive stockpiles of new machines show that the overall supply of machinery outstripped demand by a wide margin.[35] With the larger, more modern firms under the FMMB working at only 80 percent of capacity, potential machinery output in 1957 exceeded the 1955 forecast by at least 125 percent.[36]

The unexpectedness of this breakthrough in engineering is evident in Peking's response to the simultaneous appearance of unplanned output and excess capacity, the latter extending even to new plants built with Soviet assistance. Surprised planners began to scale down current and projected investments and to investigate the relation between requirements for machinery and other capital goods.[37]

Why did planners make such large errors in estimating productive

TABLE 2.1
Output Growth and Plan Fulfillment in Industry, 1952–57

Indicator (unit)	1952 Data	1957 Plan	1957 Actual	1957 Actual as Percentage of Plan
Gross output value (in million 1952 yuan)				
Industry (excluding handicrafts)	27,010	53,560	65,020[a]	121.4
Producer sector	10,730[a]	24,303[b]	34,330[a]	141.0
Machinery	1,404[a]	3,470[c]	6,177[a]	178.0
Chemicals	864[a]	2,271[d]	4,291[a]	188.9
Producer sector less machinery and chemicals	8,462	18,562	23,862	128.5
Physical output				
Coal (mmt)	68.5	113.0	130.0	115.0
Crude oil (tmt)	436	2,012	1,458	72.5
Steel ingot (mmt)	1.35	4.12	5.35	129.8
Cement (mmt)	2.86	6.00	6.86	114.3
Electric power (billion kwh)	7.26	15.90	19.34	121.6
Internal combustion engines (thousand hp)	27.6	260.2	609.0	234.2
Hydroelectric turbines (kw)	6,664	79,500	74,900	94.2
Generators (thousand kw)	29.7	227.0	312.2[e]	137.5
Electric motors (thousand kw)	639	1,048	1455	138.8
Transformers (thousand kva)	1,167	2,610	3,500[f]	134.1
Machine tools (units)	13,734	12,720	28,000	220.1
Locomotives (units)	20	200	167	83.5
Railway freight cars (units)	5,792	8,500	7,300	85.9
Merchant ships (thousand dwt tons)	21.5	179.1	54.0	30.2
Trucks (units)	0	4,000	7,500	187.5
Bicycles (thousand units)	80	555	1,174	211.5
Caustic soda (tmt)	79	154	198	128.6
Soda ash (tmt)	192	476	506	106.3
Ammonium sulphate (tmt)	181	504	631	125.2
Ammonium nitrate (tmt)	7	44	120	272.7
Automobile tires (thousand sets)	417	760	873	114.9
Sulphuric acid (tmt)	149	402[d]	632	157.2
"666" insecticide (tons)	600[d]	70,000[c]	61,000[g]	87.1

Sources: Unless otherwise noted, data are from *First Five-Year Plan*, pp. 34, 48–49, or from Kang Chao, *The Rate and Pattern of Industrial Growth in Communist China* (Ann Arbor, 1965), table C–1.

Note: mmt = million metric tons; tmt = thousand metric tons.

[a] Shigeru Ishikawa, *National Income and Capital Formation in Mainland China* (Tokyo, 1965), p. 60.

[b] Planned 1957 output for "means of production" or "type A (*chia-lei*) industry" was 2.265 times the 1952 level. Su Tai-yün, *Wo-kuo kuo-tu shih-ch'i-chung kung-yeh fa-chan su-tu ti chi-ko wen-t'i* (Shanghai, 1956), p. 33.

[c] WKKT, p. 75.

[d] Chang, *Hua-hsüeh kung-yeh*, pp. 16, 18, 22.

[e] Chu-yuan Cheng, *The Machine-building Industry in Communist China* (Chicago, 1971), pp. 250, 253.

[f] *Kung-jen jih-pao*, January 10, 1958.

[g] Miyashita Haruo, "Insecticide Industry," in *Chūgoku no kagaku kōgyō*, ed. Kambara Shū (Tokyo, 1970), p. 185.

capacity in machinery, which they regarded as "the key to the technological transformation of our economy"? Lacking detailed information on more than a handful of China's twenty-five hundred machinery plants, China's leaders apparently believed that, as in the 1930s, the inherited machinery plants were still "only able to manufacture accessories, do assembly or repair work or produce some small and simple machines."[38] Anticipating only modest contributions from old industrial bases, they diverted experienced personnel, investment goods, and raw materials to new industrial centers. When complaints of low utilization rates throughout coastal industry elicited a revision of 1956 plans to allot more working capital, investment funds, and materials to older enterprises, these units responded with an output spurt that continued into 1957.[39] In machinery, this spurt pushed production of a wide range of producer durables beyond the targets set under the FFYP.

This episode confirms the existence of productive potentials carried over from pre-1949 years. Unsuspected latent capacities were not confined to the machinery industry. Table 2.2, which provides crude measures of the output response of various segments of industry to increments of capital and labor during the FFYP years, demonstrates the abnormally high growth, relative to added resources, in machinery and chemicals, and especially in Shanghai's producer sector. With the exception of the relation between higher employment and production in the machinery industry, which is influenced by the presence of idle capacity in the terminal year, each measure of output responsiveness in these three areas is substantially above the average for the producer sector as a whole. Despite idle capacity in machinery and a steady drain of personnel from Shanghai,[40] these three segments, which turned out only 26 percent of 1952 producer output and received less than one-fifth of FFYP investment in producer industries, accounted for over 40 percent of the overall growth of producer output during 1952–57.[41]

These results demonstrate that the swift growth of producer output during the FFYP years was to a large degree a continuation of a development process begun decades earlier. Sectors and regions that had shown the greatest dynamism in prewar China again played a leading role. Their contribution to industrial advance far exceeded expectations based on the new resources placed at their disposal. As will be seen in chapter 3, this pattern of disproportionate contributions from

TABLE 2.2
Producer Sector Response to Resource Injections, 1952–57
(in million yuan)

	Producer Sector		Subsectors		Producer Sector Less Machinery and Chemicals
	National	Shanghai	Machinery	Chemicals	
1. Incremental output, 1952–57 (1952 yuan)	23,600[a]	3,177[b]	4,773[a]	3,427[a]	15,400
2. Fixed investment outlay 1953–57 (current yuan)	21,290[c]	411[d]	2,830[e]	1,300[f]	17,160
3. Incremental employment 1952–57 (thousands)	2,060[h]	—	387[g]	140[h]	1,533
4. Incremental output ÷ investment (1 ÷ 2)	1.11	7.73	1.69	2.64	0.90
5. Incremental output ÷ incremental employment (1 ÷ 3)	11,456	—	12,333	24,478	10,046

[a] Table 2.1.

[b] Shanghai industrial output (excluding handicrafts) from Robert M. Field, Nicholas R. Lardy, and John P. Emerson, *A Reconstruction of the Gross Value of Industrial Output by Province in the People's Republic of China, 1949–73* (Washington, D.C., 1975), p. 21. Share of heavy industry (assumed identical with producer goods) in Shanghai industrial output was 22.9 percent in 1952 and 36.5 percent in 1957 (Sun Ching-chih ed., *Economic Geography of the East China Region*, translated in JPRS 11438(1961):83).

[c] *Ten Great Years*, p. 61.

[d] *Kuang-ming jih-pao*, September 24, 1957, gives FFYP basic construction investment in Shanghai industry as 500+ million yuan. During 1949–57, heavy industry (assumed identical with producer goods), received 82.2 percent of Shanghai's total industrial investment (*Chieh-fang jih-pao*, September 3, 1957). FFYP investment in Shanghai's producer sector is estimated at approximately 500 × .822 = 411 million yuan.

[e] Annual state investment in machinery for 1952–56 from WKKT, p. 69. Ishikawa, *National Income*, p. 155, gives planned 1957 investment in ferrous metallurgy as 0.883 billion yuan. Ching, "Proportional Relation," p. 13, gives the planned 1957 ratio of investment in machinery and ferrous metals as 0.85:1. Investment in machinery in 1957 is estimated by assuming these plans to have been implemented.

[f] Cited by Kojima Reiitsu, "Industrial Production and the Chemical Industry," in *Chūgoku no kagaku kōgyō*, p. 38.

[g] Cheng, *Machine-building*, p. 281.

[h] John P. Emerson, *Nonagricultural Employment in Mainland China: 1949–1958* (Washington, D.C., 1965), p. 143.

older industrial sectors and centers is a continuing feature of Chinese industrialization.

Qualitative Aspects of Performance

Industrial product quality, which includes the matching of product assortment with customer requirements as well as the workmanship devoted to each item, depends on the capacity of available equipment and personnel and on the nature of incentives. In China, steadily growing ability to upgrade the quality and variety of producer output was partially offset during the 1950s by excessive concentration on raising the volume of output. Especially where central planning and control remained weak, close attention to qualitative aspects of production was not an outstanding feature of the first post-1949 decade. In the absence of close supervision from above, industrial leaders tended to ignore official pronouncements urging quality change unless there was no possibility of conflict with the crucial task of meeting quantitative targets.

In the present context, we are interested in the effect of this "output first" mentality rather than its institutional roots, which are discussed in chapter 5. Primacy of quantity over quality meant that improvements in workmanship and assortment were typically limited to what might be termed a natural rate determined largely by the development of technical and managerial skills from the low levels of the early 1950s. The resulting upward drift of quality, similar to the Horndal effect discussed by economic historians, is visible throughout most of the FFYP period.[42]

Numerous accounts illustrate the central position of output maximization in the objectives of industrial enterprises. In extreme cases, managers ignored all targets save gross output value and sales. Many firms sought to increase output value by abandoning assortment plans and concentrating on easy products, items with high output value per man-hour or, if materials were scarce, with high value per unit of material used. Inattention to detail enabled producers to raise output at the expense of customers who found themselves obliged to make do with engines that leaked oil, machines with missing parts, or other "small defects" in production ignored in the rush for higher volume.[43] At times, even lip service to quality was dispensed with; in one instance, some units at Anshan refused to join a discussion of quality problems, while elsewhere it was stated that "because of time limitations, the meeting did not adequately discuss how to guarantee quality and economy" in construction.[44]

Innovation, a task that required the attention of the same skilled personnel instrumental in maintaining high rates of output, was also neglected by unsupervised units.[45] A 1953 directive lamented the "obvious aversion to experimenting on manufacturing new products." Two years later the press attacked timid producers for "vying with each other in making old varieties" and refusing to "make new varieties with the result that old varieties of products are overstocked," and decried units "which are only interested in turning out products which can be produced on a mass scale . . . and are not interested in overcoming difficulties to do trial manufacture and manufacture of new products."[46] Despite these complaints, directives and editorials suggesting that the material shortages and idle capacity expected during 1957 could be turned to advantage by concentrating on trial manufacture and improved quality showed that central officials acquiesced in their subordinates' view of research and development as residual tasks suited for otherwise idle interludes.[47]

Inattention to quality and assortment was most evident during periods such as the "production high tide" of 1956, when many firms raised output by relaxing inspection standards, abandoning Soviet techniques, and arbitrarily simplifying designs to reduce unit consumption of scarce inputs.[48] Even when output targets were easily surpassed, there often seemed to be little pressure or incentive for qualitative improvements. Although 1956 output of the items shown in table 2.3 exceeded the 1957 targets by as much as 100 percent, progress toward the projected 1957 size standards was minimal and even negative in the case of electric motors.

Despite this evidence of resistance and backsliding, the quality and assortment of most products did show an upward trend through the FFYP years. Gradual progress was an almost automatic corollary of the accumulation of industrial experience and technical knowledge throughout industry and of consolidation within the planning system. In the steel industry, growing technical competence enabled closer regulation of the chemical and physical properties of steel products. The

TABLE 2.3
Average Unit Capacity for Selected Machinery Products, 1952–57

Item (unit)	Average Unit Capacity 1952	1955	1956	1957	1957 Plan	1956 Production as Percentage of 1957 Plan
Hydroelectric turbine (kw)	606	—	1,803	—	9,938	129.2
Electric generator (kw)	40	43	42	—	77	127.0
Electric motor (kw)	7.0	5.6	5.8	4.8[a]	7.7	102.0
Transformer (kva)	72	35	26	—	231	110.8
Internal combustion engine (hp)	18	17[b]	18	—	24	207.8
Steam boiler (tons per hour)	1.2	—	2.9	—	3.1	112.4[c]

Sources: Except as noted, WKKT, pp. 76, 95; final column calculated from table 2.1 and Cheng, *Machine-building*, app. II.

[a] First quarter figure given in ECMM 94(1957):20.

[b] Calculated from Chao, *Rate and Pattern*, p. 127, and Cheng, *Machine-building*, p. 253.

[c] Calculated from 1952 and 1956 output data shown in Cheng, *Machine-building*, p. 251, and from the planned 1957 output of 2.2 times the 1952 level as stated in Ching Lin, *Ti-i-ko wu-nien chi-hua-chung ti chi-ch'i chih-tsao-yeh* (Peking, 1955), p. 18.

share of top-grade products rose rapidly from low levels, as did the weight of heavy rails, seamless tubes, and other complex shapes in overall output.[49] Power plants succeeded in switching to lower grades of coal while reducing transmission losses and unit fuel consumption.[50] Machinery producers added new varieties to their product lines. Table 2.3 shows steady progress in raising the maximum capacity of some products; the average size of machine tools increased, while the number of models expanded from 40 in 1952 to 200 in 1957.[51]

Import substitution provides another sign of technical progress. The percentage growth in machine production between 1953 and 1957 was more than twice that of imports (including complete plants), indicating a sharp increase in the share of domestic products in total machinery supply. Substitution of domestic for imported locomotives, rolling stock, blast furnace equipment, coke ovens, and other items often entailed substantial savings.[52]

This mixed record masks important changes that greatly increased the potential for future improvements in the quality of producer output. In terms of the framework outlined in the introduction, accumulation of production and planning experience, together with new equipment and institutional development, pushed the level of attainable skills considerably beyond the requirements imposed by the tasks of the 1950s.

Growing economic sophistication in Peking was one ingredient in reversing industry's tendency to skimp on quality. By 1957 economic writers had outgrown earlier naive expectations that Soviet institutions and massive investment would quickly eliminate all obstacles to industrialization.[53] The reality of technical and marketing difficulties at the newest Soviet-built plants awakened Chinese planners to the importance of demand forecasting, an area almost completely neglected prior to 1957.[54]

Peking's new appreciation of industrial interdependence and the resulting need to extend economic analysis beyond the broad aggregates included in the FFYP were essential to future efforts to match output with requirements. The experience of 1956 showed that undisciplined expansion diverted scarce materials and manpower, and yielded a legacy of imbalance and useless inventories. At the same time, newly acquired information about machine building, the sector with the most difficult assortment problems, showed that without central guidance even the best intentioned factory executives could not keep abreast of rapidly changing demand patterns.[55]

These changes at the top were accompanied by equally significant institutional developments that created a mechanism for attacking technical problems identified on the factory floor and expanding the flow of technical data among enterprises, administrative units, and research groups.

At the factory level, the emergence of a professional inspectorate committed to maintaining national standards exemplified the growing concern for raising quality.[56] In the early 1950s, with literate and experienced personnel desperately scarce, managers assigned inspection chores to the dregs of their work force. Later on, better-educated entrants formed the nucleus of a new generation of inspectors whose dedication can be inferred from clashes with superiors intent on using substandard items to fill out production quotas.[57] Improvements in the stock of measuring devices also contributed to the development of industrial quality control.

Technical problems uncovered by factory inspectors and visiting investigation teams were referred to a growing array of research and design institutes attached to industrial ministries and enterprises.[58] Lack of experience and equipment initially confined these units to elementary inquiries. Some were criticized as paper organizations formed only "because the ministry said so" and incapable of formulating and attacking research problems. Close cooperation between researchers and production personnel was sometimes difficult to achieve. At the central level, plans for innovation were primitive; even the national twelve-year plan for science and technology was criticized for its lack of concrete suggestions.[59]

In spite of these difficulties, China's research establishment did begin to assist industrial development during the 1950s. Clark rightly emphasizes the role of Soviet models and technicians in the design and research achievements of this period,[60] but reports of independent Chinese progress are not without merit, especially with regard to technical and design modifications needed to operate Soviet processes and equipment.

It was soon discovered that without careful microeconomic analysis, the introduction of advanced techniques often created undesirable side effects. Chinese engineers undertook the complex task of preparing Soviet methods and equipment for operation under local conditions. At the Harbin Boiler Works, which received copies of technical documents from two Soviet plants, Chinese personnel spent nine months preparing a new set of plans suited to indigenous skill levels and product requirements. The Harbin group concluded that "we cannot transplant living things as a whole, but must study Soviet standards and then rationally deal with these problems according to concrete conditions in our country," a view whose wide applicability can be seen in numerous other reports.[61]

Chinese engineers also contributed to improving the quality of casting, a key element in machinery production. Since two-thirds of China's casting shops processed less than three thousand tons per year while even forty thousand annual tons is a small facility in Soviet parlance, it is hardly surprising that Soviet casting techniques were difficult to use in Chinese plants. The Soviet methods created problems even in large units such as Shenyang's #1 Machine Tool Plant, and were entirely inappropriate for small units.[62] With Soviet efforts focused on reforms that were largely counterproductive, the steady improvement in heat-treatment techniques came mainly from the efforts of Chinese personnel.[63]

Improved communication links provided opportunities for industrial units to raise the quality of output by learning from each other. In addition to information exchanged during the course of visits by planners and inspectors to individual units, industrial ministries and other agencies organized national, sectoral, and regional technical conferences on such topics as casting, machining, and quality control. These meetings served as forums for appraising new methods and popularizing the successes of advanced units. Demonstrations by individual workers and frequent intervisitation programs among factories provided similar opportunities for sharing advanced experiences at the local level.

Conclusion

The development of China's producer industries under the FFYP illustrates both the strengths and drawbacks of a big push toward industrial expansion based on massive investment, rapid import substitution, and administrative allocation of resources. With a strong government providing political and monetary stability and relaxing many constraints formerly imposed by a market economy, current output expanded swiftly. Gradual completion of industrial construction projects, many financed and equipped with Soviet and East European assistance, brought forth a steady stream of products that China had been unable to manufacture in the past.[64]

On the negative side, the concentration of ministerial and enterprise leaders on quantitative expansion meant that industrial products often failed to match requirements. Frequent lapses in coordination obliged many units to mark time or suspend normal standards while awaiting the arrival of key equipment or materials, adding to the flow of useless or flawed commodities. In general, industry's rapidly expanding production and investment activities were marked by a diminishing, but still considerable, degree of confusion.

Such difficulties are an inevitable by-product of major efforts to mobilize and redirect resources in any economy. This was recognized by Chinese planners who advocated quick entry into new fields of endeavor using any feasible methods to manufacture essential items. With production underway, attention could then be shifted to questions of cost, quality, and technical improvement. As P'eng T'ao, Minister of Chemicals, put it:

> Draw up construction plans according to the principle of existence first, then progressiveness. This is because China's industry is backward, technical levels are low, the varieties of chemical products are few, and many essential products cannot be manufactured. Accordingly . . . we must first solve the problem of existence or absence [of new products] and then move from backward to advanced [methods].[65]

The short-term costs associated with simultaneous efforts to push ahead with a wide range of new activities are especially severe in engineering, construction, and other sectors with many firms, heterogeneous products, and diverse interindustry relations. Unexpected progress in some units and unforeseen delays in others create sudden demand surges and supply bottlenecks whose effects ripple disruptively through the economy. In China, these problems were magnified by the size and scope of planned changes and by the limited competence of staff and workers throughout industry.

The key feature of industrial development during the 1950s, however, is neither the sharp rise in output volume nor the equally striking costs of this expansion. It is rather the widespread appearance, often in embryonic form, of regular channels for accumulating and applying expertise and technical information to difficulties arising from the productive process. Together with the experience acquired during the FFYP years and the new technology embodied in imported equipment, these institutional changes represent a gathering of forces with a potential for qualitative gains extending far beyond the limited achievements of the FFYP years. To realize these gains, industry would have to alter the quantitative focus that dominated factory policy throughout the 1950s. The necessary restructuring of incentives came only in response to an economic crisis brought on by the Great Leap Forward and the collapse of technical cooperation with the Soviet Union.

Chapter 3

Producer Industries since 1957

We have now traced the growth of producer industries from the turn of the century to the end of the FFYP period. Before 1949, the producer sector was too small to influence the overall course of China's economy. Rapid growth during the 1950s greatly enlarged the volume of output but did not fully develop the integration, flexibility, and innovative mechanisms needed to produce an adequate response to shifting patterns of demand. It was only in the decades following 1957 that China entered a period of self-sustaining industrialization in which redeployment of domestic resources began to satisfy the changing requirements of a growing economy by providing new products, absorbing new technologies, and restructuring the proportions among existing commodities and resources.

As the dominant source of intermediate and capital goods for all sectors of the economy, China's producer industries have played a central role in this transition to self-sustaining growth. The present chapter shows how the interaction between new industrial policies and accumulated production experience have led industry to explore previously developed technological potentials and describes the resulting improvements in responsiveness to demand, innovative performance, and integration within the producer sector.

Industrial Reforms and the Great Leap Forward

As the FFYP period drew to a close, there was widespread agreement that industry had outgrown its earlier dependence on Soviet models and advice, and that future plans would have to strike out in new directions dictated by Chinese realities and problems. Mao Tse-tung captured this spirit when he commented that

> In economic work, dogmatism primarily manifested itself . . . in heavy industry and planning. Since we didn't understand these things and had absolutely no experience, all we could do in our ignorance was to import foreign methods. . . . Now the situation has changed.[1]

Mao himself sparked an interlude of lively discussion with his April 1956 speech "On Ten Major Relationships," half of which was devoted to a probing review of past policies affecting balance among sectors, regions, and administrative levels within the economy. Encouraged by Mao's critical stance, economic journals published hundreds of explicit and detailed accounts of weaknesses in industrial planning, management, and investment programs.

Public debate and internal policy discussions led to a series of reforms carried out in 1957 and early 1958.[2] Industrial planners called for a slowdown in the growth of output and investment. Relaxation in the pace of growth was intended to give planning officials and enterprise managers an opportunity to place greater emphasis on quality, assortment, cost, balance, customer service, and innovation, areas that had suffered widespread neglect in the past, especially during the "production high tide" of 1956. Increased provincial and local authority over industry was another aspect of the 1957 reforms. Decentralization, implemented in a series of decrees beginning in November 1957, sought to reduce the burden on clogged channels of vertical communication within the planning system and to reduce the bureaucratic distance between customers and suppliers.[3] Increased investment in small-scale manufacturing was a final aspect of the 1957 reforms aimed at alleviating commodity shortages and providing customers in agriculture and handicrafts with better access to industrial goods.

These reforms sought to shift the basic character of industrial growth away from the big push approach, with its emphasis on the volume of output, toward a less hectic mode of expansion in which quality and complementarity take precedence over sheer quantity, so that user requirements rather than production competitions determine relative commodity outputs. In his studies of Hungary's economy, Janos Kornai has identified these two approaches as rush growth, which dominated China's industrial policy between 1949 and 1960, and harmonic growth which, as is argued here and in chapter 5, has replaced rushing as the basis of industrial policy and activity since 1960.[4]

The 1957 initiative in the direction of harmonic growth was swept away by the Greap Leap Forward of 1958–60, a succession of campaigns that attempted to capitalize on what Mao Tse-tung, among others, viewed as the boundless productive potential of China's masses. In industry, where the Leap is best remembered for its promotion of backyard iron smelting, central controls over funds, manpower, and materials were replaced by sweeping demands for local initiative in expanding industry. At the enterprise level, managers, technicians, and inspectors were shunted aside in favor of less conservative leaders who called for bold acceleration of production.

These pressures resulted in an interlude of decentralized rush growth in which concentration on quantity and neglect of quality were carried to new extremes. Plans were replaced by dreams, and these were reported upward as localities and enterprises vied to claim more incredible feats of "leaping forward." Developments in machine tools and ferrous metallurgy illustrate the events of this period.

Ambitious but possibly attainable targets for 1958 machine tool output were soon discarded in favor of impossibly high goals. In pursuing these new objectives, established units discarded normal quality standards, and production spilled from the factory sector into newly organized units with no tradition of workmanship or quality control. All this can be seen in table 3.1. Both the output gains for major plants and the claims of Kansu, Fukien, and other nonindustrial areas imply a drastic erosion of standards. The Talien Machine Tool Plant produced 191 lathes in August 1958, but claimed 471 units in the following month, with daily output reaching a peak of 55 lathes.[5] Abandonment of quality standards is evident from a variety of sources. Major plants in Shenyang and Shanghai used "simplified" or "native" parts, equipment, and designs to boost output. Unit value of products manufactured at the K'unming Machine Tool Plant plunged nearly 50 percent during 1957–58. One source states that 1958 output of 50,000 machine tools included 35,000 simplified items, implying that 1958 output of standard goods was far below the 1957 figure of 28,000 units. The same is probably true of 1959 and 1960, when output reportedly rose to 70,000 and 90,000 annual units.[6]

In ferrous metallurgy we again find erosion of quality and also a radical departure from initial plans, this time in the form of vast

TABLE 3.1
Machine Tool Output, 1957 and 1958

	1957 Output	1958 Target	1958 Output
National total	28,000[a]	—	50,000[a]
Provincial data			
Shanghai	4,390[a]	—	12,700[a]
Peking	1,900[a]	—	4,770[a]
Kansu	1,600[b]	—	5,000[b]
Fukien	334[a]	—	1,336[a]
Shansi	235[c]	2,770[c]	—
Kirin	38[a]	—	3,919[a]
Municipal data			
Nanking	720[d]	3,600[e]	—
Ch'angsha	434[f]	—	2,172[f]
Canton	65[g]	2,000–2,200[g]	—
Individual firms			
Shenyang #1 Machine Tool Plant	3,700[d]	8,000[b]	—
Talien Machine Tool Plant	1,210[h]	1,500[h]	—
Shenyang #3 Machine Tool Plant	1,040[d]	—	1,950[i]
Shanghai Machine Tool Plant	800[d]	1,400[j]	4,000+[j]

[a] Chen, *Statistics*, pp. 187, 200, 202, 205.
[b] JMJP, November 6, 1958, and January 7, 1960.
[c] U.S. Central Intelligence Agency, *Weekly Report on Communist China*, 18(1960):11.
[d] *Shin Chūgoku no kikai kōgyō* (Tokyo, 1960), p. 27.
[e] *Nan-ching jih-pao*, November 6, 1958.
[f] *Kung-jen jih-pao*, December 20, 1958, and January 19, 1959.
[g] *Kuang-chou jih-pao*, April 9, 1958.
[h] *Chung-kuo ch'ing-nien pao*, March 9, 1958.
[i] Annual rate based on eight months' output from JMJP, September 1, 1958.
[j] *Wen-hui pao* (Shanghai), January 1, 1959, and *Kung-jen jih-pao*, March 6, 1958.

multiplication of small-scale blast furnaces in the countryside. Following the lead of Mao Tse-tung's 1956 speech, the preliminary version of China's second five-year plan published later in that year envisioned a new balance between large and small plants and between advanced and backward regions.[7] These principles were applied to ferrous metallurgy in discussions that culminated in a decision to invest "a great deal more than before . . . on small projects that require comparatively small investment and little time to build." Work was to begin in 1958 on "medium and small-scale metallurgical plants" in Yunnan, Hunan, Shansi, Anhwei, and elsewhere; on "small iron smelting plants" in Kwangtung, Yunnan, Kansu, and Shensi; and on the Canton section of the Kwangtung #1 Iron and Steel Works.[8]

This modest program was swamped in the summer and autumn of 1958 by a tumultuous campaign to achieve universal participation in ferrous metallurgy—the famous backyard iron and steel furnaces. Although consolidation of the backyard smelters, most of which were hopelessly uneconomic, began almost immediately, prodigious amounts of materials and especially labor power were lavished on the iron and steel campaign. Apparently deceived by false reports of enormous increases in grain output, local authorities freely diverted rural labor to support the campaign to raise iron and steel output: Szechwan's Provincial Party Committee responded to a shortage of iron in Chungking by ordering nearby localities to increase the work force in transport by "another 100,000 people," while Peking authorities transferred manpower from irrigation projects to "strengthen the force in steel and coke loading and shipping."[9] Much of the output from these endeavors, however, was useless. A 1959 report by the Native Iron Utilization Inspection Group of the FMMB concluded that "not a single plant which does not use an alkaline, hot-blast iron furnace can profitably use native iron in its regular production" of machine castings, indicating that the product of small blast furnaces was more akin to iron ore than to refined metal.[10]

In terms of the model of skill formation outlined in the introduction, the weakness of the Great Leap was that existing skill potentials fell short of those required to complete the tasks attempted. An aroused political leadership supported innovation with unprecedented vigor, but skill deficiencies led to costly failures in both urban and rural industry. On the positive side, however, the Great Leap must be credited with initial experimentation along lines that later proved highly fruitful. It is in these hectic years that we first observe attempts to build rural industries with close ties to agriculture, large-scale training and consulting programs linking enterprises of widely differing technical levels, and a general effort to familiarize China's rural populace with the products and techniques of industry.

Industrial Policy since 1960

Despite possible long-term benefits, the immediate impact of the Great Leap on industry was strongly negative. Beginning in August 1958, "the Planning Commission and the central ministries. . . . dispensed with overall planning and simply made no estimates of how much coal, iron and transport would be needed."[11] This breakdown of normal planning and reporting procedures, coupled with an explosion of industrial resources due to the completion of major FFYP construction projects and a near-tripling of the industrial work force in 1958 alone, created urgent requirements for consolidation.[12] On top of this came the twin blows of Soviet technical withdrawal, which left key investment projects unfinished, and a series of disastrous harvests that signaled the need to increase industry's support for agriculture. The demand shifts resulting from these setbacks transformed an unavoidable adjustment process into a crisis in which industrial collapse became a genuine possibility.

Disruption of the statistical network and fears that factual reports would result in reprisals similar to those meted out to the cashiered defense minister P'eng Te-huai delayed recognition of the Leap's catastrophic consequences in both industry and agriculture. As the magnitude of these difficulties gradually became clear, specialists temporarily eclipsed by Mao Tse-tung's personal intervention in economic decision making gradually regained control over industrial administration. This group, whose supporters seem to have included such prominent men as Liu Shao-ch'i, Chou En-lai, Teng Hsiao-p'ing, Po I-po, Li Hsien-nien, Li Fu-ch'un, T'ao Chu, and Sun Yeh-fang, instituted a sweeping program of consolidation and reform. Their policies, which began to appear as early as 1959 and were forcefully applied from the start of 1961, are summarized in the famous and controversial "Seventy Articles Concerning Industrial Enterprises and Mines" distributed in September 1961.[13]

These directives ordered enterprises to draw up detailed information regarding capital stock, inventories, and production capacity, to curtail unauthorized construction, recruitment, and sales, and to develop systems for monitoring finances, resource consumption, labor productivity, cost, and quality—all signs of a new determination to exercise firm central control over industry. Emphasis on the "system of responsibility assumed by the factory superintendent under the leadership of the Party committee," the authority of specialist personnel over inspection, stock taking, and finance, and the provision that political study "should be cut down as far as possible" all indicated that party personnel and political activity were required to serve the needs of production, rather than vice versa.

In seeking a quick and flexible response to economic dangers, proponents of the "Seventy Articles" did not flinch from drastic measures, including a partial revival of free-market selection criteria unknown in Chinese industry since 1949. Unproductive resources were summarily dismissed from industry. Cultural Revolution sources have directed attention to the closing of small enterprises, especially ironworks, that diverted labor, materials, and funds from agriculture. But the cutbacks were not confined to small units. Thc Shih-ching-chan steel complex returned 40 percent of its 52,000 workers to agriculture during 1960–63. Shanghai Steel Plant's #1 blast furnace shop eliminated 56 percent of its labor requirements between 1959 and 1961. Shansi Machine Tool Works dismissed over 2,000 workers in July 1961. Dozens of units reported reduced employment, including some in key sectors such as Shanghai's chemical industry, which planned to raise output and profits by 15 percent during 1964-65 while reducing its overall work force by 10 to 15 percent.[14]

Peking now reversed its earlier emphasis on output maximization. The new orders stipulated that "products that are not up to standard shall not be allowed to leave the factory." This was echoed in the party journal *Red Flag*, which added that "products that fail to come up to the quality standard . . . should not be included in the output index."[15]

In contrast to earlier pleas for quality change, tough enforcement was now much in evidence; attempts by the Talien High Pressure Valve Works to attribute substandard output to the poor quality of the plant's machinery brought a curt rebuff from provincial and municipal inspectors, who uncovered design errors and ruled that unless the ministry's standards were met, output "would not be examined and accepted." Management finally promised to "adhere resolutely to the principle that accessories not conforming to standards should not be assembled, and final products not conforming with standards should not leave the factory."[16] Similar confrontations occurred throughout industry. Inspectors pulled no punches; at Shanghai, high waste rates in iron castings were "due to the incompetence of the technical management." Once again, products "which have not been inspected are not allowed to go out of the factory. This regulation is being strictly enforced." Some units were forced to suspend operation pending quality improvement.[17]

With customers now expected to scrutinize incoming shipments for quality defects, to "despatch . . . representatives to the relevant production factories where they would take care of the inspection of products about to be delivered," and even allowed to break relations with uncooperative suppliers, producers began to pay closer attention to the opinions and needs of purchasing organizations.[18] Visits to customers gave production personnel a vivid understanding of the need to meet demand conditions. Employees of one Shanghai mining equipment plant had never seen their products in operation; they were sent to the mines to observe at firsthand the damage and waste wrought by their own inferior workmanship. Within three years, successful reforms had catapulted this same enterprise into national prominence as winner of a cost and quality competition among producers of pneumatic tools.[19]

As monetary controls tightened, firms that had previously ignored financial criteria struggled to reduce costs and avoid the injunction that "except with special instructions . . . losing concerns . . . should stop operation." Large reductions in labor norms revealed the extent of latent productive capacity: Peking Sewing Machine Plant cut assembly time by 54 percent; Shenyang #2 Machine Tool Plant enforced successive cuts of 34 percent and 62 percent. Other units reported reductions in working capital, raw material consumption, and transport costs. As a result of the crackdown on waste, economic journals were filled with descriptions of falling costs and rising profits.[20]

Planners also renewed previously unsuccessful efforts to foster specialization and division of labor within the producer sector, especially in machine-building. Beginning in 1963, a barrage of articles extolled the cost advantages of specialized hardware production and subcontracting arrangements for machine parts; news media carried testimonials from skeptical executives who now supported interenterprise cooperation.[21]

With the planning system in disarray after a three-year lapse in central control, new directives could not be enforced immediately. Reinstatement of qualified managers was often a necessary preliminary; at Nanking's large Yung-li-ning Chemical Works, for example,

> the deputy head of the education section, who has special experiences in the control of technical materials and knows several foreign languages . . . is now, based on his special knowledge and the needs of technical work developments, transferred back to the control of technical materials.[22]

Lower-level opposition to the reversal of Great Leap initiatives may explain the delayed response of some units; T'aiyuan Chemical Works did not begin efforts to eliminate financial losses until late in 1962; quality upgrading at Shenyang #1 Machine Tool Plant and financial control at Peking Boiler Works began only in 1963.[23]

During the course of the early 1960s, a revitalized leadership group in Peking used these measures to reverse industry's tendency toward undisciplined expansion. The transition from rushing toward harmonic growth envisioned in the 1957 reform proposals was gradually accomplished as planners and managerial personnel at all levels began to devote less attention to raising volume alone and focused more on meeting current needs whose urgency, under near-famine conditions, was obvious to all.[24]

The initial phase of reform was marked by forceful reassertion of central prerogatives as Peking struggled to revive the framework of central planning and to channel resources into grain production. But with industry responding to the new policies and grain production improving, the center started to relax its controls as early as 1962 and 1963. Rural industry, much of which was shut down in 1961, began a vigorous expansion that continues today.[25] In the sphere of science policy, professional associations and their members gained greater autonomy, and industrial enterprises were encouraged to develop programs of applied research based on the combined skills of technical specialists and ordinary workers.[26] Provinces and localities gradually assumed control of industrial planning, supervision, and supply tasks formerly performed by central ministries and national planning agencies.[27]

In chapter 5, we will consider the administrative and organizational changes underlying these policies. For the present, it is essential to emphasize the broad continuity in economic policy that has existed since the early 1960s. Without denying the reality of periodic conflicts and shifts, stability rather than oscillation appears as the chief characteristic of the post-1960 policy environment within the industrial sector. The center has continued its stress on harmonic growth and agricultural support efforts while allowing gradual extension of regional, local, and enterprise responsibility largely unconnected with, and in fact antedating, the Cultural Revolution of 1966–68.

In industry, the Cultural Revolution witnessed radical efforts to overthrow so-called bourgeois authorities and their systems of planning, accounting, and control at both the central and factory levels. The would-be revolutionaries met with forceful resistance at all levels of industry. Perhaps because the anarchic tendencies of the insurgents stirred memories of the Great Leap and its aftermath, government and party authorities applied continuous pressure to limit the extent of disruption and maintain some semblance of industrial normality.

From December 1966, when youthful Red Guards and other protest groups were permitted to enter factories, the Central Committee of the Communist Party, *People's Daily*, and leadership groups in the provinces and major cities issued directives such as the following:

December 1966: "Stick to the eight-hour day, observe labor discipline and fulfill the production norms."

January 1967: "The revolutionary rebels in banks . . . must exercise strict supervision over the expenditures of all . . . units."

February 1967: Outsiders are barred from "The Industrial System for National Defense," national commissions for science, planning, economy and construction, the finance ministry, banks, and major new organs.

March 1967: "Exert . . . utmost efforts to fulfill the State's production plan and construction plan. . . . The majority of cadres of all factories and mining enterprises are good and relatively good. . . . The People's Liberation Army must vigorously . . . support industrial production."[28]

Premier Chou En-lai summed up what was probably the majority view in a reported statement that "production and the service trades cannot be suspended. Otherwise, what shall we eat?"[29]

These and similar exhortations did not prevent sporadic disruptions of production and displacement of planners, managers, accountants, engineers, and technicians, but the damage was temporary and quick repaired. Provincial reports indicate that after falling by 14 percent between 1966 and 1968, overall industrial output in 1969 already surpassed the 1966 peak by 14 percent.[30] As industrial routine was reestablished, it was already clear by 1970 that the demise of Liu Shao-ch'i, Teng Hsiao-p'ing, and other individuals associated with industrial reform efforts had left the policies themselves largely unscathed.

Since the growing complexity of industrial technology makes industry increasingly reliant on the services of expert personnel, it is not surprising that reinstatement of disgraced specialists began as early as

1967. As a subsequent editorial entitled "Bring Back the Industrial Experts" put it: "Without the engineers and technicians taking part" in design, trial manufacture, research, and other exacting activities, "the level of technical . . . and productive management . . . cannot be heightened."[31] Renewed emphasis on expertise was increasingly evident at the microeconomic level. The Communist party committee of Talien's Steel Mill found that "the essential management personnel were too much reduced" during the Cultural Revolution and solved this problem by increasing the number of professional managers and returning worker-managers to production jobs. Fushun's Coal Research Institute offered special encouragement to intellectuals "trained in the old schools" before 1949.[32]

Though not without substance, charges that economic planners had "placed profit in command" of industrial activity failed to alter the prevailing emphasis on financial criteria; 1970 discussions concluded that "profits are an important measure of efficiency and cost accounting and could not be ignored."[33] Even the initially successful attack on material incentives was undermined during the early 1970s and then reversed in 1977 as the Hua-Teng leadership revived interest in bonuses and piece rates.[34]

If the Cultural Revolution failed to upset the harmonic growth policies adopted during the early 1960s, the same is true of the interlude of political instability and economic stagnation that surrounded the deaths of Mao Tse-tung and Chou En-lai. This period, stretching roughly from 1974 to early 1977, saw no real challenge to past policies, but rather an absence of policy as confusion and uncertainty at the top created a climate of laxity in which provinces, localities, and even individuals managed to evade responsibilities or revise tasks to suit their own interests. The problem facing the incoming Hua-Teng administration in late 1976 and early 1977 was the restoration of discipline rather than of policy, and the new leadership seemed to encounter little difficulty in reinstituting the familiar industrial priorities favoring quality, balance, and complementarity.

Industrial Performance since 1957

Industrial growth has continued since 1957, but at a somewhat less rapid pace than was achieved between 1949 and 1957. Fluctuations in output quality make it difficult to measure the extent of the industrial boom of 1958–60 or the subsequent depression. Even at the nadir of China's economic fortunes, however, 1961 industrial output surpassed the 1957 level (see table 4.1); for producer industries the margin was quite large. Industry resumed its advance after 1962, and by 1965, producer output was approximately three times the 1957 level (see table 4.4). During the ensuing decade, which includes the disruptive Cultural Revolution years, the pace of expansion tapered off somewhat, but with annual increments regularly exceeding 10 percent, estimated 1975 output volume in China's producer industries was about three times the 1965 total and over ten times the level of 1957.

To assess the impact of new industrial policies on performance in the producer sector, we must look beyond aggregate measures of growth and examine changes in the composition of output. Given the volume of new plants entering production after 1957, continued output growth is not surprising. Nor is it impressive to discover that newly completed plants designed to produce trucks, electric power, or steel contributed to major output increases planned for these sectors. What is striking is the ability of the producer sector to initiate large-scale production of commodities whose importance was not forseen during the 1950s, and for which Soviet technical and economic assistance made little or no provision. Rapid expansion of China's petroleum and chemical fertilizer industries since 1960 provides important examples of unplanned structural change that could not have occurred without the shift from rushing to harmonic growth policies described above.

During the 1950s, China's petroleum industry remained small and weak, with 1957 output of crude oil falling well below the FFYP target of two million tons (see table 2.1). With known oil reserves spread across remote areas of China's northwest, development plans were modest as coal dominated overall energy supplies and the USSR supplied the bulk of China's small petroleum requirements.

China produced no equipment for extracting or refining petroleum before 1949. Under the FFYP, work was begun on a major Soviet-aided installation at Lanchow whose annual output was expected to equip new plants with the capacity to produce 180,000 tons of refined oil and 75,000 tons of ammonia each year. At the same time, a smaller petroleum machinery plant was begun at Paochi, Shensi.[35] While the

Lanchow plant was under construction, output of petroleum equipment lagged behind the growth of other engineering sectors. In 1957, domestic suppliers provided only 20 percent of new machinery for extracting crude oil; their share of new refinery equipment was certainly much lower.[36] During the Great Leap, some of these suppliers were diverted to new assignments, while others devoted their efforts to an abortive program of building small-scale oil refineries. As a result, Chinese sources complained that crude oil production was delayed by parts shortages even before the withdrawal of Soviet advisers.[37]

The break with the Soviet Union forced China to adopt a strategy of self-reliance for her growing civilian and military petroleum requirements. Domestic engineering firms were suddenly called upon to supply not just parts, but whole sets of equipment for extracting, transporting, and refining crude oil. Fortunately for the Chinese, the withdrawal of Soviet technical aid coincided with the discovery of the large Ta-ch'ing oil field in the northeastern province of Heilungkiang. A succession of additional discoveries in Shantung, Hopei, and Kwangtung provinces created an opportunity for vastly enlarged petroleum output in the vicinity of major industrial centers, but exploitation of these newly discovered resources was limited by the weak state of China's petroleum equipment industry.

The remarkable response of domestic equipment suppliers can be seen from the swift rise of crude oil production recorded in table 3.2. Drilling, extracting, and refining capacity increased by a factor of approximately 15 between 1962 and 1977, allowing China to dispense with petroleum imports during the mid-1960s, raise the share of oil in domestic energy consumption from about 5 percent to nearly 25 percent, and to enter world petroleum markets as a minor exporter beginning in 1973.[38]

Newly imported facilities contributed only marginally to the opening of new oil fields, refineries, pipelines, and port facilities and the expansion of older units. China has purchased several refinery plants abroad, but their combined capacity accounts for only a tiny fraction of the post-1960 output surge. Only the recent development of offshore drilling operations in the Pohai Gulf region shows major dependence on equipment imports.[39] Although the USSR and Romania may have continued to supply China with some items of petroleum machinery after 1960, there can be no doubt that the bulk of the equipment and

TABLE 3.2
Output of Crude Oil and Chemical Fertilizer, 1949–77
(in million tons)

Year	Crude Oil	Chemical Fertilizer[a]
1949	0.1	--
1952	0.4	0.2
1957	1.4	0.8
1962	5.7	2.8
1963	6.4	3.8
1964	8.6	5.8
1965	11.0	7.6
1970	28.2	14.0
1971	36.7	16.8
1972	43.1	19.8
1973	54.8	24.8
1974	65.8	24.9
1975	74.3	27.9
1976	83.6	—
1977	90.3[b]	36.8[c]

Source: Except as noted, U.S. Central Intelligence Agency, *China: Economic Indicators*, pp. 20, 22.

[a] Estimated fertilizer output based on standard units of 20 percent nitrogen, 18.7 percent phosphoric acid, or 40 percent potassium oxide.

[b] Based on a preliminary estimate showing 8 percent growth during 1976–77 (FBIS, December 27, 1977, E9).

[c] Based on an increase of 31.9 percent during 1975–77 reported in *The China Business Review* 5.1(1978):43.

supplies needed to expand petroleum output from less than ten million tons annually during the early 1960s to over ninety million tons in 1977 has come from domestic suppliers.

The Soviet-aided plant at Lanchow has provided some of this equipment. Construction of this facility, begun about 1956, took many years. In mid-1963, the plant was described as hurrying toward the start of production, but its management was "relatively chaotic" as late as December 1962, and reported completion of only 23 percent of annual construction tasks during the first five months of 1963 suggests little improvement. The Lanchow plant is ignored in several later descriptions of the petroleum equipment industry; only in 1976 is it mentioned as occupying "an important position in the national economy."[40]

The belated completion and small capacity of the Lanchow plant and the absence of information about the Paochi project suggest that much of the equipment supplied to the petroleum sector after 1960 came from units originally assigned to other tasks. Medium- and small-scale Shanghai plants, including the Ta-lung Machine Works described in chapter 1, have emerged as prominent suppliers of petroleum equipment. The nucleus of Shanghai's supply network is the Shanghai Petroleum Machinery Parts Company, a conglomerate formed in 1955 by merging a number of plants that had formerly manufactured parts for textile and printing machinery. It was these Shanghai firms that produced China's first refinery equipment in 1963. By 1964, the Shanghai consortium also had "the capability to manufacture complete sets of drills and various kinds of drill bits, hoist, cramp, pump, sleeve head and anti-gushing devices and other drilling and mining equipment."[41]

Other regions have also contributed to the growth of petroleum equipment manufacture. Chinese materials mention newly completed plants and also older units such as the Lanchow General Machinery Factory, originally built as an arsenal by the nineteenth-century official Tso Tsung-t'ang and "a number of heavy machinery factories and boiler plants which have reorganized their production, entered the petroleum equipment industry, and now produce large quantities of petroleum equipment."[42] In terms of quality and innovation, however, the Shanghai plants, whose advanced techniques provide "a tremendous contrast" with methods used elsewhere, continue to occupy a leading position.[43]

Similar developments occurred in chemical fertilizers. FFYP output of fertilizers expanded rapidly from a tiny base (table 2.1) under a rush growth policy that paid little heed to production costs, industrial safety, or to balancing the mix of products with agricultural nutrient requirements.[44] During the Great Leap, China pursued a dual policy of experimenting with domestically equipped small plants while awaiting the completion of large Soviet-aided facilities. As in petroleum, simultaneous failure of many small-scale attempts and suspension of Soviet shipments and advice at large projects threw fertilizer plans into confusion. With unfinished plants in disarray, quality problems forcing small plants to shut down, and revised economic plans demanding unprecedented emphasis on agricultural support efforts, 1961 found the chemical industry in a weak position.[45]

The fertilizer sector has rebounded from these difficulties and raised output from an estimated three million tons in 1962 to ten times that figure in 1977 (see table 3.2). Although the desire to exploit scale economies and the qualitative limitations of small-plant products have turned the Chinese toward foreign equipment suppliers for the current wave of fertilizer expansion, the output expansion of the 1960s and early 1970s was based on domestic equipment, with imports providing only a small fraction of new capacity.[46]

The discovery that despite initial setbacks, small plants can provide satisfactory fertilizers at reasonable cost has greatly eased China's fertilizer supply situation. Small plants turned out over two-thirds of incremental fertilizer output between 1960 and 1975, and unlike large-scale plants, their equipment can be produced in quantity by Chinese manufacturers.[47]

As with the petroleum industry, small- and medium-sized plants located in older industrial centers have emerged as leading equipment suppliers for the fertilizer industry. Domestic fertilizer equipment first appeared in quantity in 1962; Shanghai led the way, supplying one major plant alone with 25,000 tons of equipment, or 2.5 times the planned annual output from the Lanchow Petroleum and Chemical Equipment Plant.[48] While expanding output volume, Shanghai firms enlarged their product line by turning out China's first equipment for urea manufacture in 1965. Manufacture of equipment for fertilizer plants has spread to Shenyang, Peking, Hupei, Hunan, Kansu, Honan, Kiangsu, and other regions, but the core of the equipment industry remains in Shanghai, where a group of over four hundred factories supplied three hundred sets of equipment for synthetic ammonia plants between 1970 and 1972.[49] Shanghai's contribution is illustrated by the history of the first fertilizer plant in remote Chinghai province, commissioned in 1966:

> Some of the equipment of the new plant was manufactured by Tsinghai Province's developing machine building industry. The rest came from Shanghai. Shanghai also trained technical staff for the plant and provided technicians to help install the machinery.[50]

Petroleum and fertilizer are by no means the only industries that have been created or massively enlarged since 1960. The list of new sectors includes electronics, computers, chemical fibers, plastics, and a wide range of aerospace, nuclear, and other military-linked industries. While recent development in these sectors has benefited from the presence of equipment and techniques imported during the 1950s, the unplanned cutoff of Soviet technical aid and the subsequent and equally unplanned demand shifts toward agriculture and military preparedness have forced China's domestic producer industries to display great flexibility and inventiveness to overcome a new generation of economic problems. In engineering, the burden on domestic suppliers is reflected in the sharp post-1960 decline in the share of imports in total machinery supplies, a trend that even the recent surge of foreign purchases has failed to reverse (see tables 4.11 and 4.12).

As new industries emerged, established sectors built up an impressive record of qualitative improvement along with quantitative growth. The chemical industry raised both the volume and variety of manufactured farm inputs; its growing sophistication can be seen in its mastery of the complex techniques used for mass production of contraceptive pills.[51] In engineering, increases in the scale of domestic products shown in table 3.3 have appeared alongside rapid improvements in the quality and variety of domestic output. Machine tool producers have developed new models incorporating multiple spindles, numerical controls, and other advanced techniques. Steel plants can now be equipped with domestically manufactured basic oxygen furnaces. Design improvements are reported at many plants, including some of the new plants constructed during the 1950s. Successive cost reductions have lowered machinery prices by more than 40 percent compared with the FFYP period.[52] Information for diesel engines compiled in table 3.4, which appears typical of overall trends, shows that current products are both lighter and cheaper than engines manufactured by advanced producers during the mid-1950s.

Visitor accounts substantiate Chinese reports of qualitative development. While noting that Chinese technological sophistication cannot match the achievements of comparable industries in North America, Europe, and Japan, foreign specialists credit the Chinese with qualitative achievements far beyond the results of the 1950s. Comments by American machine tool specialists may be cited as representative of recent reports:

> Internal grinders made in Wuhsi operate well. . . . the lathes are quite old and speeds and feeds are not high. We saw several N/C 3-axis machines. . . . of very good construction. . . . Most of the machine tools [in the plants visited] are Chinese. . . . the tooling is

> well-designed; and although they cannot produce with the dynamic characteristics of U.S. equipment, their efficiency is high. . . . considering the age of the machines, a phenomenal amount of production is being achieved. . . . The appearance is that of Japan in 1959–1960 when she began her big push in the machine tool business.[53]

TABLE 3.3
Maximum Capacity of Chinese Machinery Products, 1955–77

Item (unit)	1952	1955–58	1964–66	1970s
Hydroelectric generator (kw)	3,000[a]	72,500[b]	100,000[c]	300,000[d]
Thermal generator (kw)	--	25,000[b]	100,000[c]	300,000[e]
Electric motor (kw)	940[a]	3,430[f]	—	6,300[g]
Transformer (kva)	15,000[a]	40,500[f]	220,000[c]	330,000[g]
Drilling rig (m)	500[a]	1,000[a]	3,200[h]	—
Power shovel (cu m)	--	1[a]	—	8.25[i]
Ocean freighter (dwt)	—	5,000[j]	10,000[c]	50,000[k]
Diesel engine (hp)	—	600[j]	8,820[m]	18,000[n]

[a] WKKT, p. 80.
[b] SCMP 1489(1957):16–17.
[c] Cheng, *Machine-building*, p. 134.
[d] BBC W758(1974):A15.
[e] Vaclav Smil and Kim Woodard, "Perspectives on Energy in the People's Republic of China," *Annual Review of Energy 1977* 2:307–42.
[f] ECMM 105(1957):26.
[g] SCMP 4814(1971):180–81.
[h] Hu, "Petroleum Equipment Industry," p. 15.
[i] JeNelle Matheson, *Construction Equipment: A Market Assessment for the People's Republic of China* (Washington, D.C., 1976), p. 17.
[j] *Ten Great Years*, p. 105.
[k] BBC W904(1976):A6.
[m] JPRS 35070(1966):23.
[n] BBC W879(1976):A7.

Along with these qualitative achievements by advanced firms has come a process of industrial deepening that has raised standards throughout the industrial hierarchy and also greatly expanded the number and spatial distribution of industrial enterprises. Rising standards, a topic discussed in the next chapter, are most clearly visible in the spread of new machinery models from advanced plants to lesser enterprises at the provincial, county, and even commune levels.

The spread of medium- and small-scale producer factories to small cities and rural areas throughout China is another feature of industrial deepening that has transformed industrialization from an urban to a truly national phenomenon.[54] As we have seen, the initial impetus for expanding small industry came at the end of the FFYP; premature expansion during the Great Leap led to waste and confusion, and many

TABLE 3.4
Chinese Diesel Engines, 1956–57 and 1975

Plant and Location	Horse power	Engine Weight kg	Engine Weight kg/hp	Production Cost (in yuan) per Unit	Production Cost (in yuan) per hp
A. Data for 1956–57					
Chinan (Shantung) Plant	—	—	—	—	84[a]
Shanghai Diesel Plant	—	—	—	—	89[a]
Wusih Diesel Plant (Kiangsu)	40[b]	1,202[b]	30[b]	—	91[a]
Weifang (Shantung) Plant	10[b]	260[b]	26[b]	—	117[a]
Nanch'ang (Kiangsi) Plant[a]	12	600	50	—	—
	16	580	36	—	—
Tientsin Internal Combustion Engine Plant	small	—	60[b]	—	—
Unspecified	300[c]	1,300[c]	4.3[c]	—	—
Unspecified					
Past results	—	—	—	—	200+[d]
Present (1956)	—	—	—	—	150-[d]
Advanced units (1956)	—	—	—	—	110[d]
B. Data for 1975					
Large Plants					
Peking Internal Combustion Engine Plant	45–65	—	—	3,200–4,000	60–70
Old model	55	550	10	—	—
New model	60	340	5.7	—	—
Wusih Diesel Plant (Kiangsu)	12	130	10.8	—	—
Medium and Small Plants					
T'aiyuan (Shansi)	10	126	12.6	—	—
Anyang (Honan)	12	130	10.8	800[e]	67
Hsin-hsiang #2 (Honan)	12	150	12.5	700[e]	58
Tzu-ch'i (Chekiang)	3	39	13	—	—
Wusih County Plant (Kiangsu)	4	40	10	—	—
Ch'angchou (Kiangsu)	12	130	10.8	—	—
Shanghai Power Machinery Plant	35	310	8.8	—	—
Shanghai Ma-lu Commune Plant	3.5	38–42	11.4[f]	550	157

Sources: 1975 data from Rural Small-Scale Industry Delegation, trip notes.

[a] *Chūgoku shiryō geppō* 114(1957):17, 42.

[b] Wang Hsin-min, "Opinions on Developing Our Diesel and Coal-Gas Engine Industry," CHKY 5(1957):5.

[c] JMJP, October 30, 1956.

[d] JMJP, May 13, 1956.

[e] Prices paid by purchasers. Other prices appear to be those received by producers.

[f] Midpoint of data range.

small plants were shut down during the retrenchment of 1960–62. But as agricultural conditions stabilized and the opportunity cost of rural industrial ventures declined, official policy once again began to encourage local industrial development.

The volume of resources devoted to local industry has expanded steadily since about 1963. Careful attention to pilot projects, cost reduction, and quality control has brought greatly improved results. Many small enterprises now operate profitably with selling prices below those received by major enterprises during the FFYP years.[55]

Continued investment in small- and medium-sized plants has pushed industry down to the level of China's two-thousand-odd counties, most of which are now active in one or more branches of the producer sector. In 1957, it was hoped that each province could have its own agricultural machinery plant. In 1978, there are over forty-three hundred plants that manufacture and repair farm machinery. Each province manufactures farm machinery, tractors, and power equipment. Nearly all of the two-thousand-odd counties manufacture and repair farm machinery, 80 percent possess small cement plants, 55 percent operate coal mines, 50 percent manufacture chemical fertilizers, and over half engage in a whole range of producer enterprises: machinery, fertilizer, cement, iron and steel, and coal mining.[56] Further deepening can be seen in the recent steep rise in industrial activity within China's fifty thousand rural communes, many of which now operate small-scale hydropower stations as well as workshops for repairing and manufacturing farm equipment.[57]

Table 3.5 gives an idea of the overall size of small-scale industry, a category that consists primarily of plants operated at the county level and below. Estimates for 1972 show small plants occupying a dominant position in the fertilizer, cement, and farm machinery sectors, and small-scale output in the so-called five small industries—the small-plant component of the machinery, cement, iron and steel, chemical, fertilizer, and energy (coal and hydropower) sectors—accounting for approximately 6 percent and 8 percent of gross output value for all industry and for the producer sector respectively.

Despite these modest output shares, the expansion of small- and medium-sized producer enterprises in small cities and rural areas has added a new dimension to China's industrial economy. Small plants provide a source of industrial expansion that economizes on several

TABLE 3.5
Estimated Share of the "Five Small Industries" in Aggregate Factory Output for 1972 (in billion 1952 yuan)

Product or Sector	Small-scale Share (in percentage)	Gross Value of Factory Output	
		Total[a]	Small-scale
Chemical fertilizer	60[b]	3.643	2.186
Building materials	50[c]	6.480	3.240
Farm machinery	67[e]	13.009[d]	8.716
Energy			
Electric power	6[f]	6.589	0.395
Coal	28[g]	4.834	1.353
Iron and steel	18[h]	22.108	3.979
Total for five industries	35.1	56.663	19.869
Producer sector	7.5	263.826	19.869
Total factory output	6.3	312.991	19.869

[a] Figures in this column are from Rawski, "Industrial Performance," in *Quantitative Measures*, tables 21, 27, 34, and 37.

[b] Calculated from Robert M. Field, "Civilian Industrial Production in the People's Republic of China: 1949–74," in *China: A Reassessment of the Economy* (Washington, D.C., 1975), p. 166, on the basis of tonnage.

[c] Small plant share of 1974 cement output as estimated by Ian H. McFarlane, "Construction Trends in China, 1949–74," in *China: A Reassessment*, p. 315.

[d] Agricultural machinery accounted for 6 to 7 percent of 1956 machinery output (Chao, *Hsin Chung-kuo ti kung-yeh*, p. 43). This share is assumed to have reached 15 percent by 1972. Overall machinery output from Rawski, "Industrial Performance," in *Quantitative Measures*, table 7.

[e] 1966 figure cited by Carl Riskin, "Small Industry and the Chinese Model of Development," *China Quarterly* 46(1971):271.

[f] Small plants account for 20 percent of hydropower capacity (*Peking Review* 21 [1975]:30–31), which in turn furnishes an estimated 28 percent of aggregate generating capacity (Thomas G. Rawski, "The Role of China in the World Energy Situation" [unpublished, 1973], p. 27). The output share of small plants may be generously estimated at 20 × .28, or about 6 percent.

[g] 1973 figure from BBC, W803(1974):A15.

[h] Thomas G. Rawski, *Industrialization, Technology and Employment in the People's Republic of China* (Washington, D.C., 1978), p. 122.

scarce resources: foreign exchange, highly skilled technicians, long-distance rail and truck transport, and central government financing. Rural industrialization provides a constructive outlet for regional pride and allows localities to compensate for some of the errors and oversights of a centrally directed system of economic planning. With their agricultural orientation and strong local ties, small plants have forged new bonds of integration and cooperation between farm and factory. They have brought industrial products, techniques, and skills to the heart of the farm economy, moving China's vast agricultural population toward the mainstream of an industrialization process that is now nearly a century old.

Sources of Innovative Capacity

By 1965, China's economy had left crisis behind. Industry's new ability to break technological bottlenecks by providing appropriate producer goods to agriculture, petroleum, chemicals, defense, and other sectors was the key to reversing a dangerous economic situation. Industry's responsiveness to the new and unanticipated demand patterns that emerged in the wake of the Great Leap Forward and the Sino-Soviet rift provides concrete evidence that the policy shift from rushing toward harmonic growth was widely implemented throughout the producer sector. Large-scale manufacture of equipment for the petroleum and chemical fertilizer industries, formation of manufacturing and repair networks for farm machinery, and many other achievements of the 1960s and 1970s could never have occurred unless thousands of factories and millions of employees devoted far more energy to technical improvements and cooperative efforts than had been expended during the FFYP years and the Great Leap Forward.

After 1960, the process of technological change veered back toward the pattern of incremental, skill-based improvement engineering familiar from our study of the prewar decades. Stripped of its comfortable reliance on Soviet assistance and the passage of time to overcome technical difficulties, industry had no option but to mobilize internal resources to meet the requirements of a new economic situation. The subsequent path of China's economy reflects the success of this effort. Reliance on existing resources to reshape domestic production functions in the producer industries and the prominence of inherited enterprises and prewar industrial centers in the solution of technological problems point toward our initial model of skill formation as a vehicle for understanding the forces responsible for China's recent industrial progress.

The analytic framework developed in the introduction identifies resource accumulation, incentive, and experience as probable causes of innovation. Since incentives do not vary spatially and investment policy has discriminated against older industrial centers, experience and skill accumulation offer the most likely explanation of the superior innovative performance of inherited industrial units.

Resource accumulation certainly improved industry's technical capabilities after 1957. Completion of major investment projects brought modern Soviet equipment and techniques into a capital stock formerly dominated by facilities of prewar vintage. The geographic distribution of new investment, however, was heavily skewed in favor of northeast, central, and northwest China. Available data on the provincial breakdown of industrial investment compiled in table 3.6 show how little was allocated to relatively developed coastal areas (except Liaoning) in contrast to the large sums poured into interior regions.

Neglect of Shanghai, which contributed nearly 20 yuan to the state budget for each yuan of investment funds received, was a most conspicuous aspect of the FFYP investment policy. Shanghai produced 19 percent of overall industrial output and 28 percent of machinery output in 1957, but received a mere 2.5 percent of the FFYP investment funds, a level surpassed by at least ten provinces.[58] Only two of approximately two hundred Soviet-aided investment projects were assigned to Shanghai; the three northeastern provinces of Liaoning, Kirin, and Heilungkiang received sixty-eight.[59]

Shanghai's low investment priority was shared by other centers of prewar industry. Tientsin, second only to Shanghai as an early industrial base, received no Soviet-aid projects; despite the massive scale of the FFYP investment, a 1957 report complained that only 7 percent of the city's machine tools had been installed since 1952.[60] Recommendations by Mao Tse-tung and others that coastal industry not be neglected brought some added investment to older centers, but not much; Shanghai's share of national investment rose from 2.5 percent during 1953–57 to 4.1 percent and 4.4 percent in the following two years.[61]

In the case of Shanghai, this low investment policy continued after the Great Leap. In 1961, Deputy Mayor Ts'ao Ti-ch'iu reported that economic readjustments "consisted mainly in shortening the front of capital construction." Ts'ao's list of economic tasks for 1962 makes no mention of investment activities, and his report of December 1965 notes

TABLE 3.6
National and Regional Investment Data, 1953—57
(in million yuan)

Category or Region	1957 Share[a] in Industrial Gross Output (in percentage)	Investment Outlay, 1953–57		Average Industrial Project Size
		Overall	Industry	
National total	100.0	55,000[k]	25,030[k]	—
Soviet aid projects	—	—	11,000[m]	70.512[m]
Support projects	—	—	1,800[m]	12.587[m]
Provincial data				
Shanghai	19.5	1,371[a]	500+[b]	0.200[b]
Liaoning	17.2	7,770[a]	—	—
Shantung	5.1	—	450+[i]	0.960[i]
Kwangtung	4.0	1,438[a]	550[d]	0.835[j]
Kirin	3.3	2,150[a]	1,716[h]	—
Chekiang	3.0	—	276[e]	—
Hupei	2.5	2,210[a]	802[c]	—
Hunan	2.1	1,217[a]	350+[f]	—
Honan	1.9	2,590[a]	654[g]	—

[a] Lardy, "Centralization and Decentralization," pp. 31, 40. Total 1957 industrial gross output (excluding handicrafts) was 65.02 billion 1952 yuan.

[b] *Kuang-ming jih-pao*, September 24, 1957. Average project outlay is for 600 to 700 projects undertaken in 1956.

[c] *Hu-pei jih-pao*, December 31, 1957, reported that 36.3 percent of the province's FFYP investments had gone to industry.

[d] *Wen-hui pao* (Hong Kong), October 13, 1957.

[e] Data for 1949–57, ibid., September 19, 1957.

[f] *Hsin Hu-nan pao*, September 30, 1957.

[g] Figure for 1953–56 reported in JMJP, March 31, 1957.

[h] Derived by applying the 79.8 percent share of industry in total 1953–56 investment reported in *Chi-lin jih-pao*, August 9, 1957.

[i] *Ta-chung jih-pao*, September 30, 1956; data refer to 1952–56.

[j] 177 million yuan were to be expended on 212 major units in 1957 (*Ta-kung pao* [Hong Kong], July 9, 1957).

[k] *Ten Great Years*, p. 57.

[m] *First Five-Year Plan*, p. 39. These are planned outlays.

that "no big industrial construction and expansion projects were undertaken in Shanghai over the past two years; in most cases, technological transformation was effected on the original foundation."[62] Further extension of this trend can be seen from a retrospective analysis indicating that Shanghai, which still accounts for 15 percent of overall industrial output (1975 data), received only 3.4 percent of overall state investment between 1950 and 1976.[63]

The distribution of other newly available resources did not offset the disadvantage that investment policies imposed upon Shanghai and other older centers. Graduates of China's expanding educational establishment, who swelled the ranks of technical personnel in industry and commerce by 100 percent between 1957 and 1961, were probably distributed in the same way as investment funds, with the majority claimed by the high-priority Soviet-aid projects.[64] Only the growth of research institutes, about one-tenth of which are located in Shanghai, might be said to have favored older bases rather than the newly developing industrial centers in the northeast, central, and northwest regions of the nation.[65]

Changing incentives, a factor discussed at length in chapter 5, also contributed to the shift from rushing to harmonic growth. We have already stressed the burden that poor harvests and Soviet withdrawal placed on the producer sector. The nature of China's economic crisis and the need for a wide-ranging innovative response were clearly understood in Peking, and economic leaders pushed hard to communicate the tenseness of the situation and the urgency of new priorities and requirements throughout industry.

As a result of shifting objectives, which can be assumed to have affected all producers in a similar manner, and increases in productive resources, which were not equally distributed, China's producer sector entered the 1960s with two quite distinct types of enterprises: recipients of major FFYP investment outlays and shipments of equipment from the USSR and Eastern Europe, including some firms with pre-1949 histories of Japanese ownership or management, and older, smaller units that form the legacy of prewar industrial advance in the private sector and typically received only minor infusions of imported equipment and technical aid between 1949 and 1960.

The contrasting performance of these two groups of firms since 1960, a period in which economic difficulties, unplanned demand shifts, and isolation forced Chinese industry into ambitious efforts to improve quality, variety, and manufacturing techniques, provides a clear-cut test of the relative importance of modern equipment and of industrial experience in determining innovative capacity in the producer sector. With performance now judged by the harmonic criterion of how well current output meets immediate economic needs rather than by its sheer volume, older plants clustered in Shanghai, Tientsin, and other centers of China's prewar industrial development, have established a strong leadership position as the cutting edge of Chinese technical advance. This can be seen with particular clarity in engineering and, more generally, in Shanghai's preeminent technological role in a wide range of industries.

Shanghai's Ta-lung Machinery Works, whose early history is described in chapter 1, typifies the innovative success of established Shanghai firms. After producing a variety of equipment during 1949–54, Ta-lung was asked in 1955 to specialize in producing formerly imported petroleum equipment. This shift, supported by a modest investment grant of three million yuan, transformed Ta-lung into Shanghai's largest producer of petroleum equipment. Further funds were used in 1958 to convert the plant into a manufacturer of chemical fertilizer equipment.

Since 1960, Ta-lung has supplied both the petroleum and fertilizer industries, experimented with advanced techniques for metallurgy and compressors, manufactured equipment for synthesizing diamonds, and continued its role as a job shop supplying items that customers cannot procure elsewhere. As of 1971, employment stood at forty-three hundred workers, with total output reportedly twenty-three times the 1949 level. As in the past, much of the firm's fixed capital is self-supplied.[66]

Old or self-supplied equipment is a common feature of long-established plants. Tientsin "has raised its own production capacity mainly through transforming the enterprises established before liberation." In Shanghai, "much of the existing equipment . . . is outworn and backward" so that "technical reform was not primarily achieved by building new plants or adding whole sets of new equipment, but by tapping production potentials and by innovation and renovation."[67] These claims are confirmed by accounts of skeptical outsiders who assumed that Shanghai's achievements stemmed from a superior equipment base. A Wuhan plant assigned to produce diesel engines responded by demanding several million yuan worth of machinery and several hundred skilled workers and technicians. Instead, some of the Wuhan personnel were sent

> to visit the Ch'eng-fu Power Machinery Plant of Shanghai, where they discovered that most of their machine tools were old and much specialized equipment was made by workers in the plant. The conditions at the Shanghai plant were not any better than at the Wuhan plant, but the production of diesel engines at the former was

progressing rapidly. They also noticed that the Shanghai plant had all the answers to the difficulties bothering them.[68]

Visiting Shanghai to obtain technical information is a recurrent theme in Chinese news reports of the past decade. Peking workers organized groups to "learn from the advanced and catch up with Shanghai"; "factories and enterprises of Wu-han . . . study the advanced experiences of Shanghai and other areas." During the first half of 1965 alone, over fifteen thousand visited the metropolis, which also dispatched over one thousand consultants to help other units trying to catch up. In 1970, the city established a Science and Technology Center that "helps factories solve tricky technical problems, popularizes new equipment and methods, mounts periodic exhibitions." By 1973, this Center, which employs thirteen hundred researchers and workers, had drawn a million visitors.[69] Specialized institutes perform similar functions for applications involving computers, electronics, and other new fields. The Shanghai Municipal Computer Technology Institute, for example, established in 1969,

> has solved some 1,360 problems in aeronautics, optics, hydrology, electrical engineering, architecture, surveying, textile engineering, and medicine for more than 40 cities throughout China.[70]

Like the diesel workers from Wuhan, visitors learn that Shanghai's achievements do not rest on large investments or externally supplied equipment. Innovation is pictured as the result of ingenuity, dedication, flexibility, and, above all, hard slogging effort. At Shanghai's Petroleum Machinery Parts Plant:

> When they began producing oil drills, there were many difficulties, and quality was poor. But whatever the difficulty, it could not topple this plant's workers. They penetrated individual wells, analyzed various types of rock layers, and conducted a scientific analysis of every defective drill. Only in this way did they gradually master the technique of manufacturing drills and advance product quality beyond the original specifications.[71]

These methods have produced results that oblige other industrial centers to look to Shanghai as a pacesetter in such diverse fields as machine tools, pumps, bicycles, computers, and transformers.[72] Even in steel, cable, shipbuilding, coal mining and metallurgical equipment, sectors with major Soviet-aided plants located elsewhere, the city's older units continue to make outstanding innovative contributions.[73] Shanghai's Industrial Exhibition, China's only permanent display of this sort, reveals the giant metropolis's industrial leadership to Chinese as well as foreign visitors.

As we have seen in the case of petroleum and chemical fertilizers, expansion of new industries depends heavily on Shanghai expertise. Shanghai also pioneers in new processes and techniques. Visitors occupy themselves with

> learning new techniques of recently developed fields, such as electronic spark processing, forge pressing, vacuum casting, iso-ion cutting, argon arc welding, electro-slag welding, hot riveting, chemical and unlined hearths, and many new chemical reaction processes.[74]

More recently, Shanghai's "municipal science and technology exchange centre . . . has energetically popularized laser knowledge through short-run training classes, exhibitions, science-educational galleries, publications and so forth."[75]

What accounts for the ability of older industrial centers, most notably Shanghai, to outdo newer units in terms of product development and introduction of new manufacturing techniques? Since Chinese investment policy has attached low priority to the regions and types of enterprises that have shown the highest degree of technological dynamism, capital cannot form part of our explanation. A more significant possibility is that large plants may suffer from diseconomies of scale. Smaller firms are reportedly "more compact and . . . more flexible in adjusting their production."[76] At larger units such as Shenyang's #1 Machine Tool Plant, a Soviet-aided project that has long been a favorite target for Chinese economic critics, organization is "swollen and ineffectual, technical control . . . highly complicated . . . the potentialities of equipment and personnel cannot be fully developed and utilized and production technology is not likely to advance and improve."[77]

Innovation may be especially difficult under conditions of large-scale production. Ma T'ien-shui, formerly a Shanghai party official, points out that new methods "may seem to work well in small-scale production. But when there is production in bulk, the quality begins to drop." Shanghai experience shows that the best policy toward innovation is to

> begin with small factories, concentrate forces on the speedy mastery of new technology, and build and develop new sectors of industry. Particularly in the case of newly risen industries that require more complex technology, Shanghai follows the principle of going from the small to the large-sized . . . medium and small-sized factories always have to shoulder a greater share of the task of developing new varieties.[78]

The great strength of Shanghai, Tientsin, and other established industrial centers lies in experience. With their "skilled veteran workers and experienced technical persons, old industrial bases and old enterprises . . . find it easier to tackle . . . complicated technical problems than new enterprises and new industrial bases."[79]

Personal experience alone, however, appears inadequate to account for the superior performance of established units. Tens of thousands of veteran workers, engineers, and managers have been reassigned from old to new plants and from established to emergent industrial centers. Even if Shanghai has managed to hoard the cream of the pre-1949 trainees, the priority given to newer centers in assigning fresh graduates means that at the very least, newer units at Anshan, Shenyang, Loyang, Ch'angch'un, and other locations can match the smaller Shanghai units in terms of sheer technical and engineering talent.

The experience that appears most relevant to innovative success is the experience of regrouping available resources to cope with unforseen production problems or shifts in market conditions. In the words of one Chinese observer, "Shanghai has . . . many years of experience in organizing large joint projects and tackling major problems."[80] This is the common element shared by survivors of the unstable and ruthlessly competitive market economy of the republican era, by enterprises that have made the transition from repair work to manufacturing after 1949, and by small, low-priority units that have found themselves bounced around from product to unfamiliar product with distressing frequency ever since 1949. For all these firms, opportunism, flexibility, and problem solving offered the key to survival and expansion both before and after 1949.

The carryover of organizational behavior patterns developed prior to 1949 has propelled the Ta-lung Machinery Works, Hopei's K'ai-lan Coal Mine, Talien's Locomotive and Rolling Stock Works, and other older units into positions of technical and innovative leadership intended for newer, better equipped enterprises.

This factor is especially apparent in Shanghai, a city whose function in China's economy resembles that of New York in America's. Already in the 1930s, there was an abundance of small, modestly capitalized enterprises specializing in what Vernon calls "producing the unpredictable."[81] Revolution thrust these firms into a new, but once again harsh and unstable, economic climate. Inherited industry was neglected by investment and supply planners, while party propagandists branded China's established industrial centers as irrational, bourgeois, and parasitic legacies of imperialism. Under these circumstances, local pride, patriotism, and self-interest together impelled industrial staff and workers to convince Peking that they, too, could help build socialism.

When summoned during the 1950s to raise output, older enterprises responded by shattering the performance targets set for them. After 1960, when quality and complementarity rather than sheer quantity were stressed, the same organizations, drawing once again on patterns of cooperation and competitive enterprise traditions inherited from the past, responded with supplier behavior appropriate to business downturns: innovation, customer service, cost reduction.[82]

It is this legacy of experience in the industrial art of responding to duress that, more than any other factor, stands behind the superior ability of established industrial centers to copy and modify foreign equipment samples, to extract useful information from foreign technical publications, and to apply it to current domestic problems. This explains Shanghai's unplanned but vital role as technological intermediary between the mass of Chinese producers who strive to attain advanced national levels of productivity, quality, cost, and technique, and the outside world whose standards become the target of Shanghai's own technological aspirations.

The lessons of experience are by no means unique to Shanghai. Lesser centers of prewar development have encountered the same combination of urgent new demand components and limited access to new resources that have led to wide-ranging innovations in Shanghai industry. Beneficiaries of China's post-1949 investment drive have by now accumulated nearly three decades of experience in grappling with numerous and difficult problems involved in adapting imported plant and equipment to domestic economic conditions, ironing out bugs in unfamiliar processes, and responding to shifting customer requirements.

Under these conditions, learning theory would predict the gradual emergence of new centers of innovation and technological dynamism outside of Shanghai. This is exactly what has occurred during the 1970s. Coastal provinces, which are comparatively rich in industrial experience but lack modern large-scale enterprises, have followed Shanghai in converting repair shops into production facilities and organizing small plants for joint manufacture of complex new products.

Kiangsu province illustrates this trend. In Ch'angchou, a pre-1949 railway repair works has developed into a manufacturing operation that "turns out 4,000 waggons and repairs and makes more than 300 locomotives a year," while the city's first machinery plant, founded in 1913, has now become "a large enterprise which produced 33,000 top-quality diesel engines for farm use in 1974."[83] Nearby Wusih county established a power tiller plant

> by amalgamating two handicraft co-operatives which then had only 280 workers and 24 pieces of simple equipment. Later, the workers manufactured more than 200 sets of highly efficient special purpose equipment, designed and installed six streamlined production lines and thus raised annual production capacity from 500 tractors in 1970 to 10,000 at present.

With the exception of some gear cutters and heating equipment made in nearby Shanghai, this plant's equipment comes entirely from Kiangsu suppliers. The plant itself has fabricated a substantial proportion of its machinery, including lathes, automatic gear cutters, and grinding machines. In July 1975, the plant was making a batch of twenty automatic lathes to replace simpler equipment in machining tractor parts.[84]

Joint efforts among Kiangsu firms closely resemble the tactics used to manufacture petroleum and fertilizer equipment in Shanghai:

> Under a unified plan, Kiangsu has organized cooperation among different enterprises in making a given machine. Each plant produces one or several specific parts of the machine and one particular plant is

> in charge of assembling them. . . . When the construction of Chingchiang tractor works started in 1973, 227 factories in the province combined forces to produce special equipment. . . . With more than 2,000 workers and over 1,000 machine tools, it is now able to turn out 5,000 tractors a year.[85]

Shantung and other regions report similar progress.[86]

Regions favored by post-1949 investment policies have become increasingly prominent in experimentation with new technologies during the 1970s. Peking reports advances in machine tools, electronics, and chemical instruments.[87] New products displayed at the Canton Trade Fair now come from Peking, Harbin, and Shensi as well as traditional industrial centers.[88] Research institutes and manufacturers in Talien, Harbin, Lanchow, Yümen, Tach'ing, Ch'engtu, T'ienshui, and even Ninghsia now cooperate with enterprises in Shanghai, Shenyang, Peking, and Tientsin to produce new types of instruments and refining apparatus for the petroleum industry.[89]

As a result of these changes, producers formerly dependent on Shanghai's innovative leadership now form their own networks of cooperation and mutual support:

> In cooperation with the Capital Iron and Steel Works, Anshan Iron and Steel Company and the Luchou [Szechwan] gasfield, the Southwestern Iron and Steel Research Institute has successfully made petroleum drill pipes in the 55 kilogram class. A start has thereby been made in filling the gap in the production of steel for oil and natural gas drill pipes in China.[90]

This gradual extension of innovative activity shows that China's producer sector is beginning to develop a degree of depth, flexibility, and in-built progressiveness that is more akin to the features of industry in advanced economies than to China's embryonic, disintegrated industry of the 1930s and 1950s. The cumulative strengthening of industrial skills that accompanies innovative efforts provides a key ingredient in expanding industrial potential. This is widely recognized by Chinese, from Mao Tse-tung, whose writings are sprinkled with such epigrams as "knowledge is gained through difficulties" and "there won't be success without failure," on down to the reporter whose visits to power tiller and diesel engine factories in Ch'angchou, Kiangsu, led him to observe that:

> In the course of increasing the output and improving the quality of these two products, other factories working on coordination to make gears and springs and do the casting and forging have naturally moved ahead at the same time. Thus conditions have been created for the production of other machinery products.[91]

With Harbin, Shenyang, Peking, and other large cities now joining Shanghai and Tientsin in supporting a full panoply of scientific and industrial endeavor, with dozens of secondary industrial nodes springing up across the country, and with industrial products, equipment, and techniques taking firm root throughout wide areas of the countryside, China's producer sector seems well prepared to move toward the ambitious goals outlined in Chou En-lai's final address: "to accomplish the comprehensive modernization of agriculture, industry, national defense, and science and technology before the end of the century, so that our national economy will be advancing in the front ranks of the world."[92]

Chapter 4

Producer Industries and China's Economic Development

Chinese accounts often describe industry as the leading force in developing the nation's economy. In the following pages, we inquire into the nature of the producer sector's contribution to overall growth from the perspective of output, technology, and intersectoral linkages.

The Growth of Industrial Output

China's reluctance to issue comprehensive industrial performance data has led foreign observers to prepare a variety of independent estimates of output growth. In recent years, the accumulation of published data and intensive discussion among specialists have greatly reduced the differences among various outside estimates and between the outside estimates as a whole and performance indicators obtained from Chinese sources. This new consensus allows us to present an overview of quantitative trends in industry and in the producer sector without undertaking a detailed evaluation of Chinese industrial statistics.[1]

Table 4.1 displays three estimates of industrial output growth. Although each series measures gross (or sales) value rather than value added, there is considerable evidence that for China, unlike the Soviet Union, gross value data provide a valid measure of real output growth.[2] The series in columns 1 and 2 are estimates of the gross value of factory output (GVFO), a concept that includes the products of modern factories and handicraft factories employing four or more hired workers, but excludes the output of individual handicraft operations employing fewer than four hired workers. The two remaining series measure the gross value of industrial output (GVIO), a broader category encompassing GVFO, individual handicrafts, and since 1957, certain agricultural processing and handicraft activities formerly classified with agricultural rather than industrial output.[3]

The series in the first three columns of table 4.1 originate with commodity output estimates, which are aggregated into performance indices for machinery, steel, textiles, and other industrial branches using 1952 price weights. The branch indices are combined into an aggregate index by means of interbranch weights based on officially estimated sectoral shares in 1957 gross output value (columns 1 and 2) or on independently estimated sectoral shares in the 1956 industrial wage bill (column 3).

The series shown in the final column of table 4.1 results from compiling Chinese reports on the growth of GVIO at the provincial and national level. This series provides the best available approximation to an official measure of industrial growth for the years since 1957.

The most striking feature of the output series shown in table 4.1 and the implied growth rates that appear in table 4.2 is the close agreement among estimates calculated with widely different methodologies. Some of the differences are predictable: estimates of GVFO should grow faster than the others because GVFO excludes the relatively slow-growing handicraft and farm processing components included in GVIO; the Field/CIA estimates should lag behind the others because Field uses an independently derived series of machinery production that grows less rapidly than the official totals incorporated into the other series; and the use of successively later price bases reduces the measured rate of growth because of the inverse correlation between sectoral output growth and relative price changes displayed in table 4.3.

If industry is narrowly defined to exclude handicrafts and farm processing, the estimates in tables 4.1 and 4.2 show that the gross value of factory output has grown at a pace somewhat above 10 percent per annum during the quarter-century beginning in 1949. There have been cylical downswings associated with the aftermath of the Great Leap Forward (1958–60) and to a lesser extent with the Cultural Revolution (1966–68) and the political unrest before and after the death of Mao Tse-tung in 1976.

TABLE 4.1
Estimates of Gross Industrial Output, 1912–76

Year	Rawski-GVFO[a] 1952 prices	Rawski-GVFO[a] 1975 prices	Field/CIA-GVIO[b] 1952 prices	FLE-GVIO[c] 1957 prices
		A. Billion yuan		
1912	1.251[e]	—	—	—
1933	10.510[d]	—	—	—
1936	12.822[e]	—	—	—
1949	10.781[f]	—	14.020	—
1952	27.014	24.896	34.330	—
1957	65.020	55.189	78.390	70.400
		B. Index numbers, 1957=100		
1958	—	—	142	—
1959	—	—	173	—
1960	—	—	181	—
1961	—	—	105	—
1962	128	121	111	—
1963	149	140	134	—
1964	180	164	161	167
1965	228	205	199	204
1966	—	—	232	249
1967	—	—	202	—
1968	—	—	221	217
1969	—	—	266	283
1970	—	—	316	344
1971	441	369	349	381
1972	481	401	385	416
1973	571	473	436	463
1974	—	—	455	491
1975	—	—	502	538
1976	—	—	502	—

[a] Rawski, "Industrial Performance," in *Quantitative Measures*, table H–10, except as noted.

[b] Methodology for this series and data for 1949–57 are from Field, "Civilian Industrial Production," pp. 164–68; data for 1958–76 are from U.S. Central Intelligence Agency, *China: Economic Indicators*, p. 15, where the series is labeled "value added in industrial production." The figure for 1976 is preliminary.

[c] Field, Lardy, and Emerson, *Provincial Output*, p. 17.

[d] Sum of gross output value in factories, utilities, and mines as estimated in Liu and Yeh, *Economy of the Chinese Mainland*, pp. 141, 157.

[e] Derived from the 1933 total using an index of industrial gross output shown in Chang, *Industrial Development*, pp. 60–61.

[f] Chen, *Statistics*, p. 210.

TABLE 4.2
Average Annual Growth of Industrial Gross Output, 1912–73
(in percentage)

Period	Rawski-GVFO 1952 Prices	Rawski-GVFO 1975 Prices	Field/CIA-GVIO 1952 Prices	FLE-GVIO 1957 Prices
1912–33	10.7	—	—	—
1912–36	10.2	—	—	—
1912–49	6.0	—	—	—
1949–73	15.9	—	14.2	—
1952–73	13.3	11.8	11.6	—
1957–73	11.5	10.2	9.6	10.1
1965–73	12.2	11.0	10.3	10.8

Source: Calculated from table 4.1.

TABLE 4.3
Sectoral Output and Price Changes, 1952–75
(1952=1)

Sector	1972 output[a]	1975 Price Index
Petroleum	76.4	0.574
Machinery	61.8	0.577
Chemicals	35.4	0.821
Ferrous metals	16.0	0.609
Electric power	15.2	1.269
Building materials	10.4	0.487
Paper	6.3	1.244
Coal	5.8	1.600
Consumer manufactures	3.0	0.924
Timber	1.5	1.244

Sources: Price data from Rawski, "Industrial Performance," in *Quantitative Measures*, tables H–1 and H–10. Output data for 1972 from ibid., tables 27 and 34; for 1952, from Ishikawa, *National Income*, p. 60. Petroleum output value for 1952 is extrapolated from the 1956 figure on the basis of changes in crude oil output shown in Chen, *Statistics*, pp. 186–87.

[a] Sectoral indices based on gross output totals calculated in terms of 1952 prices.

Comparing the estimates for GVFO and GVIO shows that enlarging the scope of industry to include handicrafts and agricultural processing reduces annual growth rates by one to two percentage points. Despite major price reductions in the most dynamic sectors of industry (table 4.3), recalculating output growth in terms of 1975 prices lowers the measured growth rate of GVFO by no more than 1.5 percentage points. This result shows that high rates of industrial growth are not, as some have argued, a function of price distortions favoring machinery and other fast-growing producer branches. Although we lack the cost data to cast sectoral performance data in net rather than gross terms, there is considerable evidence that value added has grown more rapidly than the gross value indicators shown in table 4.1.[4]

Turning to the growth of producer output, table 4.4 presents estimates of GVFO in both 1952 and 1975 prices for the years 1949–74; average rates of growth are compiled in table 4.5. The data for 1949–57 are from widely accepted Chinese statements. For later years, output estimates are derived from commodity-based sectoral performance indices for steel, machinery, chemicals, and other industries. These

TABLE 4.4
Estimated Producer Output and Share in Industrial Total, 1912–74

	Producer Sector GVFO (in billion yuan)		Producer Share of Overall GVFO (in percentage)	
Year	1952 Prices	1975 Prices	1952 Prices	1975 Prices
1912	.528[b]	—	42.2	—
1933	3.450[a]	—	32.8	—
1936	7.017[b]	—	54.7	—
1949	3.100[c]	—	28.7[c]	—
1952	10.730	9.850	39.7	39.6
1957	34.330	26.831	52.8	48.6
1962	59.048	44.679	71.1	66.9
1963	70.274	52.628	72.4	68.1
1964	84.177	60.124	72.1	66.6
1965	109.032	76.574	73.4	67.7
1966	137.045	95.427	—	—
1970	200.522	134.571	—	—
1971	237.426	158.290	82.8	77.6
1972	263.826	176.000	84.3	79.5
1973	311.854	206.269	84.0	79.0
1974	328.016	216.700	—	—

Sources: Except as noted, Rawski, "Industrial Performance," in *Quantitative Measures*, tables 17, 34, H–10, and H–12; and table 4.1 in this book.

[a] Factory output of producer goods plus gross output of mines and utilities from Liu and Yeh, *Economy of the Chinese Mainland*, pp. 141, 157.

[b] Derived from 1933 total using an index of gross output value for steel, soda ash, cement, power, and coal. Quantity data from table 1.1 in this book, 1952 prices from Liu and Yeh, *Economy of the Chinese Mainland*, pp. 462, 569, 578.

[c] Chen, *Statistics*, p. 210.

TABLE 4.5
Average Annual Growth Rates for Producer Output, 1912–74
(in percentage)

Period	Based on 1952 Prices	Based on 1975 Prices
1912–33	9.4	—
1912–36	11.4	—
1912–49	4.9	—
1949–74	20.5	—
1952–74	16.8	15.1
1957–74	14.2	13.1
1965–74	13.0	12.3

Source: Calculated from table 4.4.

indices have been combined, using officially reported 1957 sectoral gross output totals as weights.

These data and estimates show that the producer sector has consistently surpassed industry's overall growth performance throughout the post-1949 years. Average growth rates have declined gradually, but remain well above the 10 percent level associated with aggregate industrial growth, resulting in a steady rise in the share of producer goods in total industrial production.[5] Once again, we find that shifting from 1952 to 1975 prices reduces estimated growth rates by less than two percentage points. Unfortunately, shifts in prices and industrial classification make it difficult to match these results with recent Chinese statements regarding output growth in the producer sector.[6]

Comparison of performance indicators for the producer sector with measures of overall industrial growth shows that China's post-1949 industrial expansion has generated steady and rapid structural change. Textiles and food processing, which accounted for half of factory output in both 1933 and 1952, together comprise only 13.9 percent of estimated GVFO for 1973.[7] In their place stand the greatly enlarged engineering, metallurgical, and chemical industries that now account for a combined total of roughly two-fifths of gross output value.

The rise of newly prominent industries within the producer sector also can be seen in table 4.6, which describes the composition of producer output for benchmark years between 1952 and 1972. These data reveal a pattern of structural change, again insensitive to relative

TABLE 4.6
Composition of Gross Value of Factory Output in the Producer Sector, 1952–72
(in percentage)

	1952	1957	1965	1972
A. In terms of 1952 prices				
Machinery	13.1	18.0	28.4	32.9
Ferrous metals	12.8	15.2	11.0	8.4
Building materials	5.8	4.7	3.2	2.4
Chemicals	8.0	12.5	12.6	11.6
Petroleum	2.3	1.9	4.3	7.1
Electric power	4.0	3.2	2.7	2.5
Coal	7.7	5.2	2.7	1.8
Timber	11.8	3.4	1.4	0.7
Paper	6.0	4.9	2.6	1.5
Others	28.4	31.0	31.0	31.0
Total	100.0	100.0	100.0	100.0
B. In terms of 1975 prices				
Machinery	8.2	13.3	23.3	28.4
Ferrous metals	8.5	11.8	9.5	7.6
Building materials	3.1	3.0	2.2	1.8
Chemicals	7.2	13.1	14.7	14.2
Petroleum	1.4	1.4	3.5	6.1
Electric power	5.6	5.2	4.9	4.8
Coal	13.5	10.6	6.2	4.4
Timber	15.9	5.3	2.4	1.4
Paper	8.2	7.8	4.7	2.9
Others	28.4	28.4	28.4	28.4
Total	100.0	100.0	100.0	100.0

Source: Rawski, "Industrial Performance," in *Quantitative Measures*," table H-9.

Note: Column totals may not check because of rounding. Constancy of the share of "others" arises from the methodology of estimating total output. Natural gas, nonferrous metals, rubber, nonmetallic minerals other than building materials, electronics, and an unknown portion of defense production are the principal sectors included in this residual category.

price changes, in which metallurgy, metal fabricating, chemicals, and, most recently, petroleum expand their shares of total output at the expense of older industries based on an earlier generation of natural resources: coal, power, timber, paper, and nonmetallic minerals.

These broad conclusions, like those regarding trends in overall industrial growth, are not controversial. Machinery manufacture is the only major sector for which foreign analysts seriously question the Chinese progress reports that form the basis for the estimates in table 4.4. Yet even if Robert M. Field's estimates of machinery production are substituted for Chinese data showing higher output value, the average annual growth rate of producer output during 1952–73 declines by only one percentage point, and the terminal share of producer goods in aggregate industrial output falls only three percentage points below the figures reported in tables 4.4 and 4.5.[8]

Inspection of the pre-1949 output totals included in tables 4.1 and 4.4 reveals that rapid and sustained industrial growth did not begin with the formation of the People's Republic in 1949, but can be traced back as far as 1912. Industry not only grew rapidly prior to World War II, but also contributed a larger share to the modest prewar increment in China's total output than any sector except agriculture.[9]

Since 1949, the producer industries have supplanted agriculture and consumer manufacturing as the leading source of increases in output. This can be seen from table 4.7, which uses Perkins's estimates of gross domestic product to show that nearly 60 percent of incremental output during 1957–71 originated in industry. Since the figures in tables 4.1 and 4.4 imply that producer goods accounted for about 90 percent of incremental gross output in industry during this period, we may conclude that producer industries were responsible for approximately half of the increase in China's aggregate output during 1957–71, a share that is double that of the services sector and three times that of agriculture.[10]

TABLE 4.7
Estimated Growth of Gross Domestic Product by Sector, 1957–71
(in billion 1957 yuan)

	Contribution to GDP		Average Annual Growth Rate 1957–71	Contribution to Incremental GDP	
Sector	1957	1971	(in percentage)	Amount	Share (in percentage)
Agriculture	43.93	60.37	2.3	15.44	16.8
Industry[a]	24.22	81.73	9.1	57.51	58.9
Services	27.56	51.26	4.5	23.70	24.3
Gross domestic product	95.71	193.36	5.2	97.65	100.0

Source: Dwight H. Perkins, "Growth and Changing Structure of China's Twentieth-Century Economy," in *China's Modern Economy in Historical Perspective* (Stanford, 1975), p. 161.

[a] Includes factories, mining, utilities, and handicrafts.

Technology

How are producer goods manufactured in China? During the FFYP years (1953–57), the restoration of political and monetary stability, rapid increases in utilization of fixed assets, and policy emphasis on raising output volume allowed output to grow much faster than employment or fixed assets and led to rapid growth of total factor productivity.[11] Data gaps make it diffcult to extend estimates of sectoral investment, capital stock, and employment into the 1960s and 1970s, but partial data, qualitative information, and visitor accounts provide a clear picture of changes in factor proportions and trends in the overall technical level of the producer industries.

In the broadest terms, Chinese industrial technology is developing along lines reminiscent of patterns established by the advanced industrial nations of North America, Europe, and Japan. There is an unmistakable trend toward capital deepening involving rising labor productivity, increased capital-labor ratios, and growing automation. This, in turn, has created a large and growing gap between labor productivity in industry (including rural industry) and the rest of the economy, especially agriculture.

The advance of industrial labor productivity emerges clearly from data and estimates assembled in table 4.8. If the 1952 and 1957 totals for factory industry are combined with 1975 data for the state sector, the most comparable aggregate, we see that gross output per worker has risen by an average of 3.4 percent annually during 1957–75 and even faster during 1952–57. Estimated labor productivity in the five small industries exceeds the 1952 total for all factories. In collective industry, which consists mainly of commune-run enterprises, output per worker has reached the level attained by all factories in 1950. In agriculture, however, gross output value per man-year has risen by less than 1 percent annually since 1957, reaching a 1975 total well under 300 yuan.[12]

The process of capital deepening is visible from several perspectives. With output rising fastest in sectors with relatively high initial ratios of capital to labor (table 4.9), structural change alone has caused a significant rise in capital intensity. Capital per worker has risen in individual industries as well. New plants built during the 1950s, especially those equipped with Soviet machinery, were highly capital-intensive and have remained so; three leading machinery enterprises, for

TABLE 4.8
Industrial Labor Productivity, 1933–75

Year	Sector	GVFO Billion 1952 Yuan	Employment (in millions)	Gross Output per Worker 1952 Yuan
1933	Industry	10.510[a]	1.94[b]	5,417
1949	Industry	10.781[a]	3.1[c]	3,478
1952	Industry	27.014[a]	5.3[c]	5,097
	Producer sector	10.730[a]	2.7[c]	3,974
	Consumer sector	16.284[a]	2.6[c]	6,263
1957	Industry	65.020[a]	7.9[c]	8,230
	Producer sector	34.330[a]	4.7[c]	7,304
	Consumer sector	30.690	3.2[c]	9,591
1975	Industry	431.038[d]	39.3[g]	10,967
	State sector	370.693[e]	24.8[g]	14,947
	Collective sector	60.345[e]	14.5[g]	4,162
	Five small industries	25.909[f]	4.7[g]	5,513

Note: The output and employment estimates in this table exclude handicrafts.

[a] Taken or calculated from tables 4.1 and 4.4.

[b] Liu and Yeh, *Economy of the Chinese Mainland*, p. 69.

[c] Emerson, *Nonagricultural Employment*, p. 143.

[d] Obtained by applying the 16.1 percent rise in GVIO estimated for 1973–75 by Field, Lardy, and Emerson, *Provincial Output*, p. 17, to the 1973 estimate given in table 4.1.

[e] Chang Ch'un-ch'iao, in "On Exercising All-Round Dictatorship Over the Bourgeoisie," *Peking Review* 14(1975):6, states that the 1973 output shares of state and collective industry were 86 and 14 percent. The same figures are used to decompose 1975 output.

[f] Obtained by applying the 30.4 percent rise in producer output estimated for 1972–75 by U.S. Central Intelligence Agency, *China: Economic Indicators*, p. 15, to the 1972 estimate shown in table 3.5.

[g] Rawski, *Industrialization, Technology and Employment*, p. 39.

example, reported construction costs of 18,000–28,000 yuan per worker.[13] Data for small plants shown in table 4.10 also indicate high levels of capital per worker; even with substantially reduced machinery prices, capital per worker in recently built or designed chemical, cement, and machinery plants often exceeds the industrywide averages for the 1950s shown in table 4.9.

The trend toward automation can be seen in the enthusiasm with which Chinese commentators welcome the labor-saving potential of mechanization throughout the economy, a theme amply confirmed by visitors. A group studying rural industry reports that "time and again we

TABLE 4.9
Sectors Ranked for Capital Intensity and Output Growth, 1952–72

Order of Decreasing Capital-Labor Ratio, 1952–53	Productive Fixed Assets per Production Worker (in yuan)	Order of Decreasing Output Growth, 1952–72	1972 Gross[c] Output (1952=1)
1. Electric power	51,197	1. Petroleum	76.4
2. Petroleum	24,945[a]	2. Machinery	61.8
3. Paper	9,528	3. Chemicals	35.4
4. Ferrous metallurgy	9,251	4. Ferrous metallurgy	16.0
5. Chemicals	8,120	5. Electric power	15.2
All Industry	5,656	*All Industry*	11.6
6. Coal	5,029	6. Building materials	10.4
7. Textiles	4,806	7. Paper	6.3
8. Machinery	4,750[b]	8. Coal	5.8
9. Food processing	3,373	9. Food processing	2.9
10. Building materials	2,431	10. Textiles	2.8
11. Timber	1,210	11. Timber	1.5

Sources: Ishikawa, *National Income*, pp. 60, 125–26; Rawski, "Industrial Performance," in *Quantitative Measures*, table 33; and tables 4.1 and 4.3 in this book.

[a] Crude oil extraction.

[b] Data refer to metal processing, which includes manufacture of metal products and repair work as well as machinery manufacture.

[c] Calculated in terms of 1952 prices.

were told by factory representatives of the efforts they were making to eliminate manual, highly labor-intensive processes and to substitute mechanized methods."[14]

The movement toward capital deepening does not mean that Chinese industry has found no opportunities for fruitful deviation from technological patterns developed in more advanced economies. On the contrary, Chinese engineers and workers have successfully produced unique products, such as ammonium bicarbonate fertilizer, substituted small plants for large units and local materials for standard items in construction and manufacturing, and developed ingenious processes to manufacture sophisticated products with unsophisticated equipment.[15] Expansion of small plants and experiments with new combinations of productive factors have increased industrial output and accelerated the spread of industrial products, techniques, and experience into rural as well as urban regions.

But even though today's small enterprises often match or exceed

TABLE 4.10
Small Plant Data on Capital per Worker, 1970s

Enterprise (province)	Construction Cost (in million yuan)	Number of Workers	Construction Cost per Worker (in yuan)
Chemicals			
Hsiyang (Shansi) Fertilizer Plant	7.5	450	16,667
Lin (Honan) Fertilizer Plant	6	520	11,538
Chia-ting (Shanghai) Fertilizer Plant[a]	8	630	12,698
Wusih (Kiangsu) Electrochemical Plant	3.8	600	6,333
Cement			
Lin (Honan) Plant[a]	0.33	250	1,320
Ts'un-hua (Hopei) Plant[a]	0.27	97	2,784
Nan-hai (Kwangtung) Plant	5[b]	549	9,107
Hsi-yang (Shansi) Plant	0.35	144	2,430
Electric power			
Lin (Honan) County Plant	1.46	43	33,953
Lin (Honan) Brigade Plant[c]	0.017	4	4,250
Hsun-te (Kwangtung) Project[d]	9.7	96	101,042
Machinery			
Lin (Honan) Tung-fang-hung Plant	1.5	300	5,000
Consumer products			
Lin (Honan) Cotton Textile Plant	0.5	186	2,688
Lin (Honan) Fluorescent Bulb Plant	0.3	180	1,667

Source: Except as noted, Perkins et al., *Rural Industry*, pp. 64–70.

[a] Sigurdson, *Rural Industrialization*, pp. 235–36.

[b] Excludes value of self-made machinery without which total cost would have reached eight million yuan.

[c] Plant operates on a part-year basis with part-time employees.

[d] This is part of an integrated project that includes navigation and flood control as well as power generation.

the performance standards set by large plants during the 1950s,[16] there can be little doubt of their inability to match current standards of cost and quality at larger plants whose techniques and operations more closely resemble those found in large Western or Japanese enterprises. In the fertilizer and cement industries, for example, Sigurdson presents design specifications showing that small plants typically use more capital and materials, as well as more labor per ton of product, than larger facilities; product quality also poses problems for smaller plants in these industries.[17]

Recent Chinese import decisions and policy discussions show that the weakest industrial sectors are precisely those that have failed to advance in the direction of capital-intensive world technologies. In chemicals, ferrous metallurgy, petroleum refining, petrochemicals, and electric power, the inability of domestic producers to fabricate large-scale equipment has restricted domestic output growth to what can be gained from the combined efforts of large plants built during the 1950s and small and intermediate facilities built thereafter. The inadequacy of domestic production has led to growing imports of steel and fertilizers, shortages of electric power and petroleum refining capacity, and substantial imports of large-scale components or complete plants in each of these sectors.[18]

Even mining, a field that appears to offer considerable opportunity to substitute labor for machinery, seems to have suffered from limited access to capital-intensive techniques. Evidence of declining labor productivity in coal production suggests that reliance on a labor-intensive approach to mining operations may be responsible for the present situation in which "the prominent problem in current industries is that the raw material, fuel, and power industries are falling behind the processing industries."[19] The solution, as articulated by Teng Hsiao-p'ing and others, is to launch a "Great Mining Campaign" to construct new mines, assign capable leaders to key management positions, and "aggressively develop advanced and large mining equipment, transportation equipment and other mining machines"—a capital-intensive prescription that specifically rejects the alternative of large employment increases in this sector.[20]

These observations suggest that, despite its capital intensity, Western industrial technology is so productive that it often maintains an advantage in cost as well as quality over alternative methods, even when, as in China, the ratio of capital to labor costs is enormously higher than it is in the countries for which the technology was originally intended.[21] China's experience in the producer sector offers only limited support for the view of Fei and Ranis that

> in spite of the easy availability of imported technology, the underdeveloped country is well advised to select that [technology] which is more suitable for substantial modification or adaptation, or even better, to innovate on the basis of a completely indigenous production function, by streamlining or modernizing traditional production functions.[22]

The negative experience of the Great Leap Forward (1958–60), during which peasant communities with little knowledge or experience of industrial operations were encouraged to manufacture iron, steel, machinery, and other producer items, demonstrated the impossibility of converting China's traditional production functions to industrial use.

Modification of foreign technologies, which is most visible in the proliferation of small- and medium-sized machinery, cement, metallurgy, and fertilizer plants in small cities and rural areas, is most effective when the presence of complementary facilities of varying technical levels permits a division of labor in which demanding tasks are reserved for more sophisticated enterprises, leaving semimodern units to concentrate on relatively simple operations.

China's agricultural machinery industry illustrates how this complementarity can work.[23] The industry consists of a large, closely integrated network of plants ranging from national-level units such as the Loyang Tractor Works, a Soviet-built enterprise employing twenty-three thousand workers and producing an annual total of over twenty thousand tractors, to smaller factories and workshops, some with only a few dozen workers and several machine tools, now operated by 98 percent of China's approximately two thousand counties, 90 percent of 50,000-odd agricultural communes, and many of the roughly six hundred thousand agricultural production brigades.[24] The degree of enterprise technological sophistication varies with a unit's position in the administrative ladder, with national-level plants displaying the highest and brigade and commune shops the lowest levels of technical development.

Production responsibilities are distributed within this technological and administrative hierarchy on the basis of plans designed to match tasks with capabilities. Parts for a particular machine may come from separate units with widely varying technical capacities, as when county plants use diesel engines and ball bearings from regional or provincial units to manufacture power tillers. Alternatively, the input from higher levels may take the form of advanced machinery, as when "modern and even semi-automated machine tools" appear "even at the lowest organization levels" alongside primitive hand methods of fabrication and assembly.[25]

The result is a mixed technology that uses capital-intensive methods to obtain crucial tolerances or physical properties and assigns labor-intensive methods to assembly work and other peripheral tasks, even at the largest enterprises. In China, this approach has nurtured a rapidly growing equipment industry that supplies the farm sector with large quantities of tough, inexpensive, and functional machines. This successful experience has arisen not from abandoning capital-intensive production techniques, but by systematic grafting of labor-intensive operations requiring conventional machine tools (often in large numbers) onto a core of highly specialized and capital-intensive operations. And even here, it is important to bear in mind the gradual but universal shift toward capital-using innovations, even in assembly and other operations in which mechanization has no apparent impact on product quality.

The entire engineering sector operates with a similar mix of capital- and labor-using technologies. In some fields, foreign visitors unexpectedly encounter advanced factory operations; bearing production at a Peking automotive plant is "indistinguishable from a whitemetal strip mill in a typical UK factory—the various processes . . . being comparable and operating at about the same speed."[26] Visitors to Shanghai's #1 Petroleum Equipment Plant, a former textile factory, were surprised to encounter a fully automated, numerically controlled production line.[27]

Elsewhere, primitive methods are used, giving rise to sharp contrasts between technical levels at different plants or even within individual plants. At a Peking vehicle repair works employing twelve hundred workers, "there was a considerable contrast between operations, with some being done in a very elementary way while others were tooled with highly sophisticated machinery."[28] As one foreign engineer observed, "The best is very good . . . but there is an incredible mixture of modern and ancient" production techniques.[29]

Electronics is another area of rapid development based on a combination of sophisticated and manual techniques, the former predominating in large-scale units and in what Heymann calls "scientific laboratory industry," the latter in subcontracting enterprises that rely on the manual dexterity of urban housewives to provide components for more sophisticated firms.[30]

In both engineering and electronics, the nature of manufacturing technology enables Chinese producers to raise the overall technical level of factory operations by piecemeal absorption of crucial elements of foreign technology. This absorption process takes a variety of forms, including imports of individual machines or occasionally of whole plants, mastery of technical information gleaned from foreign publications, factory visits, trade negotiations, licensing agreements or industrial exhibitions, and replication of imported prototypes.

As in the prewar years, progress toward world technical levels is most evident in sectors in which the lack of scale economies and indivisibilities permits the Chinese to decompose modern techniques into central and peripheral components and then use indigenous methods in the latter without undercutting essential features of the final product. Since some techniques are easier to reproduce, adapt, and integrate with existing facilities than others, technological advance is highly irregular. In some areas, such as large-scale integrated circuitry, foreign manufacturers report that China is "fast approaching world's highest performance levels," while in others, such as machine tool manufacture, even the best Chinese plants do not approach the tolerances and quality control standards demanded in world markets.[31]

Quite different conditions prevail in cement and petrochemicals, industries in which continuous-flow processes offer little room for technological decomposition, and in ferrous metallurgy and electric power, where scale economies figure prominently in advanced production methods. In these industries, Chinese technology appears homogeneous rather than uneven. The inability of domestic engineering producers to build plants to the scale required by advanced technologies means that technical levels, while progressing, are uniformly obsolete; foreign visitors do not report the technological peaks and valleys found in machinery and electronics manufacture.

In the cement industry, for example, output from large-scale plants has lagged because of China's inability to follow the world trend toward enlarged plant size and because Chinese plants lack basic technological improvements that are now standard in other countries.[32] In petrochemicals, an American visitor reports that

> everywhere [at several petrochemical plants and three oil refineries visited] the situation was about the same: from our point of view the equipment was outmoded and the processes are not up to date (continuous and automated) but an abundance of human labor . . . makes it possible to produce materials which have acceptable properties.[33]

Thus the level of technological sophistication at leading producer enterprises depends on the degree of technological separability as well as on investment levels and the accumulation of experience in different activity areas. China's high investment levels, continued growth of industrial experience, and post-1960 policy emphasis on technical development have resulted in a steady absorption of new techniques. Intersectoral differences in the degree to which advanced technologies can be decomposed into central components requiring advanced methods and peripheral elements allowing for the replacement of capital with labor without affecting product quality have permitted leading enterprises in some sectors, notably engineering and electronics, to make major advances toward world technological levels. In industries facing closely integrated technologies, advanced units have made important gains, but have not succeeded in approaching international technological frontiers.

The performance of enterprises below the national technological frontier is also relevant in assessing a nation's technical development. In China, technical advance spreads from centers of innovation, adaptation, and technological absorption along well-developed lines of communication that link leading enterprises and research institutes with distant rural workshops. Exchanges of personnel among units of differing technical levels, national and local meetings focused on particular problems or on "exchanging advanced experiences," and a massive flow of scientific and technical publications serve as vehicles for disseminating new methods throughout the industrial system.[34] Horizontal links also appear highly developed; one county-level fertilizer plant displays tokens of thanks for assistance rendered to enterprises in nine different provinces![35]

Together with the growth of experience and enlarged supplies of key inputs provided by advanced units, this inflow of technical knowledge has enabled regional and local enterprises to achieve notable advances in technique, product quality, and cost reduction. County plants now turn out lathe models that were highly regarded innovations when first introduced by advanced producers during the mid-1950s. Diesel engines produced in county plants are now lighter and cheaper than earlier products of larger plants. Rural fertilizer and steel plants earn substantial profits even with selling prices that are lower today than in 1957. Commune plants now use techniques such as powder metallurgy that were formerly confined to large and technically sophisticated units.[36]

The achievements of all types of enterprises in improving their operations show that despite the obvious limits to technical sophistication, limits of which China's present leaders are keenly aware, China has developed effective methods for implanting foreign innovations into domestic industry, for spreading new techniques and products from advanced to backward enterprises and regions, and for designing unique approaches to current technological problems in some fields.

Intersectoral Linkage

Growth and technical development in the producer sector have played key roles in the process of expanding and restructuring China's entire economy. Manufacture of consumer products, including some export lines, now depends on regular supplies of plastics, artificial fibers, and other nontraditional materials furnished by the producer industries. China is in the midst of shifting her energy base from coal to petroleum and natural gas, which now provide one-third of China's primary energy supplies as opposed to only 5 percent in 1957 and 14 percent in 1965.[37] This, too, is a result of developments within the producer sector.

Investment and agricultural development are two major areas that illustrate the essential contribution of producer industries to the overall process of economic growth. The dependence of investment programs on imports of machinery and whole plants from the Soviet bloc during the 1950s is widely recognized. After 1960, reduced supplies of foreign exchange and rising food imports obliged the Chinese to curtail machinery imports and rely primarily on domestic sources of producer durables. The recent surge of machinery purchases has obscured the reality of China's continuing reliance on domestic suppliers for the overwhelming bulk of her requirements for producer durables.

The reduced importance of machinery imports is evident from table 4.11, which presents constant price series for machinery imports and for major indices of domestic production and investment activity. Despite the recent expansion of equipment imports, examination of a longer period beginning in 1957 shows that construction activity, machinery output, industrial production, gross capital formation, and gross domestic product have all grown more rapidly than imports of machinery and whole plants. The large gap between the growth of machinery production and imports means that the share of imports in China's machinery supplies is now far below the 40 to 45 percent range reported in Chinese publications for 1957.[38]

TABLE 4.11
Growth of Machinery Imports and Economic Activity, 1957–75
(index numbers, 1957=100)

	1957	1965	1971	1973	1975	Average Annual Growth Rate 1957–75 (in percentage)
1. Imports of machinery (includes complete plants), 1957 prices	100	52	74	101	242	5.0
2. Aggregate output, 1957 prices	100	140	202	239	264	5.5
3. Industrial production						
A. GVFO, 1952 prices	100	228	441	571	—	11.5[a]
B. GVIO, 1952 prices	100	199	349	436	502	9.4
4. Machinery production, 1952 prices						
A. High series	100	501	1,300	1,642[b]	2,042[b]	18.2
B. Low series	100	257	711	930	1,156	14.6
5. Gross domestic fixed capital formation, 1957 prices	100	182	291	348	—	8.1[a]
6. Construction activity	100	182	300	369	404	8.1

Sources: Line 1: Imports for 1957–73 in current and 1957 dollars are compiled in U.S. Central Intelligence Agency, *Foreign Trade in Machinery*, pp. 1, 6. Estimated current dollar value of 1975 imports (including machinery, transport equipment, precision instruments, and watches and clocks) shown in U.S. Central Intelligence Agency, *China: International Trade, 1976–77* (Washington, D.C., 1977), p. 13, is converted to 1957 dollars by assuming an 8 percent annual rate of price increase during 1973–75.

Line 2: Figures for 1957–71 are GDP estimates by Perkins, "Growth and Changing Structure," p. 161. Subsequent figures are obtained by applying percentage changes in GNP as estimated in U.S. Central Intelligence Agency, *China: Economic Indicators*, p. 3.

Line 3: table 4.1.

Line 4: Row A is for Rawski, "Industrial Performance," in *Quantitative Measures*, table 7. Row B is from U.S. Central Intelligence Agency, *China: Economic Indicators*, p. 15.

Line 5: Robert M. Field, "Real Capital Formation," in *Quantitative Measures*, table 19.

Line 6: U.S. Central Intelligence Agency, *China: Economic Indicators*, p. 5.

[a] Growth rate covers 1957–73.

[b] Percentage growth during 1972–75 assumed equal to that of the series shown in line 4B.

Measurement of import dependence in producer durables is complicated by the inconvertibility of the Chinese yuan. Use of official exchange rates to convert import totals valued in dollars appears to understate the share of imports both before and after 1960.[39] R. M. Field has used calculations of purchasing power parity to estimate the yuan value of machinery imports. The resulting estimates of the share of domestic supplies in apparent consumption of producer durables—58 percent for 1957, 90 percent for 1965, and 92 percent for 1973—are more plausible, especially since the 1957 figure tallies with Chinese statements.[40]

A final method, based on the same Chinese reports and on subsequent trends in the estimated real value of imports and domestic machinery production, was used to obtain the results shown in table 4.12. These figures show that the recent import surge has not reversed the shift toward self-reliance in producer durables that occurred during the 1960s. The 1975 ratio of imports to imports plus production falls in the range of 7 to 9 percent or 12 to 15 percent depending on which output series is chosen. In neither case is the share of imports significantly larger in 1975 than it was ten years earlier.

Each of these calculations supports the conclusion that domestic firms supply most of the producer durables as well as the entire construction component of China's current investment programs. Imports are certainly more significant as carriers of new technology than might be inferred from table 4.12, but a 10 percent volume share severely limits even the qualitative impact of imported machinery on China's overall level of industrial technology. Furthermore, equipment imports are concentrated in a small number of industries: fertilizers, petroleum refining, petrochemicals, ferrous metallurgy, and electric power. Only in fertilizers is the scale of imports large enough to cause major changes in industrial size and structure. With this exception, the role of equipment imports is now confined to breaking bottlenecks and introducing particular types of capacity needed to obtain essential product characteristics—a far cry from the overall dominance of Soviet equipment in industrial investment plans of the 1950s.

Unless the real value of equipment imports reaches a large multiple of its recent level, the impact of imported machinery will continue to be episodic and microeconomic rather than broad and macroscopic as during the 1950s. If we look at the whole economy, and not just fertilizer or petrochemicals, the trade data in tables 4.11 and 4.12 show that, despite recent increases in technology-bearing imports, China's overall technical progress will continue to depend primarily on the ability of the domestic producer industry to absorb, imitate, and modify foreign technologies, to increase the number of enterprises that can master

TABLE 4.12
Share of Imports in Apparent Consumption of Machinery, 1957–75

Year	Share of Imports in Apparent Consumption	
	Low	High
1957	0.40[a]	0.45[a]
1965		
High domestic output series	0.065	0.078
Low domestic output series	0.119	0.142
1971		
High domestic output series	0.036	0.044
Low domestic output series	0.065	0.079
1973		
High domestic output series	0.039	0.048
Low domestic output series	0.068	0.082
1975		
High domestic output series	0.073	0.088
Low domestic output series	0.122	0.146

Source: Calculated from data in table 4.11 using the formula $a_t = \dfrac{M}{M + Q\left(\dfrac{1-a}{a}\right)}$

where a = imports divided by the sum of imports and domestic output during 1957.
a_t = the same quotient for a later year t.
M = imports (in constant prices) in t divided by imports in 1957.
Q = domestic machinery output (in constant prices) in t divided by output in 1957.

These calculations ignore China's small exports of machinery.

[a] Chinese statements reported in Cheng, *Maching-building*, p. 66, and SCMP 3392(1965):21.

progressively more advanced products, materials, and techniques, and to provide growing volumes of improved products to all sectors of China's economy.

Economic difficulties brought on by the Great Leap Forward convinced China's leaders that improved performance in the farm sector was essential to further industrial growth and that agricultural growth, in turn, required strong industrial support. New policies that identified agriculture as the "foundation" and industry as the "leading sector" of the economy have achieved considerable success in reducing the variance and increasing the normal level of the harvest. Agricultural output has grown at an average pace of 2 to 2.5 percent annually since 1957, with higher growth rates of 3 to 3.5 percent recorded since 1965. In addition, the farm sector has expanded both incomes and employment opportunities for a peasant labor force that has absorbed some eighty million new entrants since 1957.[41]

These achievements can be traced to two sets of innovations: organizational changes brought about by agricultural collectivization, and technological shifts permitted by a growing flow of industrial products into the rural economy. Average annual growth rates for stocks and flows of agricultural producer goods illustrate the expansion of these inflows:[42]

rural power consumption, 1957–75	32%
small-scale cement output, 1958–76	19%
chemical fertilizer output, 1957–75	21%
equipment stocks (horsepower):	
irrigation and drainage equipment, 1957–76	26%–27%
tractors, 1957–76	18%
power tillers, 1970–76	46%

The addition of growing quantities of chemical fertilizer, much of it manufactured in county-level plants, to traditional organic fertilizers has pushed China into "a class with some of the world's highest users of fertilizers including Japan."[43] Chemical manufacturers also provide the farm sector with large quantities of pesticides and plastic sheeting. Rural construction projects, including annual winter works campaigns that involve over 100 million peasants, depend on cement, steel, explosives, and other manufactured construction materials.[44]

The expansion of farm machinery production has led to a significant degree of mechanization in Chinese agriculture. Table 4.13 presents inventory estimates for three types of farm equipment: irrigation and drainage machinery, tractors, and power tillers. These figures show that these types of equipment alone provide Chinese farmers with mechanical power roughly equivalent to the 0.69 horsepower per hectare of cultivated land available to Japanese farmers from *all* types of power machinery in 1955. Since Chinese farms are equipped with large numbers of threshers as well as lesser amounts of other varieties of machinery, we can see that, despite the evident labor intensity of Chinese farm practices, agriculture will soon approach Japanese mechanization levels of the early 1960s. Under these conditions, China's present objective of achieving "basic mechanization of farm work by 1980" does not appear unrealistic.[45]

The impact of industrial inputs on rural labor requirements is quite

TABLE 4.13
Inventory Estimates for Selected Farm Equipment
(in million horsepower)

Year	Irrigation and Drainage Equipment	Power Tractors	Tillers	Total for Three Items: Million Horsepower	Total for Three Items: Horsepower per Cultivated Hectare[b]
1957	0.6[a]	0.4[c]	--	1.0	0.01
1962	3.6[a]	1.5[c]	--	5.1	0.05
1963	5.2[a]	1.7[c]	--	6.9	0.06
1964	7.0[a]	1.8[c]	--	8.8	0.08
1965	9.1[e]	2.0[d]	--	11.1	0.10
1966	10.0[c]	2.2[c]	--	12.2	0.11
1970	16.9[c]	4.5[c]	0.3[c]	21.7	0.20
1971	20.0[c]	5.5[d]	0.4[c]	25.9	0.24
1972	24.0[c]	6.6[c]	0.7[c]	31.3	0.29
1973	30.0[c]	8.5[c]	1.1[c]	39.6	0.37
1974	36.0[c]	10.9[c]	1.6[c]	48.5	0.45
1975	43.0[c]	12.3[c]	2.2[c]	57.5	0.54
1976	46.5[d]	14.6[c]	3.2[c]	64.3	0.60
1977	50+[e]	—	—	67.8+	0.63+

[a] Dwight H. Perkins, "Constraints Influencing China's Agricultural Performance," in *China: A Reassessment of the Economy* (Washington, D.C., 1975), p. 360.
[b] Calculated from the inventory totals for three items and a constant figure of 107 million hectares for cultivated acreage cited in Perkins, ibid., 353.
[c] U.S. Central Intelligence Agency, *China: Economic Indicators*, p. 13.
[d] Interpolation between previous and subsequent figures.
[e] FBIS, December 28, 1977, E3.

complex. Electrification and mechanization of crop processing, irrigation, transport, and other operations have eliminated the demand for millions of man-years of human labor. But increased supplies of water, nutrients, and motive power have simultaneously permitted cropping cycles to be intensified in many directions. In some regions, for example, machines capable of replacing human labor formerly devoted to irrigation, harvesting, threshing, transport, plowing, and transplanting during seasonal labor peaks have eliminated bottlenecks that formerly restricted the spread of multicropping. In Hsin-chou county, Hupei:

> the "two-way rush" [rushing through harvesting and planting] has for years been the critical period of time in which cotton and rice fight for labor power, fertilizer and water supply. But in 1964, because machines were used to lift water, abundant labor power was saved. The

> pressure of the "two-way rush" on paddy fields was reduced, and there were special shifts responsible for fighting the drought and guarding against insect pests in cotton fields.[46]

Mechanization led to unprecedented harvest results and also to increased overall labor requirements in Hsin-chou and in many other regions.

On balance, the labor requirements created by various forms of intensification, land improvement, and water conservancy projects, all of which depend heavily on industrial supplies, have far outweighed the labor replacing effect of mechanization. As a result, estimated labor requirements per farm worker rose from 160 to 250 annual days between 1957 and 1975. Industrial inputs have played a key role in absorbing new workers and in raising the utilization of existing farm labor. Increased supplies of complementary inputs have actually raised farm output per man-year during 1957–75 despite a 34 percent increase in the labor force and no growth of cultivated acreage.[47]

Finally, we must consider the long-run impact of increased local production and consumption of industrial farm inputs on the process of rural development:

> a reasonably strong argument can be made that the major contribution of the agricultural machinery industry to Chinese society has not been through any direct impact on agricultural production, but has been through an indirect process of "scientification" of the rural masses. A hand tractor imported from Japan would have the same physical productivity as one made in China, but it would certainly not have the same impact as one made in a brigade or commune machine shop where every peasant knows someone who helped build it. By pushing the production of particular agricultural machinery all the way to the brigade level, China has removed the "foreignness" from new technology.[48]

Bearing in mind the finding of Inkeles and Smith[49] that participation in factory work and in agricultural cooperation facilitate the emergence of modern character traits, opinions, and interests, we must conclude that the agricultural support activities of China's producer sector have contributed not just to higher farm output and employment, but to a broader process of rural modernization as well.

Some International Comparisons

Serious comparison of China's post-1949 economic achievements with those of other developing nations has hardly begun. The brief discussion here does not attempt to fill this void, but seeks to establish two points: first, that China's producer sector has expanded at a relatively swift pace, and second, that China's industrial sector is an essential component in national economic development rather than an artificial creation arising from forced-draft import substitution.

Meaningful comparisons involving China must focus on large nations in which the scale of economic problems as well as aspirations begins to approach the enormous magnitudes that characterize Chinese economic life. India and Brazil are states that share with China the problems and opportunities associated with large national size. They also aspire to many of the same economic goals as China: creation of a large, comprehensive, and technically progressive industrial sector; strong military capability; and amelioration of interregional disparities in income and wealth. The policies of all three governments point to growth of producer output and its intersectoral linkages as reasonable tests of industry's contribution to national economic goals.

In terms of output growth, China's performance is outstanding among the three countries. In table 4.14, sectoral output indices for Chinese and Indian two-digit industries are aggregated into overall series for the producer sector using both Chinese and Indian intersectoral weights. All variants of the Chinese output index outgrow all variants of the Indian series throughout 1952–73. Over two decades, Chinese producer output has grown at approximately twice the Indian rate. Substitution of Indian for Chinese intersectoral weights does not alter, and indeed reinforces, this conclusion.[50]

Information on the growth of value added in Brazilian manufacturing and on the share of output originating in the textile, food, and beverage sectors may be used to construct a rough index of value added in producer manufacturing spanning the years 1939–73.[51] The average annual growth rate of this index is 9.3 percent for 1939–73, 10.8 percent for 1949–73, and 12.3 percent for 1965–73. Comparison with table 4.5 shows that the pace of growth matches China's performance only after 1965.

Assessing the relative impact of industrial development on overall

TABLE 4.14
Growth of Producer Output in China and India, 1952–73
(1952 = 100)

	1957	1965	1970	1973	Average Annual Growth Rate 1952–73 (in percentage)
Chinese output					
1. Chinese weights					
A. 1952 prices	320	1,016	1,869	2,906	17.4
B. 1975 prices	272	777	1,356	2,094	15.6
2. Indian weights	421	1,301	2,420	3,748	18.8
Indian output					
3. Chinese weights	171	448	574	674	9.5
4. Indian weights	158	374	525	591	8.8

Sources: For China: Output indices for electric power, coal, petroleum, ferrous metals, machinery, chemicals, building materials, timber, and paper are compiled from the sources cited in table 4.3. For machinery, the 1972 output level is used for 1973. Chinese intersectoral weights are based on sectoral shares in Chinese 1957 GVFO computed from Ishikawa, *National Income*, p. 60, panel B. Gross output for the coal and petroleum industries in 1957 is extrapolated from Ishikawa's 1956 figures, using percentage changes in physical output of coal and crude oil derived from Chen, *Statistics*, p. 187.

For India: Sectors are the same as for China except that metal processing replaces machinery. Sectoral output indices for 1952–70 are from Subraminian Swamy, "Economic Growth in China and India, 1952–1970: A Comparative Appraisal," *Economic Development and Cultural Change* 21.4, pt. 2(1973):43–44. These indices have been extended to 1973 using sectoral value data found in UN Economic and Social Council for Asia and the Pacific, *Statistical Yearbook for Asia and the Pacific, 1975* (Bangkok, 1976), p. 142. Where sectoral data were not found, values were projected on the basis of physical output of coal and lignite (for coal), cement (for building materials), and roundwood removals (for timber) reported in *Statistical Yearbook, 1975*, pp. 142–45. Indian intersectoral weights are computed from data on the structure of value added in 1956 shown in Swamy, "Economic Growth," p. 39.

Note: Each index takes the form $I_t = \sum_i w_i I_{it}$, where I_{it} is an output index for the *ith* sector in year t (1952=100) and w_i is the intersectoral weight attached to the *ith* sector.

economic performance raises complex issues that cannot be adequately treated without straying far beyond the confines of this study. Available evidence does, however, create the impression that China has outstripped both India and Brazil in creating fruitful linkages between industry and other sectors. In Brazil, industry's isolation, both in geographic and input-output terms, has meant that industrial expansion has contributed only marginally to raising output and productivity in other sectors, notably agriculture, or in nonindustrial regions.[52]

India's producer sector often appears sluggish and unresponsive to shifting patterns of domestic demand. One observer finds "little evidence that progress of import substitution in production was accompanied by an increase in designing and product development." Even experienced firms make "few adaptations and improvements of foreign designs" with the result that machine tool models, for example, show no change over periods of ten to fifteen years.[53] In terms of intersectoral links, Mellor's employment-oriented strategy for India, "a strategy that uses technological change in an initially dominant agriculture as a major stimulus to a broadly participatory pattern of rural and urban development," points to the superiority of Chinese performance, for Mellor's proposals include many features that Chinese leaders have implemented with great vigor since the early 1960s.[54]

These observations depicting Brazilian and Indian industry as largely self-contained and preoccupied with replication of existing product types rather than with technological upgrading, innovation, and service to nonindustrial customers recall the state of Chinese industrial operations during the 1950s and emphasize the extent to which Chinese industry has improved its demand responsiveness over the past two decades. In China, unlike Brazil, the continuing growth of agricultural output, amounting to approximately 40 percent since 1965, is inextricably linked with the injection of fertilizer, pumps, power tillers, steel, cement, and other industrial goods into the rural sector. And in contrast to India, the absence of international competition has not prevented Chinese enterprises at all levels of sophistication from turning out a steady flow of new products, quality improvements, and process innovations in response to changing requirements and competition induced by administrative exhortations.

Some economists have argued that the policies of import substitution pursued by all three countries may give rise to false or hothouse industrialization. Balassa, for example, writes that

> We cannot accept as a criterion of success the fact that the structure of manufacturing industry in countries following an inward-looking strategy approaches that of the industrial nations. While the former group of countries has established a wide range of industries . . . they generally use backward technical methods, manufacture products of low quality, and have not achieved the extent of intra-industry specilization that is desirable under modern conditions.[55]

These strictures are certainly applicable to most branches of industry in China as well as in India and Brazil. But Balassa fails to consider that producing inferior goods in excessively integrated plants using backward techniques is an indispensable component of long-term processes, which, as we have seen in the case of China, can lead to improved technique, product quality, and productivity, not only in industry, but throughout the economy.

In developing an economy of China's size, large injections of manufactured intermediate and capital goods are needed to help feed and employ a growing population and to begin the dauntingly difficult task of enlarging the share of employment in highly productive nonfarm activities. The volume of goods required for these purposes could not conceivably come from normal international exchange. In addition to the diffiiculty of financing such enormous imports, a trade-linked industrialization strategy would quickly encounter supply problems. China's annual absorption of machine tools, for example, now exceeds United States output by a large margin!

The history of Japan's relatively open economy illustrates the importance of an early shift toward domestic manufacture of producer goods. The share of imports in total supplies of producers' durable equipment dropped steadily from about 1890. By 1900, these imports had fallen to less than one-third of domestic machinery output; in 1930, the ratio of imports to domestic machinery output was only one-eighth.[56] The remaining supplies came from domestic producers whose operations embodied the precise elements of backwardness lamented by contemporary observers and, more recently, by Balassa and other trade-oriented development economists.[57]

Japan's experience, and China's as well, shows that the production and consumption of inferior producer goods may ignite and later sustain an ongoing process that results in successive improvements in quality, technology, and productivity along with the growth of output. In China, as in the case of earlier industrializers, it is this improvement process, rather than the enlarged output volume itself, that constitutes the producer sector's greatest contribution to the development of the national economy.

Chapter 5

Organization, Administration, and Efficiency

The preceding chapters describe the expansion and technical maturation of the producer sector and show how this group of industries has influenced the evolution of the whole economy. Improved performance in the producer sector arises not only from higher resource inputs and technological levels, but also from changes in the structure and functioning of industry's planning and administrative systems. These shifts are the focus of the present chapter. They have led to notable increases in economic efficiency during the post-1949 period and have played a central role in the transition from rushing to harmonic growth that characterizes the 1960s and 1970s. Organizational and administrative developments are also responsible for certain unique features that distinguish Chinese industrial operations from similar activities in other nations.

Chinese industrial reform has focused on administrative rather than organizational measures. Despite the importance of territorial decentralization, which has transferred formal authority over many enterprises from the central to the provincial level, most reform measures have affected the operation of existing administrative structures rather than the structures themselves. Reduced plan tautness, informal delegation of authority from higher to lower administrative levels, and a shift from direct to indirect supervision of industrial enterprises are among the most significant operational changes.

The desire for reform as well as the skills needed to implement new methods have arisen through a process of administrative development that in some ways parallels the technological evolution outlined in earlier chapters. Experience gained during the first decade of socialism showed the high and rising costs of rushing and of detailed central control over industry. The same experience, however, was essential in creating skills and building institutions without which neither decentralization nor a shift from rushing to harmonic growth could occur. Thus we find that in administration as well as in production, the experience gained during periods of weak performance can be an essential ingredient in a discontinuous process of development.

As in production, the accumulation of experience in planning and administration can only create opportunities for improved performance. Incentive as well as skill is essential if opportunities are to be translated into actual gains. Motivation is an area in which the Chinese have attempted unique approaches to problems of industrial control.

In China, as elsewhere, socialist systems encounter difficulty in specifying appropriate decision rules for managers. Ordering managers to maximize output, profit, or any other single criterion inevitably leads to undesired side effects. Expanding the list of compulsory targets forces managers to evade some requirements to satisfy others. The Chinese have tried to meet this problem by providing managers with basic performance targets of the traditional variety and by supplementing them with general rather than specific instructions that allow considerable leeway to provinces, localities, and enterprises in allocating resources at the margin of production. Substitution of general for specific instructions limits the usefulness of profit, output growth, or other statistical indicators in measuring results outside the basic plan targets. The absence of specific instructions and success indicators makes China's industrial performance highly dependent on mutual trust, understanding, and common interest among industrial leaders up and down the administrative hierarchy.

The following pages describe the evolution of China's industrial administration from a pattern of tight central control during the FFYP years into a revised system that retains much of the formal structure adopted from Soviet practice of the 1950s, but now incorporates elements of lower-level authority and entrepreneurship into the original framework of strong central control. These modifications, based on mutually reinforcing policy insights and administrative skill development, have contributed to a substantial upward trend in efficiency. At the same time, the unchanging Soviet foundations of Chinese industrial organization are reflected in the continued presence of characteristically Soviet weaknesses that persist in cycles of their own alongside the overall upward trend in planning and administrative performance.

Chinese Industrial Organization: Basic Features[1]

The present organization of Chinese industry is a hybrid, combining major features of Soviet institutions adopted in the early 1950s with subsequent modifications made in response to changing political and economic conditions. These changes have not altered the basic elements of industrial hierarchy and planning procedures as outlined here.

The State Council, which stands atop the hierarchy of industrial planning and administration, holds formal responsibility for issuing targets to all sectors. Once ratified by the State Council, economic plans carry the force of law. Actual plan preparation is centered in the State Economic Commission and its provincial counterparts, which cooperate with the State Statistical Bureau, the State Construction Bureau, the People's Bank, and other economic agencies subordinate to the State Council.

The State Council gives final approval to output plans for major commodities and value targets for various branches of industry. These norms are then transmitted to the provinces and to the central government's industrial ministries for metallurgy, machine building, chemicals, and so forth—which allocate tasks among constituent enterprises to ensure fulfillment of their portion of the national plan.

The fundamental unit of industrial activity is the enterprise, defined as an independent accounting unit with its own allocation of fixed and circulating capital.[2] The enterprise is led by a director or manager. In addition to the technical functions of procurement, production, and sales, directors enjoyed broad latitude over personnel and wage matters during the FFYP period. This system of one-man management, based on Soviet practice, was soon challenged, and executive authority partially supplanted by enterprise branches of the Communist party. Party power reached a peak during the Great Leap, declined during the early 1960s, and may have rebounded under the system of revolutionary committees that, since the Cultural Revolution, exercise nominal control over enterprise operations.

The chief obligation of the firm, and of the managers and party personnel in key posts, is to fulfill annual economic plans issued by the State Council and other government organs. Despite periodic changes in the list of norms and in the priority attached to particular items, plan targets have always included figures for total output value and physical output of major commodities, financial quotas involving wages, costs, and profit, and subsidiary requirements concerning input coefficients, research, and innovation. Enterprises may also receive additional assignments such as expanding productive capacity, training workers for other firms, or meeting special orders outside the plan.

Enterprise plans are not imposed by fiat from above. They are hammered out by enterprise managers and planning officials in negotiations that may be protracted. In 1975, officials at Peking's Capital Iron-Steel Works reported that

> Plans are made once a year during the fourth quarter, based on capacity and past results. We receive targets from the state based on the need for planned development of the national economy. The targets are discussed in the plant's Party Committee, then we draw workers and staff into discussions of the targets. In these discussions we must consider equipment capacity, supply of raw materials, labor force, renovation of equipment. Therefore we have large scale discussions. On the basis of these discussions, we draw up a plan within the factory and submit it to the Ministry. Worker-staff suggestions are usually accepted by the Ministry. If we agree with them, the plan is fixed on this basis of pooling the wisdom of leaders and workers. If we do not agree, the procedure of plan, discussion and revised plan is repeated, sometimes two or three times.[3]

As this statement indicates, the center compiles preliminary plans on the basis of the State Council's overall policy objectives and of detailed information collected from below. Enterprise leaders and, more recently, workers receive opportunities to study and discuss these drafts and to suggest modifications before the State Council's final approval. This bargaining process provides ample scope for enterprises to resist excessive output targets or to request additional materials, labor, or equipment before accepting difficult assignments. The use of enterprise statistics as the foundation of all projections enables managers to influence the planning process even before negotiations begin.

This summarizes the basic institutional framework of Chinese industry. Producers are subordinate to a dual network of government and party organizations, now complicated by the enlarged role of provincial and local governments and their industrial and planning bureaucracies. Industrial enterprises are charged with fulfilling economic plans but participate actively in their formulation. Within the enterprise, authority is shared among professional managers, engineers, party members, and other groups subject to varying degrees of party control, including trade union branches and workers' councils. The relative strength of these groups is not constant but shifts with the political and economic climate.

It is important to recognize the high degree of continuity and stability in the formulation and administration of industrial plans. Although the decentralization reforms discussed below have substituted provincial (territorial) for ministerial (vertical) lines of authority in some areas of decision making, neither the list of enterprise targets nor the process of plan formulation has changed significantly during the past quarter-century. Concrete accounts of the planning process may refer to the FFYP period, the Cultural Revolution years, or the 1970s, but they invariably emphasize the features noted earlier.[4]

Industrial Administration under the First Five-Year Plan

Beginning in 1949, China gradually built up a system of industrial administration modeled on contemporary Soviet practice. As the central government's industrial ministries extended their control over an increasing range of activities, growing numbers of enterprises were given lists of detailed performance targets, assigned specified supplies of labor, materials, equipment, and funds, and graded on the extent to which results met or exceeded plan targets.

In theory, this system aspired to furnish each enterprise with precisely enough resources to support plan fulfillment if all inputs were used with the utmost economy. If attained, the goal of making every input a bottleneck for each firm maximizes output at the microeconomic level and simultaneously exposes the incompetence of managers who lack the skill to utilize available resources fully and whose units therefore fall short of their objectives.

In practice, however, Chinese economic planning fell far short of this ideal. As we have seen in chapter 2, inexperienced planning agencies found themselves unable to exercise close supervision over a substantial, if declining, segment of industry. Even within the sectors included in planning operations, paucity of trained and seasoned personnel and absence of established statistical routines made it impossible to obtain the detailed studies of average and marginal input-output coefficients needed to predict the effect of shifting the resource mix allotted to each enterprise.

Under these circumstances, Chinese planning of necessity was a heavy-handed operation that could only aim to achieve roughly consistent patterns of input supplies and output targets for key enterprises. Even these units complained bitterly of planning errors, while lesser units invariably found themselves obliged to scramble for resources using methods picturesquely described as "four gropes and seven seeks."[5]

The combination of strong pressure to raise production— the gross value of producer output rose at an average annual rate of 35 percent between 1949 and 1957—and limited competence within nascent planning agencies led to frequent inconsistency between targets and supplies. Shortfalls of resources, in turn, created sharp conflicts of interest between the state, represented by planning offices and industrial ministries, and the managers of industrial enterprises. The state expects producers to fulfill all aspects of their plans with the resources assigned them. Victims of tardy planning, egregious supply breakdowns, or switches in priorities can hope for a sympathetic hearing from their superiors, but the center has no real choice but to insist on the fundamental soundness of economic plans and to interpret non-compliance as evidence of incompetence at lower levels.

Factory executives must maintain a high probability that plans can be met despite the likelihood of unexpected changes in the balance between goals and means of production. Otherwise, the fabric of national plans will be endangered, as will their personal careers. It is to reduce the chance of failure that factory managers enter into a search for slack, either through evading or relaxing certain plan targets or by enlarging the volume of resources at their command.

Since all targets are compulsory and major inputs are generally limited to those provided by the state, the creation of slack calls for deception, concealment, and even outright illegalities on the part of enterprises and their leaders. This explains the vulnerability of factory executives to charges raised during political campaigns: most managers are criminals, and many times over, if violations committed in the service of national economic goals are viewed as breaches of the law.

The search for slack is not a random process. Any planning system that imposes ambitious output targets along with central allocation of major inputs gives rise to characteristic difficulties resulting from managerial efforts to offset actual or potential imbalance between targets and resources. In China, as elsewhere, participants in such a system tend to focus their attention on quotas dealing with the volume of physical output and the total value of production. Quality, cost, balance among product types, and preparations for future production are often disregarded in the interest of ensuring the planned flow of current output.

Disproportionate attention to output volume is deeply rooted in the Soviet system of economic planning adopted in China during the 1950s. The fundamental goal of material balance planning is to ensure supplies of predetermined quantities of commodities needed at various points for current production, investment, consumption, and export. The primacy of output volume follows directly from this foundation. If insufficient quantities of goods are produced, the intended recipients of the missing products cannot meet their obligations, and the resulting disruption will reverberate through the economy. If, on the other hand, quantity targets are met by skimping on quality or variety, customers have less cause for complaint. Their task of meeting ambitious targets with less than ideal resources is not unusual in an economy perpetually straining to squeeze more output from limited means.

In any system based on physical commodity flows, leaders must be willing to accept high costs to avoid delay.[6] If these costs become unbearable, a general reduction in the pace of growth is needed. But so long as the pressure to raise output remains intense, exhortation alone will not suffice to direct managerial efforts toward cost, quality, assortment, and other desirable but secondary criteria.

Chinese economists were quick to grasp these matters:

> Since the general indices of our government's plans and statistics are based on quantities, attention has thus been concentrated in these with little or no regard to quality in the distribution of missions and conducting of examinations on the part of responsible organizations *on the upper level.*[7]

As long as Peking's eyes are riveted on quantity, factory managers must follow suit. Disputes between managers and inspectors reveal the institutional grounds for emphasizing quanitity:

> Factory manager Chao demanded that inspector Li certify rejects to enable the plant to meet its output quota. Li refused. Chao then appointed Li assistant shop chief and ordered him to see that the plan was fulfilled. Li immediately changed his tune and demanded that the rejects be certified, but another conscientious inspector refused to give in and Chao's plan failed.[8]

Innovation may also suffer as energies are focused on raising the quantity of output. Research and experimentation require the attention of skilled and experienced personnel whose services are also needed to maintain high levels of production. This confiict tends to be resolved in favor of higher output, leading to complaints that "many enterprise leaders who are otherwise very concerned about plan fulfillment pay little attention to new product work."[9]

Ambitious and rigidly enforced output quotas also encourage a cycle of alternate intervals of relaxation and storming or shock work that is difficult to break. At the start of each plan period, holidays, repairs, and other routine chores postponed during the rush to complete the previous plan divert resources from current production, as does the need to replenish stocks of materials and spare parts. When attendance, inventories, and equipment return to normal, it is already time to begin rushing to fulfill the next target.

Since assistance to outsiders is among the routine activities neglected during periods of peak output, interenterprise cooperation becomes least reliable just when it is most needed. Managers learn from bitter experience that emergency supplies or repair services are seldom available during periods of peak production, and take steps to ensure their operations against disruption by means of vertical integration and stockpiling, activities that often involve false reporting and misappropriation of funds.

This organizational framework and the problems and deviations that it fosters will make familiar reading to students of Soviet industry. Indeed, Soviet cooperation and advice failed to shield the Chinese from any of the major problems of plan implementation that have plagued Soviet industry for decades. Exaggerated attention to production volume, weak quality control, neglect of innovation, uneven output flows, excessive integration, illicit hoarding, and other difficulties appeared during the 1950s as nearly exact replicas of the prewar Soviet situation.[10]

Studies of industry in the European socialist countries attribute these problems to a short-term, output-oriented managerial philosophy that results from rapid turnover of executives and from their pursuit of large monetary premiums awarded for completing certain plan targets. But Chinese industry encountered similar problems during the FFYP years even though both mobility and bonuses appear far less prominent in Chinese than in Soviet factory life.[11] The strong parallels between deviant managerial behavior in China, the USSR, and Eastern Europe—regions with widely varying income levels, technical development, and industrial traditions—offer striking support for Granick's thesis that institutional factors, particularly the use of target planning, contribute substantially to the problems as well as the achievements of industries organized along Soviet lines.[12]

Industrial Reforms

The experience of the FFYP years awakened Chinese economists to the institutional roots of rush growth, with its emphasis on quantity, excessive vertical integration, compulsive hoarding of resources, and other difficulties that grew along with, and then began to obstruct, industrial expansion. With their emphasis on relaxing the tempo of output and investment growth to pursue balance and qualitative objectives, the reform proposals advanced in 1956 and 1957 essentially amounted to an espousal of harmonic growth as a new objective for industrial policy.

Many of these proposals, including a major transfer of industrial units from central to provincial control, were implemented in late 1957 and early 1958. Their impact, however, was dwarfed by the Great Leap Forward of 1958–60, during which the personal intervention of Mao Tse-tung directed industry away from the path of harmonic growth. With Peking's authority and vision blurred by the decentralization policy, by Mao's emphasis on local initiative, and by a deluge of euphoric progress reports from below, industrial activity slipped into a new mode of decentralized rushing that pushed the drive for quantity, neglect of quality, and waste of resources to new extremes.

As we have seen in chapter 3, the post-1960 period has witnessed a relatively stable policy climate in which the center presses strongly for harmonic growth and resists the tendency to revert to rushing. Central support for these policies has ebbed on two occasions—in the Cultural Revolution years of 1966–68 and again during the period of political instability surrounding the deaths of Mao Tse-tung and Chou En-lai, roughly from 1974 to early 1977. In neither case was existing policy replaced, as in the Great Leap, by new directives favoring all-out pursuit of growth. As a result, the return of political stability and consequent revival of active central policy in 1969–70 and again in 1977 led to quick and relatively easy reaffirmation of the basic strategy of harmonic growth on both occasions.

The key reform, one that crucially affected the viability of other administrative and structural changes, was a reduction in the tautness of industrial plans. This began with the appearance of idle labor and excess capacity throughout industry in 1961. By 1966, there was a clear-cut policy of allocating planned reserves of material inputs in excess of expected requirements; Richman found that the surpluses "typically range from roughly 2 to a maximum of 7 or 8 percent of total planned output value."[13] This policy was also evident in 1972 when visitors noted year-end slowdowns in units that had fulfilled their plan targets and heard from planning officials at the Anshan steel complex that "it was explicit policy not to fix targets too tightly. . . . the state tends to provide enough raw material and fuel to over-fulfill the production plan by 5 percent."[14]

Reduced plan tautness slackens the pressures compelling managers to force the pace of output and makes them more receptive to administrative proposals for qualitative change. High-level advocacy of quality, innovation, and customer service did not, of course, begin in 1961. Throughout the FFYP years, China's press carried thousands of exhortations similar to the following 1957 warning:

> it behooves the various production, construction, transportation departments when they sum up the works of the year and plan for the next to place in an important position the question of quality, to establish a rigid system of inspection over the quality of production and construction and to help cadres of lower strata to build up and improve on skills and raise the technical standard. We will encourage and reward those departments effective in raising the quality, and criticize those that have fallen short of the quality stipulation, thereby creating an atmosphere in which importance is attached to quality.[15]

Until the center made systematic provision to ensure that most units could meet the quantitative plan stipulations without straining to beat the system by shaving standards in one direction or another, quality could never occupy an important position in the constellation of managerial goals. In China, as in Eastern Europe, "some slack is essential to carry out reforms."[16]

Unlike earlier efforts to promote harmonic growth, which had foundered in the face of lower-level resistance to change, the post-1960 campaign against rush growth evoked strong support at the enterprise level. Encouraged by reduced plan tautness and undoubtedly shocked by the disastrous short-term consequences of the Great Leap Forward and the sudden withdrawal of Soviet technical assistance, enterprise leaders now realized that the shortcomings of rush growth could not be blamed solely on the inadequacies of planning and supply agencies. Enterprises now began to conduct searching reevaluations of their own operations.

Leaders at the large Kirin Chemical Corporation spent several years in combating internal opposition to the quality-first approach. During 1961 and 1962, this firm gradually learned to understand the errors of rushing; the next year was devoted to organizing for overall plan fulfillment by improving balance, stability, safety, economy, and rationalizing production operations. Only in 1964 were officials able to claim success in smoothing the flow of production and reducing unit input coefficients. Industrial journals of the mid-1960s are filled with similar reports stressing the depth and duration of reform efforts at a wide variety of enterprises.[17]

Increased managerial attention to qualitative considerations is reflected in subsequent administrative changes as well as in improved performance. The revival of individual monetary bonuses and piece rates in the early 1960s and again in 1977 demonstrates the confidence of a quality-minded leadership that these reward systems no longer engender the disregard of quality that contributed to their earlier removal from the industrial scene.[18]

Gradual substitution of indirect for direct monitoring of enterprise operations is another administrative shift that shows Peking's new confidence that managers will implement new priorities without close supervision. The rationale for indirect control based largely on financial performance was laid out as early as 1962:

> Whether or not an enterprise returns its loan to the bank in equal amount and by the date fixed is a very good yardstick for measuring its operations management and economic accounting. If an obstacle has been encountered at any of the links of production and circulation, it will be reflected here. Such a method of inspecting the operations management and economic accounting of an enterprise is simple and direct and can provide clues to many complicated economic problems.[19]

The frequency with which enterprises and regions publicly relate industrial profits to previous investment grants offers further evidence of the extent to which planners use financial measures to allocate investment funds and to assess the overall performance of production units.[20]

China's industrial reform includes structural as well as administrative shifts. The most notable institutional development has been the gradual and limited decentralization of authority over industrial planning and operation from the central government's industrial ministries to the provinces, municipalities, and counties. Decentralization began with a series of directives in 1957 and 1958 that transferred primary authority for most industrial units from the ministries to the provinces. Local authorities acquired added influence over enterprises retained under Peking's direct control through a system of central-local dual leadership, which was enlarged during the late 1960s with the transfer of the Anshan steel complex, Shanghai Machine Tool Plant, and other key enterprises from central to dual control. A further initiative in 1970 shifted "an overwhelming majority of enterprises to local control" and gave lower levels of administration "greater power to run and build certain enterprises."[21]

While these measures have aroused considerable discussion and debate among foreign observers, their impact on industrial planning and administration remains somewhat obscure.[22] There is no doubt, however, that decentralization has substantially expanded provincial and local-level participation in the formulation and administration of industrial plans. It has also raised the degree of aggregation in provincial reports to the center and in Peking's directives to the provinces. Provinces now take responsibility for many transactions, including a portion of interregional and even foreign trade, formerly directed from the center. Provincial governments have also made vigorous efforts to improve the balance between plan requirements and supplies by organizing distribution conferences and operating commodity banks as legitimate alternatives to illicit barter and black-market arrangements.[23]

Increased participation of lower-level governments in industrial planning and administration is now a well-established feature of China's industrial system. Vice-Premier Teng Hsiao-p'ing, previously attacked for favoring excessive central control, now praises decentralization for having "played an outstanding part in industrial development and in supporting agriculture with industry" and insists that "enterprises that should be decentralized must be resolutely transferred to the localities." Yü Ch'iu-li, a like-minded economic administrator and vice-premier, states that the key to raising industrial standards to the level set by model units "lies in provincial and municipal party committees," again showing that central leaders intend to maintain or perhaps enlarge the scope of provincial and local government initiative in industrial planning and management.[24]

Increased provincial and local participation has not, however, reduced the overall authority of China's central government in industrial affairs. This can be seen from a variety of sources. Barnett, for example, finds that

> Chinese Communist cadres make it very clear that central authorities again exercise effective and extensive overall control of the economy. One obtains the impression . . . that even though major annual targets are supposed to be set through a process that begins with proposals "from the bottom," in reality the crucial decisions about the most important targets are handed down "from the top."[25]

Barnett's impression is explicitly confirmed by a 1975 report that the State Council initiates the planning process by setting tentative output targets for key commodities.[26] The same source enumerates major items and policies determined by the center; the list is echoed and expanded in a subsequent report by Teng Hsiao-p'ing, who insists that the following decisions "must be centralized":

> (1) orientation and policies of national economy; (2) key industrial . . . and agricultural production quotas; (3) investment in basic construction and major . . . projects; (4) distribution of essential materials; (5) purchase and allocation of vital commodities; (6) national budgetary outlays and issuance of currency; (7) numbers

> of additional . . . workers, and the total sum of wages; (8) prices of industrial and agricultural products.[27]

Implementation of these provisions is frequently visible at the microeconomic level. Meisner reports that after semiannual consultations with Peking, the Shenyang Transformer Factory receives a plan that "specifies quantity, quality, variety, cost relationships, labour productivity, profits, and funding" and "also determines the total number of workers and the total amount of the wage bill."[28] Officials at Shanghai Machine Tool Works, another large unit, report that transfer from central to dual leadership has made little difference to the plant's operations, with targets for output, cost, profit, quantity, and gross output value still coming directly from the First Ministry of Machine-building.[29] Joan Robinson finds that new industrial hiring "has to be sanctioned by the Planning Commission," and that "the province carries the proposals of all its enterprises to the Planning Commission," evidently to secure approval, while in the sphere of investment, "every province has put in schemes of investment and the centre has to ration them out."[30]

Central authority is most evident in the financial sector. Neither the transfer of most tax collections from the center to the provinces nor the assignment of specific shares of industrial profits, the chief source of revenues, to the provinces has curtailed Peking's ability to enforce a continuing pattern of fiscal transfers from industrial to nonindustrial regions.[31] Central control over the composition as well as the size of provincial outlays may be inferred from the following interview material:

> Our constitution stipulates that provincial budgets be determined by the provincial-level National People's Congresses. Before this body receives the proposed budget, it has to be forwarded to the State Council as a component part of the state budget. If the State Council gives the green light to the figures, then the province has the right to submit the budget to the provincial NPC for formal approval. The province can also make minor changes, but major changes must be approved by the State Council.[32]

At the enterprise level, budgets are established by the center and supervised by the People's Bank. According to Cassou, "all financial needs relating to industrial investments are directly controlled by the state budget" and "the People's Bank rigorously controls the financial situation" of industrial units.[33]

Decentralization has meant a gradual devolution of authority from the center to the provinces and, more recently, to localities active in promoting rural industry, but without curtailment of the center's power to step in when local allocation decisions contravene Peking's wishes. The need for central approval of provincial budgets and economic plans allows Peking to keep abreast of local developments, and the intelligence compiled by bank personnel who are expected to make "a point of always knowing the production and management conditions of enterprises, how they use their funds and how they implement financial and economic policies," provides a ready source of details concerning suspected malfeasance.[34]

The outcome of these administrative and organizational changes is an industrial system still structured along basically Soviet lines but now operating in a fashion that differs markedly from earlier Chinese practice as well as recent Soviet and Eastern European patterns. As in the past, provincial and local administrators and enterprise leaders participate in arranging plans that their units are then expected to fulfill. Now, however, industry functions in a modified environment resulting from the universal growth of planning skills and experience, the gradual transfer of authority to increasingly competent provincial and local administrations, and above all, the reduced tautness of industrial plans.

Because the system retains its institutional similarity to Soviet industry, a turn toward taut planning immediately encourages a revival of rushing, as can be seen from 1971 conditions at the Hung-ch'i shipyard:

> under the condition of the urgency of the task of production, there were some people, including some members of the basic level revolutionary committee [i.e., leading personnel], who said "The task of production is already so heavy, where is the time for carrying out innovation?" There were even some who said "The task of production is a 'hard target,' but the task of scientific research is a 'soft target.' "[35]

Commodity shortages have a similar impact, as in the case of China's lagging coal industry:

> For many years, the output of many coal mines was sometimes high and sometimes low. The monthly output "was low in the first 10 days,

> had to be caught up in the second 10 days and required a desperate effort in the last 10 days." This situation almost became the "normal practice." In the past few years . . . this situation worsened. With a desperate effort in the last 10 days, they did manage to boost the monthly output. However, people were deadly tired and the mechanical equipment often broke down. No sooner had the output gone up than it came down again.[36]

Organizational continuity preserves the system's susceptibility to the rushing syndrome. Even though performance standards have risen, the danger of recidivism evokes high-level warnings couched in the same language used decades earlier, creating a misleading impression of stagnation. We thus find Teng Hsiao-p'ing stressing quality in a 1975 report that echoes concerns voiced ten and even twenty years earlier:

> We must give top priority to quality, variety and specifications. Products which are below the quality standard should not be allowed to leave the plant. Commodity departments and commercial departments have the right to refuse to purchase things that cannot be used. Where defective products have left the plant, the enterprise concerned must guarantee repair, replacements, and compensation. Attaching first priority to quality is a major policy.[37]

Despite episodic reappearance of rush growth in certain time periods and in particular sectors and enterprises, the administrative and structural changes outlined above have created an environment in which most factories and mines can complete their assigned quotas for quantity, cost, and productivity without the ruthless concentration on narrow performance goals that formerly produced familiar social costs in the form of shoddy goods, resistance to innovation, and widespread concealment of resources from higher authorities. With managerial energies no longer consumed by the struggle to fulfill quantitative targets, a quality-conscious leadership has made considerable gains in reshaping management objectives to encompass not only the standards of workmanship applied to individual product units but also a much wider range of economic and social considerations as well.

This shift in objectives has come about not through modification of success indicators or relative prices, but through a system of propaganda and information in which centrally controlled media alert audiences to key bottleneck areas (power shortage, lax financial supervision, inability to manufacture large-scale mining machinery, etc.) and publicize the success of model units in alleviating these problems. In addition to carrying out their assigned tasks, industrial units are now expected to study and discuss the issues and approaches emphasized in the national media. These preparations furnish guidelines under which industry "takes the initiative in its own hands" by identifying and grappling with sectoral or local bottlenecks without awaiting specific instructions from above and demonstrates self-reliance by scrambling to assemble materials, improvise equipment, and develop skills without excessive requests for outside aid.

The potential of this system, which grafts territorial decentralization and administrative exhortation onto a framework of vertically layered planning and administration, can be seen from the considerable achievements of China's producer sector in the wake of industrial reform. Its weakness lies in its reliance on the morale of lower-level personnel and on their responsiveness to imprecise instructions from the center, features to which we shall return. Before doing so, we consider the impact of reform on the efficiency of China's producer industries.

Paretian Efficiency

Paretian efficiency is a concept applied to economies in which resources, technology, tastes, and income distribution are constant. A configuration of outputs, inputs, incomes, and consumption is optimal or efficient in the Pareto sense if it is impossible to reshuffle existing resources to benefit one individual without harming another.

To attain full Paretian efficiency, every economic unit must attach identical relative values to all inputs and outputs. This immediately reveals the presence of substantial inefficiency in Chinese industry. We have already seen, for example, that central planners, factory managers, quality inspectors, and customers do not necessarily impute identical relative values to standard and defective products, or to identical goods with higher or lower costs. The following case studies of vertical integration and inventory management illustrate the extent and persistence of inefficient behavior patterns and describe the impact of industrial reforms in reducing the degree of Paretian inefficiency.

Historically, industrialization has brought with it a growing specialization and division of labor. The supply rigidities common in backward economies lead to an inverse relation between the degree of vertical integration and the level of development. We therefore expect to find more extensive integration in Chinese factories than in comparable American or European plants.

By 1957, however, Chinese economists were increasingly aware that integration had outstripped all reasonable bounds. A succession of writers attacked the surfeit of expensive, high-cost, underutilized ancillary facilities throughout the producer sector. These critics found no shortage of targets, for even field geological and mining groups had built their own repair works instead of using local machine shops.[38] The new industrial city at Loyang was a favorite target. Three large machinery plants had simultaneously expanded their repair, machine shop, and tool production capacity; by 1957, these ancillary units housed over one thousand machine tools. Neither the two electric furnaces at the tractor works nor the similar furnace at the mining equipment plant operated near capacity, and the utilization rate of a huge and costly Soviet lathe installed at the tractor works was only 7 percent.[39]

Survey results such as those described in tables 5.1 and 5.2 illustrate the high cost of integration. Forging equipment was almost universally underutilized, and production of hardware without special equipment wasted time, materials, and money even at Shenyang's #2 Machine Tool Plant, a unit noted for managerial efficiency.

TABLE 5.1
1957 Utilization Rates for Forging Equipment in Machinery Plants

Plant	Percentage
Talien Crane	35.00
Shenyang Heavy Machinery	105.81
T'aiyuan Heavy Machinery	50.82
Shanghai Mining Machinery	44.76
Shenyang Mining Machinery	47.38
T'aiyuan Mining Machinery	53.38
Talien Shipyard	53.00
Kiangnan Shipyard	34.80
East Shanghai Shipyard	77.04
Wuch'ang Shipyard	30.21
China Shipyard	38.52

Source: CHKY 6(1958):6–8, cited in *Chūgoku sangyō bōeki sōran* (Tokyo, 1963), pp. 25, 27.

TABLE 5.2
Cost and Input Comparisons in Hardware Production
(per hundred units)

Product	Shenyang Screw and Nail Plant (using special equipment)	Other Plants (using lathes)
M10×10 hexagonal bolt		
materials	4.0 kg	12.0 kg
machine time	21 minutes	480 minutes
M12 hexagonal nut		
materials	3.4 kg	7.25 kg
machine time	21 minutes	300 minutes
Production costs (yuan)		
6 mm screw	14.85	414.82[a]
8 mm screw	27.30	539.93[a]
10 mm screw	54.58	869.84[a]
12 mm screw	86.56	1,211.47[a]
8 mm hardened screw	73.42	250.51[a]
double-headed screw	146.8	939.56[a]

Source: "Concentrating Production of Standard Parts Is Economically Rational," CHKY 22(1957):18.

[a] Data from Shenyang #2 Machine Tool Plant.

Managers preferred to make rather than buy inputs because they found that integration enhanced the probability of plan fulfillment by limiting dependence on potentially unreliable suppliers. Complaints by Tientsin's Power Machinery Plant that forgings received from outside were overweight, overpriced, and defective were echoed in hundreds of press reports.[40] There were also reports of production stoppages caused by supply failures.[41] Worst of all, suppliers behaved most selfishly just when customers required the quickest service—in the tense weeks preceding the close of annual and quarterly plan periods.

From the firm's viewpoint, additional integration is nearly costless. Funds for fixed investment, if available, bear no interest; only depreciation is charged. Even if integration raises production costs, accounting quirks may raise profit as well![42] While managers see only the benefits of integration, a wider view reveals its costs as well, and this divergence signals the presence of Paretian inefficiency. With enterprises leaning toward self-supply, firm official backing for cooperation is needed to curb excessive integration. This has not always been forthcoming. Despite the criticisms published in 1957, the following years saw further increases in integration as the Great Leap campaign placed unprecedented emphasis on self-supply. The giant Ch'angch'un #1 Truck Plant was one of many units that inaugurated efforts to raise its level of self-sufficiency during 1958–60.[43]

Advocacy of specialization and interenterprise cooperation reappeared after 1960. In 1964, a vigorous press campaign sought to promote cooperation in engineering. Earlier themes were repeated: specialization would conserve investment funds by raising capacity utilization and could increase productivity and quality while reducing cost and material consumption. Once again, favorable results were publicized: special methods used at Shenyang's Standard Parts Plant halved waste of metal used in making hardware; machine tool works could buy wrenches for one-eighth the cost of self-made tools; specialist plants lowered casting costs by 20 percent.[44]

As in the past, the drive to promote "socialist cooperation" was received with suspicion:

> When at first Tsinan Automobile Works planned to give the job of casting iron parts to other plants . . . cadres . . . feared that factories in cooperation would not be able to deliver the goods in time. After three major debates . . . some cadres still insisted on having a part of the products manufactured in their own plant. Later, the Party committee of the plant decided to have three months of stock ready before resolutely cooperating with other plants.[45]

Customers were especially leery of suppliers reputed to be merely after production value and output in a one-sided manner or unwilling to accept special orders.

Fears that cooperation might disrupt production schedules point to the institutional roots of managers' desire for integration. Once again we see the key role of slack, here in the form of stockpiles of materials or parts, in persuading managers to go along with reform proposals. This anecdote also illustrates the links between quality consciousness and other reforms; a general rise in qualitative performance will erode opposition to specialization based on fears that outside suppliers will ignore their customers' needs.

During the mid-1960s, strong pressure from above combined with the reality of improved qualitative performance overcame managerial hesitation sufficiently to bring about a major increase in specialization and cooperation, particularly in engineering. Reports from Shenyang,

Tientsin, Shanghai, Canton, and Kiangsu province document the growth of subcontracting arrangements for machine parts and for the services of casting, repair, and heat treatment specialists, and describe the resulting gains in cost, productivity, and quality.[46] More recently, the proliferation of small urban plants has further increased the scope of specialization and division of labor in leading industrial centers.[47]

Despite these changes, the overall degree of vertical integration remains high. A typical comment comes from a British automotive specialist who reports that "vertical integration is a feature of the individual factories, which make a much higher proportion of the vehicle components than the small production volumes would seem to justify."[48] Large enterprises in all industries continue to operate a wide range of ancillary facilities, and the frequency with which visitors encounter well-equipped machine shops in smaller enterprises indicates that self-supply continues to occupy an important role in Chinese industrial life.

With its emphasis on self-reliance and local initiative in overcoming technical problems and supply imbalances, China's industrial strategy requires a wide dispersion of mechanical capabilities, which is in part achieved by allowing many units to maintain their own machine shops. This practice adds greatly to the flexibility of enterprise operations and eliminates communication problems that might otherwise arise between producers and consumers of machinery and parts. Yet the continuing flow of instructions that

> it is mandatory to oppose the erroneous tendency of regarding the means of production . . . as possessions of the department, of the locality or of the enterprise and that of being unwilling to take up tasks of coordination and cooperation while willingly letting . . . facilities lie idle.[49]

points to the survival of the old logic of integration and, with it, of Paretian inefficiency.

Management of circulating capital is another area in which reform has reduced but not eliminated the substantial inefficiency observable during the 1950s. Although working capital needs, like integration, should vary inversely with the level of overall development, the levels of circulating funds required by enterprises in China's producer sector often include elements of surplus or waste.

TABLE 5.3
Financial Performance of Selected Sectors and Enterprises

Category	Year	Ratio of Annual Gross Output to Working Capital	Turnover Period for Working Capital[b] (in days)
Industry	1952	6.5	
(excluding handicrafts)[a]	1955	7.8	
Ferrous metallurgy[a]			
Anshan Iron and Steel Works	1953	—	109
	1954	—	105
	1955	—	88
	1956	—	90
Enterprises under Iron-Steel Bureau	1953	—	121
	1954	—	101
	1955	—	96
	1956	—	82
Electric power[a,c]	1953	—	56
	1954	—	51
	1955	—	38
	1956	—	25
	1957	—	29
Machinery enterprises			
(1957 data unless otherwise specified)			
Shanghai Machine Tool[d]	1953	—	371
	1954	—	308
	1956 (plan)	—	238
Chinan #1 Machine Tool		4.1	125
Talien Machine Tool		3.5	171
Shenyang #3 Machine Tool		1.7	236
Shanghai Tool		3.4	160
Harbin Measuring and Cutting Tool		3.4	158
Harbin #1 Tool		2.4	203
Talien Crane		2.6	279
Shenyang Crane		2.3	208
T'aiyuan Heavy Machinery		1.7	274
Shanghai Mining Machinery		2.7	150
Shenyang Mining Machinery		2.9	157
T'aiyuan Mining Machinery		2.6	194
Ch'ich'ihar Locomotive		5.0	138
Szufang Locomotive and Rolling Stock		2.8	184
Wuch'ang Locomotive and Rolling Stock		1.9	253
Talien Locomotive and Rolling Stock		3.6	188

TABLE 5.3—*Continued*

Category	Year	Ratio of Annual Gross Output to Working Capital	Turnover Period for Working Capital[b] (in days)
Machinery enterprises (cont.)			
Talien Shipyard		1.0	785
Kiangnan Shipyard		2.2	547
East Shanghai Shipyard		1.8	281
Wuch'ang Shipyard		2.5	975
China Shipyard		1.7	448
Talien Electric Machinery		10.0	209
Hsiangt'an Electric Machinery		4.6	148
Shanghai Electric Machinery		2.9	71
Harbin Electric Machinery		2.8	228
Shanghai Cable		8.5	68
Harbin Electric Wire		11.7	46
Shenyang Cable		6.4	96
Tientsin #1 Electric Wire		8.4	65

Source: Except as noted, data are from CHKY 6(1958):6–9, cited in *Chūgoku sangyō bōeki sōran*, pp. 24–28. Data are grouped as in the source.

[a] Calculated from data in Chen, *Statistics*, pp. 153, 210, 282.

[b] Turnover period is defined as 360 times the average volume of working capital divided by annual sales (ibid., p. 52).

[c] Data refer to normalized working funds (ibid.).

[d] JMJP, October 30, 1955.

Available data on industrial working capital appear in table 5.3. Large differences in the turnover rates for metallurgy, power, and machinery plants presumably arise from technological and demand conditions: coal requirements of power plants are easier to predict than the amounts of various steel shapes needed to manufacture and repair locomotives. Industry as a whole, and steel and power plants in particular, achieved significant economies in the use of liquid assets during the course of the FFYP. The 1957 data for engineering, the only sector for which I have found interenterprise comparisons, shows that some firms used far more liquid assets than others with similar product lines, showing obvious scope for improvement.

In addition, there can be little doubt that the average firm held far more liquid assets during the 1950s than was technically necessary. Circulating funds are intended solely for financing current output, but enterprises also use these funds to hoard labor, to supplement grants for fixed capital formation, and to maintain stockpiles of unsold goods.[50] The most significant diversion of funds, however, comes from stockpiling of raw and semifinished materials in excess of current needs. The extent of hoarding is suggested by table 5.4, which presents information on engineering inventories for 1957, a year of strong emphasis on cost cutting, and confirmed by voluminous anecdotal material.

To build illegal stockpiles, managers play it safe by using inflated input coefficients to request materials and then neglect to report the resulting accumulation of inputs. In 1953, Anshan required 1.05 tons of

TABLE 5.4
Inventories Held in 1957 by Enterprises under the FMMB Industry
(in days)

Enterprise	Steel Materials	Pig Iron	Wooden Materials
Chinan #1 Machine Tool	185	—	—
Talien Machine Tool	104	—	—
Shenyang #3 Machine Tool	174	—	—
Shanghai Tool	131	—	—
Harbin Tool and Measuring Instrument	208	—	—
Harbin #1 Tool	175	—	—
Talien Crane	159	526	—
Shenyang Heavy Machinery	131	152	—
T'aiyuan Heavy Machinery	327	268	—
Shanghai Mining Machinery	120	31	—
Shenyang Mining Machinery	153	192	—
T'aiyuan Mining Machinery	111	118	—
Ch'ich'ihar Locomotive	130	—	64
Szufang Locomotive	167	—	113
Wuch'ang Locomotive	209	—	94
Talien Locomotive	120	—	67
Talien Shipyard	284	—	261
Kiangnan Shipyard	351	—	410
East Shanghai Shipyard	237	—	293
Wuch'ang Shipyard	283	—	117
China Shipyard	256	—	189

Source: CHKY 6(1958):5–8, cited in *Chūgoku sangyō bōeki sōran*, pp. 25–27. Data are grouped as in the source.

metal to smelt one ton of steel, but officials reported figures of 1.07 in the production and 1.09 in the supply plan for that year.[51] During the 1950s, this insurance typically amounted to 2–6 percent of actual needs, but fear of shortage led to bold demands:

> When . . . units hear of strained supplies . . . they double the quantities in their requisitions. . . . It is not possible for the Bureau to know exactly what the true conditions are. So . . . the Bureau swings a uniform axe . . . units that had applied for materials in accordance with the true conditions have also had to receive a cut. From this they have learned a lesson and will double requisitions in the future with 50% especially reserved for the cut by the commodity distribution bureau.[52]

With demand swollen by the fictitious claims of would-be hoarders, scarcities of industrial supplies were worsened, and at times perhaps even created by efforts to accumulate illicit inventories.

These practices result in distributions of materials that are uneven, as is obvious from table 5.4, and worse yet, not fully known to the authorities. Factories may be forced to halt production for want of materials that are not really in short supply. Expediters seek out hoards of needed items, but may be unable to make an exchange without offering scarce goods sought by others. Managers begin to hoard all scarce materials, not just those needed in their own plants.[53]

This situation is an obvious source of Paretian inefficiency; reduced hoarding could eliminate output-restricting bottlenecks in some sectors without disrupting operations elsewhere. During the 1950s, official action was limited to exhortations and inspection campaigns that met with some success, but also evoked spirited resistance. Some enterprises resorted to deceptive accounting to protect their stockpiles, while others "concealed their materials in underground chambers, covering them with scrap lest their 'wealth' should be revealed and transferred elsewhere."[54]

Improvements in supply planning, a notoriously weak aspect of economic administration during the 1950s, and reduced plan tautness can lessen the incentive for managers to build illegal stockpiles; reform measures have occurred in both of these areas. It is no coincidence that the excess reserves of materials now incorporated into industrial plans correspond almost exactly to the insurance margins previously attained through deception and subterfuge. Legitimizing these reserves of materials may not reduce the consumption of working capital, but it does improve the allocation process by increasing the planners' knowledge of actual distributions of materials and actual unit input requirements.

A flurry of organizational changes, including the creation of a General Bureau for the Supply of Raw Materials (1956), the bureau's transfer to the State Economic Commission (1958), and the creation (1963) and abolition (1964) of a Ministry of Allocation of Raw Materials, demonstrates Peking's concern with administering the allocation of materials and suggests the extent of difficulties encountered in this area. The Chinese have also developed several types of conferences and meetings that convene periodically to encourage exchange of materials and final products at the sectoral and regional levels.[55] These meetings, like the material reserves now built into annual plans, appear to be legitimate substitutes for illegal black-market or barter transactions. Local governments also work on an ad hoc basis to relieve particular shortages, as in the following instance:

> On the basis of stock-taking and check-ups in warehouses, various places including Peking, Paoting, and Changchun have organized exchange of supplies, tackling the supply problem of 13,000 tons of machine parts required by mining and metallurgical equipment.[56]

These reforms have not succeeded in eliminating hoarding of materials and other improper uses of circulating capital. This can be seen from a 1972 article that obliquely reveals the extent of recidivism by praising a small group of regions that

> set aside the departmentalist idea of "retain more supplies and report less stocks in order to make them more readily available when needed" as well as the erroneous idea that "stocktaking has reached the limit" and "all potentials are exhausted"

and also from Teng Hsiao-p'ing's 1975 warning against misappropriation of funds.[57] The reforms have, however, succeeded in weakening the pressures that cause managers to build concealed stockpiles of materials and parts. Inclusion of planned reserves in regular allocations, provision of legitimate alternatives to the black market, and active intervention of provincial and local authorities in alleviating supply difficulties have undoubtedly reduced the scope and magnitude of hoarding, and consequently of Paretian inefficiency.

These case studies of integration and inventory management reveal parallel developments that seem representative of overall changes in Paretian efficiency within the producer sector. In each case, substantial inefficiencies developed during the FFYP years. Both the problems and their institutional links were clearly recognized by 1957, but effective remedial action did not begin until after 1960. Since 1960, a combination of administrative change, territorial decentralization, and forceful information campaigns aimed at injecting concepts of social cost into discussion and decision making at all levels have raised expected performance levels. Dysfunctional management practices continue to exist, but at reduced levels, leading to a general increase in Paretian efficiency.

Is the degree of Paretian efficiency in industry larger or smaller in China than elsewhere? Since inefficiency is as difficult to measure as it is easy to detect, this question defies a simple answer. No economy approaches the Paretian ideal. The search for growth, profit, and security often leads American and European firms to deceive customers and public officials, hoard scarce resources, neglect quality, invest irrationally, and generally pursue microeconomic gain to the detriment of macroeconomic welfare. Organizational parallels between Western corporations and socialist-bloc industries suggest similar degrees of economic inefficiency.[58] Bernard Baruch's observations on the extent of Paretian inefficiency written in 1921 seem valid today:

> experience . . . has clearly demonstrated that there are many practices in American industry which cost the ultimate consumers in the aggregate enormous sums without enriching the producers.[59]

Industrial inefficiency is also common in developing countries. The widespread combination of extensive trade barriers and elephantine rationing of foreign currency creates domestic sellers' markets for industrial products and leads manufacturers toward poor quality, neglect of innovation, hoarding, and systematic efforts to deceive and manipulate government agencies. Elsewhere, inflation lowers the real cost of capital toward or even below the zero level observed in China, providing familiar incentives for excessive integration and mechanization.[60]

One specific comparison suggests a favorable view of Chinese performance. In table 5.5, we see that, despite a weak performance in the sphere of inventory management, Chinese engineering firms are far more economical of working funds than their Indian counterparts. Twenty-eight Indian enterprises surveyed during 1960–66 required more than three times the working capital (per unit of output value) for inventories alone than Chinese machinery firms used for all purposes in 1957.

Even if individual Chinese firms create no more inefficiency than their foreign counterparts, the rigidity embodied in the requirement that each unit fulfill its plan on the same date leads to uniform deviations that can, as became evident during the 1950s, create quantitatively significant problems at the national level. Here, too, relaxation of plan tautness and encouragement of local initiative in breaking bottlenecks has limited the susceptibility of China's industrial system to difficulties encountered in the past.

TABLE 5.5
Ratio of Annual Output Value to Value of Inventories, Indian Public Sector Firms, 1960–66

Firm	Output to Inventory Ratio
Hindustan Aircraft	0.4
Hindustan Shipyard	0.4
Bharat Electronics	0.6
Indian Telephone Industries	0.8
Praga Tools	0.8
National Instruments	1.5
Hindustan Machine Tools	1.0
Mazagon Dock	2.0
Hindustan Cables	1.7
Bharat Earthmovers	0.6
Heavy Electricals	0.6
Average for above firms	0.9
Average for 28 firms in several sectors	1.0
Average ratio of output to working capital for 29 Chinese machinery plants, 1957	3.8

Sources: Indian data from Bhagwati and Desai, *India, Planning for Industrialization*, p. 167. Chinese data from table 5.3 in this book.

Note: Bhagwati and Desai present inventory values in terms of number of months' production value for each of six fiscal years starting with 1960–61. The data for each firm are averaged, divided by 12, and inverted to obtain average ratios of annual output to inventory holdings.

X-Efficiency

Paretian efficiency cannot tell the whole story about any economy. The Pareto concept explicitly assumes fixed and immutable technical relations between inputs consumed and commodities produced. Leibenstein has emphasized the artificiality of this postulate, arguing that given inputs may generate varying quantities of output because

> contracts for labor are incomplete; the production function is not completely specified or known; not all inputs are marketed or, if marketed, are not available on equal terms to all buyers; and the *effective* utilization of an input depends on the degree of motivational pressure.[61]

A review of Chinese factory conditions suggests that, with a given volume of resources, output tends to cluster near the upper end of Leibenstein's range of production possibilities, indicating a relatively high degree of X-efficiency.

Incompleteness in Chinese labor contracts tends to be resolved in favor of increased effort. Recent industrial disturbances indicate that foreign observers exaggerate the passivity of Chinese workers, but it remains true that trade unions and workers' councils are more likely to push for higher output than to promote featherbedding.[62] Individual workers are strongly encouraged to come forward with ideas for productivity-enhancing job modifications. Managers are required to pay careful attention to workers' suggestions, and every worker knows the names of Anshan's Wang Chung-lun, oilfield worker Iron Man Wang, and other stalwarts whose inventiveness and dedication have earned them promotion, party membership, and national recognition.

Informal output restriction undoubtedly exists—Peking's New Year's editorial for 1978 speaks of the problem of "work evaders"—but the chance of exposure and censure by fellow workers as well as managers is far greater in China than elsewhere.[63] As a result, one might expect that the utilization of potential labor input is higher in China than it is in the United States, for example, where output restriction "is a widespread institution, deeply rooted in the working habits of American laboring people."[64]

Strenuous efforts to overcome problems arising from incomplete specification of technologies have been an outstanding feature of

Chinese industrial life since the 1950s. Regular stints of manual labor for leadership personnel, originally intended to counter elitism, are now seen as keeping executives in close touch with production operations, and receive strong endorsements from technocrats concerned with maintaining industrial standards.[65] As noted above, workers' suggestions receive close scrutiny and are often modified or improved by innovation squads composed of managers, technicians, and manual operatives. Factories maintain a wide range of educational services to expand the technical and intellectual as well as political horizons of their employees. Workers are urged to study technical publications, which are widely available at nominal prices, and to visit local libraries in search of information bearing on current production problems.

Studies of industry in the United States and elsewhere have established that workers can suggest valuable improvements even in complex and sophisticated plants; that executives immersed in commercial matters may lose contact with production operations; that productivity and worker morale respond positively to personal contact with management; and that intimate managerial knowledge of production processes is an important source of innovation.[66] With this in mind, there is every reason to believe that unless carried to foolish extremes—as it was during the Great Leap, the Cultural Revolution, and possibly during 1974–76—Chinese insistence on frequent interchange among managers, engineers, and workers and on periodic stints of manual labor for executives can improve technical performance as well as morale.

China's industrial system is one in which important resources, including managerial skills, new equipment, and perhaps most of all, industrial experience, are not equally available to all firms. The Chinese are keenly aware of internal gaps between advanced and lagging enterprises and have achieved great success in devising substitutes for missing inputs. We have already encountered the wide range of conferences, training programs, and consulting arrangements that permit backward units to draw on the human and technical resources of sophisticated research institutes and national-level firms, and we have seen how subcontracting and technical decomposition allow poorly endowed firms to contribute to manufacturing operations that require elements of advanced technology.

In addition to these methods for sharing specific resources, regular administrative comparisons among similar enterprises followed by detailed study of poor performers provide a more general method of identifying and assisting weak units and maintaining standards at better-endowed firms. Tables 5.1 to 5.4 illustrate the types of data used in these comparisons. The consequences of such observations can be seen from the following example:

> In Shanghai municipality, several financial and tax collecting personnel noticed that there was a great difference in the production cost of several factories engaged in the production of electronic components. They therefore went deep into the relevant enterprises to make investigation. . . . some . . . were thrifty while some were extremely wasteful in their use of raw materials. Together with the broad masses of workers, they exposed the contradiction, found the difference and assisted the backward factories to adopt more effective technical measures, saved a large amount of single crystal silicon, raised the acceptance rate of the product, promoted productivity and increased income.[67]

Because of such efforts, Chinese industry displays a ratchet effect which militates against increased unit consumption of labor and materials. Although this mechanism does not always work—the experience of 1956 and 1958–60 shows that intense pressure for higher output can generate increased unit costs—table 5.6 reveals a pattern of declining costs that appears typical of most branches of industry.

All of these measures contribute to reducing the gap between realized and potential output with fixed resources. Examination of the Chinese materials gives the impression that such gaps are smaller and the degree of X-efficiency correspondingly higher in Chinese industry than in many other countries. Technical and managerial improvements spread throughout China's industrial sector and are not limited to a few dynamic enterprises. The existence of regular mechanisms for improving performance of second- and third-echelon firms distinguishes China from many developing countries. In comparing China with advanced industrial nations, one suspects that Chinese waste of raw materials, the largest cost component in most Chinese industries, is smaller than European or American excess consumption of labor, the dominant cost component in their industries.[68] Comparing China with the socialist economies of the USSR and Eastern Europe again gives an

TABLE 5.6
Coke Consumption in Pig Iron Production, 1949–75
(kg/ton)

Date	National Data	Major Enterprises: Anshan	Major Enterprises: Shoutu (Peking)
June 1949–51	—	1,000[b]	—
1952	—	881[d]	—
1953	941[a]	918[d]	—
1954	893[a]	920[d]	1000[b]
1955	804[a]	851[d]	—
1956	791[a]	737[d]	—
1957	—	711[d]	—
1958	—	655[d]	690–750[d]
December 1959	999[c]	643[c]	846[c]
March 1960	870[c]	656[c]	731[c]
1962	740[f]	649[e]	—
1963	730[f]	606[c]	—
1964	720[f]	554[c]	571[e]
1965	710[f]	547[c]	—
1966	700[f]	—	400[c]
1970	680[f]	—	—
1974	650[f]	—	—
1975	—	—	500[g]

Note: American Iron and Steel Institute, *Annual Statistical Report* (New York, annual) gives the following coke ratios for U.S. producers: 1940, 892; 1950, 897; 1960, 726; 1975, 611.

[a] Data for pig iron used in steelmaking from Chen, *Statistics*, p. 268.

[b] Naikaku sōri daijin, *Chūkyō tekkōgyō*, 1: 47, 313. The figure for Shoutu refers to late 1953 or early 1954.

[c] Kojima Reiitsu, "Iron and Steel Industry," in *Chūgoku keizai no chōki tembō* IV (Tokyo, 1971), ed. Ishikawa Shigeru, 2: 82.

[d] Clark, *China's Steel Industry*, pp. 14, 18.

[e] SCMP 3219(1964): 14.

[f] Alfred H. Usack, Jr., and James D. Egan, "China's Iron and Steel Industry," in *China: A Reassessment of the Economy*, p. 271.

[g] Author's notes as a member of the Rural Small-Scale Industry Delegation, June 14, 1975.

impression of superior Chinese performance in terms of industrial X-efficiency. Given the broad similarity of industrial organization in all of these socialist countries, unequal performance must raise questions about differences in administrative methods and motivation. These issues form the subject of the following section.

Unique Features of China's Industrial System

This study has reached favorable conclusions regarding the performance of China's producer industries since 1949. Output has grown rapidly. New industries have appeared. Older industrial branches have mastered a wide range of new technologies. Improvements in quality and variety have brought supply into better balance with requirements. Paretian efficiency has improved, and the level of achievement in terms of X-efficiency is high. All these gains have occurred in an environment of declining dependence on imports and foreign technological advice.

Institutional changes provide little help in explaining the factors underlying these achievements. Despite the impact of territorial decentralization, it is clear that China is in no sense a leader among socialist states in terms of industrial reform. Gradual price changes have increased the correspondence between relative prices and relative scarcities, but China has never moved far in the direction of substituting a price mechanism for administrative guidance of industrial activity.

This focuses attention on issues of administration and motivation within a relatively static institutional framework. As we have seen, administrative changes have played an important role in stimulating performance improvements during the 1960s and 1970s. Reduced plan tautness limits dysfunctional behavior by plant managers and encourages them to devote more attention to qualitative considerations than was done during the 1950s. This shift draws further support from Peking's new awareness that time, materials, and human capital are essential ingredients in any sort of industrial innovation and from administrative shifts affecting supply work and relations between producers and customers.

There are also certain long-standing features of the industrial system that have contributed to China's distinctive performance. The limited significance of monetary bonuses for industrial managers, coupled with low turnover in executive positions means that Chinese managers must live with the long-term consequences of current decisions. This militates against the extreme short-run outlook common in the Soviet Union. Chinese plans appear to be relatively flexible, allowing scope for revisions during the plan period.[69] In science policy, the Chinese practice of insisting on close ties between research and production has undoubtedly avoided some of the obstacles encountered in the Soviet Union, where organizational ties between factories and research institutes are weak.[70]

All of these factors, however, are passive elements that can only support a preexisting drive toward better performance. This drive must come from a highly motivated corps of leaders at the microeconomic level. China has devoted enormous efforts to training grass-roots leaders who are technically competent, sensitive to priorities laid down by the national leadership, flexible in implementing these priorities in their immediate environment, and capable of exercising the entrepreneurial skills needed to bring local resources to bear on the key problems of the day.

The growing strength of Chinese industry, not just in raising output volume, but in supporting the growth and technical development of the entire economy, is inextricably bound up with the emergence of dedicated, responsive, and aggressive leaders in provincial and county economic hierarchies and within several million industrial enterprises. The present system in which the center holds broad economic decision-making powers but in fact allows many issues to be decided far down the administrative ladder operates on the basis of the central leadership's trust in the competence, reliability, and energy of millions of industrial planners, managers, engineers, foremen, and activist workers.

Keesing has analyzed these matters with clarity and insight. "China has cut this Gordian knot" of trying to invent microeconomic decision rules that do not encourage dysfunctional behavior patterns

> by trying to build a socially appropriate balance of goals into the decision-makers themselves. In this way the Chinese get around the problem of specifying success indicators and decision criteria to meet all circumstances. The aim is to get decision-makers who are so able, socially motivated, and effectively criticized by those around them that they achieve socially appropriate decisions and policies at all levels in a complex, decentralized economy.[71]

If this system works well, and there is ample reason to believe that it has worked well through most of the 1960s and early 1970s, it is certainly capable of outperforming an orthodox Soviet system of industrial management. Subordinates not only implement their instructions, but exceed them in ways that superiors, if cognizant of local conditions, would applaud. In the hands of a competent and energetic administrative hierarchy, this Chinese system, combining features of command and atomistic economies, can develop into a formidable vehicle of economic change.

Because this sytem draws its strength from the enthusiasm, entrepreneurship, and shared goals of personnel at all administrative levels, its performance can be upset by incompetence or indecision at the top or by demoralization or passive resistance from below. If the informal ties between superior and subordinate are strained or severed, the system can lose coherence and momentum as lower-level leaders either pursue their own interests or abandon entrepreneurial behavior and seek the security of time-serving routine. Thus we see that dependence on lower-level initiative and on mutual trust up and down the administrative ladder is the weakness as well as the strength of China's industrial system.

The present Hua-Teng administration is keenly sensitive to the importance of industrial morale, for it has assumed control of the economy following an interlude of conflict, confusion, and slackness at the top and of uncertainty and disaffection throughout industry. The new leadership complains of industrial sabotage, but since retrospective criticism of the ousted "Gang of Four" contains no references to destruction of facilities or unauthorized institutional change, the charge of sabotage obviously reflects damage to enthusiasm, mutual trust, and entrepreneurship.

In assessing the industrial situation, the Hua-Teng group finds that leadership in some units has fallen into the hands of incompetent political hacks. The main problem, however, is that in many groups

> leadership squads have, in different degrees, the problems of "softness, laziness, and laxness." Some of the leadership of these units put fear before everything else and are afraid to persist in principles. They dare not publicly praise the good and criticize the bad. . . . the revolutionary will of others has withered away, and they are just muddling along, acting like hypochondriacs and moaning for nothing, following the beaten track in doing work and being bogged down in passivity.[72]

Faced with stagnant industrial output and low morale, the new leadership has raised wages in an effort to secure worker support. The wage increases are limited to personnel earning less than 90 yuan per month, a restriction that excludes most experienced managers, engineers, and technicians.[73] For these groups, exhortation rather than money holds the key to better performance, at least in the eyes of the Hua-Teng group. Resounding declarations of national will to industrialize, highly publicized meetings intended to rekindle enthusiasm for professionalism and entrepreneurship, and widespread acclaim for units and regions whose leaders initiate decisive programs to overcome economic problems are the means by which Peking seeks to regain the support of key industrial personnel.

Progress reports emphasize improved morale as well as the estimated 14 percent rise in industrial output during 1976–77:

> Labor discipline in factories vastly improved after the great political revolution to expose and criticize the "gang of four" and the wage increases. Now there are more people who arrive on time and leave on time and work much harder than before. An atmosphere of studying theory and mastering skills after work has prevailed. The number of work evaders has greatly decreased.[74]

Although it is too early to predict the outcome of these efforts to restore internal cohesion and morale to China's industrial sector, recent developments confirm our emphasis on the contribution of managerial morale to China's industrial achievements. If Peking fails to recapture the loyalty and stimulate the enthusiasm of lower-level industrial leaders, only a return to taut planning can regain strong forward momentum, and this would certainly bring about a recrudescence of dysfunctional tendencies that industrial planners have worked diligently, and on the whole successfully, to overcome.

Chapter 6

China's Producer Industries in Perspective

China's producer industries have grown rapidly since 1900. Along with expanded volume and range of output has come a growing capacity to select, absorb, and reshape elements of foreign and domestic scientific and engineering knowledge to meet the needs of a changing economy. The producer sector has developed from a thin layer operating on the economy's geographic and sectoral fringes into a large and cohesive system that spans China's vast landscape and influences every branch of economic endeavor.

These advances do not mean that Chinese industry can soon approach world technical levels. Some producers, mostly in the machinery industry, claim to have reached world standards, but even the leading units in most sectors lag well behind international developments in technology, with other enterprises often falling considerably short of the performance standards of domestic leaders.[1]

Gaps between existing and best practice, domestic or international, exist universally, even in the most advanced economies. Industrial progress requires the ability to lessen these disparities. Here we find the achievement of China's producer industries. Beginning with the activities of late Ch'ing officials and obscure private entrepreneurs, these industries have gradually developed systems for identifying, analyzing, and ameliorating an ever-growing range of obstacles to continued economic growth. The evolution of this problem-solving mechanism is most visible in the history of Shanghai's engineering industry, where the experience accumulated over a span of nearly a century has created a beneficent circle in which solutions to individual difficulties enhance both the technical skills and the confidence that can be brought to bear on subsequent tasks. As we have seen, the recent emergence of new innovative poles outside Shanghai and outside the machinery industry has widened the geographic and sectoral breadth of domestically generated technical advance.

Although some new industrial methods, such as the widespread manufacture of chemical fertilizer in the form of ammonium bicarbonate, are unique to China, most of industry's achievements have come from studying, imitating, and then modifying processes and products initially developed in foreign countries. The important role of imitation in technological progress does not detract from the magnitude of China's industrial achievements, for this study and many others have shown that absorbing and adapting foreign technologies to new economic environments is a task that both requires and creates highly productive skills.

In China, this process of technological absorption has stimulated rapid output growth, given birth to many new industries, created a skilled labor force, and perhaps most important, facilitated a notable expansion in industrial flexibility that has allowed the transfer of skills and resources from one task to another in response to shifting economic requirements. The cutting edges of some producer industries now come surprisingly close to world technical standards, while lagging elements also show clear signs of technical advance, often surpassing earlier standards of leading Chinese enterprises.

The Development Process

The development process in China's producer sector reveals a number of characteristics whose significance extends beyond the Chinese scene. One such feature is the long-term and discontinuous nature of the process by which industry's skill frontier expands. Unpredictable and often lengthy intervals during which techniques are absorbed and experience is built up alternate with sudden innovative bursts such as those observed during the late 1920s and, on a much broader scale, the mid-1960s, in which industry suddenly becomes capable of supplying whole new product lines.

Shanghai's continuing technological leadership demonstrates that a legacy of productive experience can make older firms more innovative and responsive than better-equipped newcomers in the face of unforeseen changes in patterns of scarcity and demand. This illustrates the contribution of early industrialization to future as well as current output. China's present comparative advantage in the petroleum sector is in part the outcome of earlier efforts to replace imports in entirely different branches of industry. More generally, the key contribution of older firms to China's post-1960 economic achievements indicates that the nonmarket benefits of early industrialization may be large indeed. This is especially true of engineering, a sector that, as we have seen, is both technologically amenable to sequential development and, through its widespread forward linkages, of central importance as a carrier of new technology into all sectors of the domestic economy.

Since these benefits may accrue neither to industrial pioneers nor to their employees, there appears to be scope for government intervention in a market economy to support fledgling enterprises likely to generate such external gains. Infant industries may deserve protection or subsidy not only because their production costs are expected to decline, but also because their operations will enhance the technical and economic prospects of industries whose infancy may lie years or even decades into the future.

This study has stressed the interplay among experience, physical resources, and entrepreneurship as joint determinants of the pace and pattern of technical development. Apparent opportunities may be ignored because of inadequate technical skills, as seems to have occurred during the hiatus in imports resulting from World War I, or because entrepreneurial attention is directed away from innovation toward other objectives, which may range from output volume, as during China's FFYP, to political security, as during the industrial pause of 1974–76.

Although economists have long stressed the benefits of international and interregional specialization, the experience of China's producer sector shows that development may at times be enhanced by partially curtailing access to outside suppliers, domestic as well as foreign. Chinese history, and also the wartime history of more advanced economies, shows that isolation and crisis may serve as fruitful stimuli to industrial innovation.

Relying on external supplies usually offers the quickest and cheapest method of injecting new activities into a backward economy. China, for example, could not have begun mass production of tractors, ball bearings, chemical fertilizers, and many other products during the 1950s without massive imports of equipment and expertise.

But outside supplies may be a mixed blessing. The time and expense needed to adapt foreign equipment and techniques to the peculiar features of local skills and materials may sharply reduce the cost and productivity advantage of imports. More fundamentally, trade-dependent industrialization attenuates the process of skill formation that accompanies the search for internal solutions to technical difficulties. Imports may solve today's problems, but only at the cost of slowing the growth of skills needed to overcome future obstacles without outside assistance.

A new appreciation of the costs as well as the benefits of trade stands behind the retrospective Chinese belief that Khruschev "did us a good turn" by pulling Soviet technicians out of China in 1960.[2] The potential efficacy of economic independence can be seen from China's experience during the 1960s, a decade in which a combination of international isolation and domestic crisis stripped industry of its comfortable reliance on foreign support and drove domestic producers to attempt tasks formerly thought to lie beyond their technical capabilities. It was the desperation of China's economic situation rather than the repetition of familiar slogans praising quality and innovation that cleared the way for implementation of harmonic growth policies and led to palpable and enduring improvements in product development, quality control, cost consciousness, customer service, and other qualitative aspects of industrial performance.

In view of the pessimism common to most appraisals of the qualitative potential of Soviet industry, it is essential to emphasize that these changes occurred without major shifts in pricing policy, in the framework of economic planning, or in the degree of administrative control over resource allocation. Administrative changes within a relatively stable institutional framework are largely responsible for recent qualitative gains in the operation of China's producer industries.

The strong forward momentum with which industry emerged from the difficulties of the early 1960s appears to have created a broad consensus within Chinese leadership circles favoring a high degree of self-reliance at the national, regional, and even enterprise level. Shanghai and other advanced industrial centers limit their dependence on foreign suppliers to situations in which domestic products cannot meet the cost, quality, or time requirements of current demand. Other localities strive to reduce their reliance on outside purchases of materials and equipment, and individual plants continue to maintain high levels of vertical integration.

But self-reliance is not autarchy. On the national level, self-reliance is not inconsistent with a rising flow of technology-bearing imports concentrated, as we have seen in chapter 4, in sectors that domestic engineering firms have been least successful in equipping. Self-reliance also provides for downward transfers of key items of machinery, chemical catalysts, and other essential inputs from higher to lower levels of domestic industry, and may even include seemingly paradoxical calls for greater specialization within provincial networks of farm machinery manufacturers to improve product quality and maintain technical momentum without turning to external suppliers.[3]

The economic rationale for each of these policies lies in the widely shared conviction that excessive division of labor masks hidden technical potentials. The obvious short-term costs of trade restriction may be smaller than the long-run gains obtainable from exploiting these unsuspected capabilities. The resulting strategy is one of planned and partial truncation of commodity exchange designed to force regions, communes, and enterprises to muster latent skills in planning and administration and to foster the growth of problem-solving capabilities that come only from sustained grappling with technical difficulties. In seeking to link the degree of reliance on external support to levels of sectoral and regional as well as national development, Chinese planners are attempting to apply a criterion that goes beyond Hirschman's suggestion that

> in order to maximize growth the developing countries could need an appropriate alternation of contact and insulation, of openness to the trade and capital of the developed countries, to be followed by a period of nationalism and withdrawnness. In the period of openness, crucial learning processes take place, but many are of the latent kind and remain unnoticed and misperceived. They come to fruition only once contact is interrupted or severely restricted: the previous misperceptions are then swept away. Thus both contact and insulation have essential roles to play, one after the other.[4]

Some International Comparisons

The cumulative process of output expansion and technical development in China's producer industries during the present century closely parallels the earlier experiences of other industrial nations. The following examples highlight the common features of the industrialization process.

In many advanced economies, the origins of a wide range of manufacturing activity can be traced to obscure, ill-financed repair works initially serving the textile industry. These plants move from repair work to the manufacture of cheap and shoddy imitations of foreign machines, an activity that eventually serves as a springboard for the growth of modern engineering industries. In Europe,

> textile manufacturers needed repair shops to adjust their machines; gradually the experience gathered there, together with the growth of specialization in the textile industry itself, led to their transformation into machine and machine tool making establishments and from these centres a whole engineering industry would be born. It happened in New England, in Leeds, in Manchester, in Mulhouse, in Switzerland.[5]

In Europe and America, as in China, this technical development process

> tended to be cumulative, since the successful application of machinery to one field of activity stimulated its application to another, and the accumulation of knowledge and skill made it easier to solve technical problems and sense out the points where the potentialities of further technical progress were brightest.[6]

Discontinuity is another common feature of technical advance. Periods of economic boom produce strong emphasis on expanding the quantity of output, while "most research activity and significant changes in tool design" occur "during slack periods," when technicians have "the chance of devoting more time to innovations" and competitive pressures favor sellers whose machines meet the precise needs of equipment purchasers.[7]

Japan's experience provides particularly clear parallels with China's. As late as 1930, Japan's engineering sector was small and, by international standards, technically weak. Yet within only ten years, the forces of depression, growing international isolation, reflation, and war preparation transformed machine building into the largest branch of manufacturing and one now able to compete on a world level in sophisticated fields such as military aviation. The experience and skills acquired before and during the Pacific war were subsequently transferred to civilian manufacturing, where they formed the basis for Japan's emergence as a world leader in the manufacture of machinery, transport equipment, and electronics. As one writer observes, "The most remarkable feature of the period was the appearance of trades that had hardly existed or were of minor importance before the war or even in the early 1950s."[8] Ohkawa and Rosovsky attribute these advances to Japan's growing "social capability to import technology," and assign particular significance to the cost-reducing and skill-enhancing effects of "improvement engineering," or systematically upgrading the performance of equipment and techniques based on core innovations developed overseas.[9]

Commonality between Chinese and foreign factory operations appears at the microeconomic level as well. Intimate familiarity with day-to-day production activity on the part of engineers and, to a lesser extent, of other managers; provision of training facilities for blue-collar workers; participation of manual workers in planning and trial manufacture of new or modified products; temporary assignment of workers to sales organizations to teach them the importance of serving customers' needs; and organized promotion of worker morale—each of these familiar Chinese policies exists to varying degrees throughout the advanced countries, and most noticeably in Japan.[10]

Policy Implications

Whether we consider geography, resources, history, culture, politics, or socioeconomic patterns, China is obviously different from most developing countries. Yet the presence of definite parallels in the industrial history of China and of other nations suggests that Chinese experience is not entirely without value as a guide to policy problems facing underdeveloped nations.

To begin with, China's postwar industrial achievements demonstrate that import substitution and administrative allocation of resources can help build a vigorous, technically progressive, and forward-looking industrial system without the benefit of domestic or international price competition. China's experience suggests that economists may be in danger of exaggerating both the virtues of outward-looking development policies and the weaknesses of central planning.[11]

Any system of resource allocation and any pattern of investments leads to difficulties, shortages, and waste. In many ways, China seems to have made the most of a system of industrial administration and resource allocation that was established for essentially noneconomic reasons. Chinese industry performs well, not because socialist planning represents a superior form of industrial organization, but because Chinese planners, managers, and workers have devised effective methods of limiting the shortcomings inherent in China's economic environment while taking advantage of its considerable strengths. All this indicates that the way in which an economic system is operated may be more significant than its structural features in determining overall performance.

Despite its comparative independence of foreign aid and trade, the presence of a considerable domestic research establishment, a huge engineering industry, and a strong preference for avoiding slavish imitation of foreign methods, Chinese industry has rarely created production functions that depart radically from the main lines of Western technology. Like Japan, China has concentrated her technical resources on absorbing foreign techniques and then modifying them to suit local resource and demand conditions. This is true even of small-scale industry, in which production is dominated by substantial plants embodying high ratios of capital to labor and using materials and processes that offer few surprises to Western engineers.[12]

If China, being well endowed with both the means and desire to develop labor-using industrial technologies, has largely failed to do so, it seems unlikely that other low-income countries will move rapidly in this direction without massive resource injections from outside. This view leads to the expectation that, even with rapidly growing output and investment, industrialization is unlikely to offer a direct solution to the employment problems of populous developing countries.

China's experience reaffirms the complexity of economic growth. The significance of discontinuity, learning effects, technical thresholds, and conflicts between short- and long-run advantages severely limits the usefulness of neat economic concepts, plans, and models. What meaning can be attached to efficient growth or balanced growth, if we believe that errors, shoddy goods, and stopgap methods may be integral components of the development process?

Motivation and morale, factors with little place in standard economic analysis, have emerged as important determinants of industrial performance in China. Similar findings reported in studies of other nations suggest that the emphasis that Chinese economic policy places on spurring the human factor to extract maximum results from existing resources is not misplaced.[13] Motivation deserves more attention from economists.

Finally, a study of China's postwar experience leaves the impression that both the theory and practice of development economics devote too much emphasis to cautious planning and weighing of alternatives and too little to plunging ahead and taking calculated risks. Any development program will produce blunders, bungling, and errors. Since success typically hinges on the capacity to provide ad hoc adjustments to unforeseen contingencies, there is much to be said for the Chinese philosophy of immediately pushing for solutions to the "problem of existence or absence" of some desired product or technique, and then considering the "problem of advanced or backward"—meaning improvements in quality, technique, economic indicators, and so on. Indeed, had the Chinese not rushed ahead with their First Five-Year Plan, a patchwork arrangement that strained the economy's absorptive capacity in many directions, much of the progress recorded in this book would not have occurred.

Abbreviations

BBC W	British Broadcasting Corporation. *Summary of World Broadcasts: Pt. 3, The Far East, Weekly Economic Report.*
CB	United States Consulate General, Hong Kong. *Current Background.*
CHKY	*Chi-hsieh kung-yeh* [Machinery industry], Peking.
CKKY	Ch'en Chen and Yao Lo, eds. *Chung-kuo chin-tai kung-yeh shih tzu-liao* [Materials on China's modern industrial history], collection I.
CKYTH	*Chung-kung-yeh t'ung-hsün* [Heavy industry bulletin], Peking.
ECMM	United States Consulate General, Hong Kong. *Extracts from China Mainland Magazines.*
FBIS	United States Foreign Broadcast Information Service. *Daily Report, People's Republic of China.*
FFYP	First Five-Year Plan (1953–57).
FMMB	First Ministry of Machine-building.
GVFO	Gross (sales) value of factory output.
GVHO	Gross (sales) value of handicraft output.
GVIO	Gross (sales) value of industrial output from factories and handicrafts.
HHKY	*Hua-hsüeh kung-yeh* [Chemical industry], Peking.
JMJP	*Jen-min jih-pao* [People's daily], Peking.
JPRS	United States Joint Publications Research Service.
SCMP	United States Consulate General, Hong Kong. *Survey of China Mainland Press.*
SMR	*Minami Manshū tetsudō kabushiki gaisha* [South Manchurian railway company].

SSCK — SMR Tenshin jimusho chōsaka. *Shina ni okeru san sōda oyobi chisso kōgyō* [China's acid, soda, and nitrogen industries].

WKKT — *Chūgoku no tekkōgyō to kikai kōgyō* [China's steel and machinery industries].

Symbols and Units of Measure

Symbols Used in the Tables

— indicates data which are not available

-- indicates amounts which are nil or negligible

Units of Measure

One Chinese yuan was equivalent to approximately U.S. $0.26 in 1933, $0.38 in 1957, and $0.50 at the official exchange rates of the mid-1970s. The post-1949 exchange rates do not necessarily reflect the relative purchasing power of the two currencies.

All weights are in terms of metric units.

Notes

Introduction

1. Wang Hu-sheng, "Several Problems of Classifying Heavy and Light Industry," *Ching-chi yen-chiu* 4(1963):18.
2. These considerations may be formalized as follows: the initial task T requires skill levels $S_{1t}, S_{2t}, \ldots, S_{nt}$ in each of n areas. Repetition of T raises potential in these skill areas to new levels $P_1, P_2, \ldots, P_n$, which describe industry's skill frontier ($P_i \geq S_{it}$ for $i = 1, 2, \ldots, n$). Entrepreneurs will attempt new tasks T^* if they believe them to be both feasible ($P_i \geq S_{it^*}$ for $i = 1, 2, \ldots, n$) and profitable. D. J. Teece, "Technology Transfer by Multinational Firms: The Resource Cost of Transferring Technological Know-how," *Economic Journal* 87(1977):242–61 demonstrates the relevance of learning theory to industrial firms.

Chapter 1

1. Illustrations drawn from U.S. economic history abound in such works as George S. Gibb, *The Saco-Lowell Shops* (Cambridge, 1950); W. Paul Strassmann, *Risk and Technological Innovation* (Ithaca, 1959); and Nathan Rosenberg, "Technological Change in the Machine Tool Industry, 1840–1910," *Journal of Economic History* 23.4(1963):414–43. The importance of technological thresholds was brought to my attention by John C. H. Fei.
2. *Ta-lung chi-ch'i-ch'ang ti fa-sheng fa-chan yü kai-tsao* (hereafter *Ta-lung*) (Shanghai, 1959), pp. 2–3. Albert Feuerwerker kindly supplied me with a copy of this source.
3. Ch'en Chen and Yao Lo, eds., *Chung-kuo chin-tai kung-yeh shih tzu-liao* (hereafter CKKY) (Tokyo, 1966), collection I:597, 618. Examples of engineering entrepreneurs with foreign training also appear in CKKY

I:593 and in *Chung-kuo kuo-huo kung-ch'ang shih-lüeh* (Shanghai, 1935), pp. 143, 213–14.

4. *Chung-kuo kuo-huo*; CKKY I:593–631.
5. Minami Manshū tetsudō kabushiki gaisha (hereafter SMR), Chōsabu, *Kita Shina kōjō jittai chōsa hōkokusho—Tenshin no bu* (Dairen, 1939), pp. 589–640. Ta-lung's access to external finance is inferred from the existence of bank records describing the financial condition of an associated textile plant (*Ta-lung*, p. 53).
6. Nung-shang pu, *Nung-shang t'ung-chi piao*, no. 1 (1912) (Shanghai, 1914), pp. 24–25, and *Manshū kaihatsu yonjū nenshi* (hereafter *Manshū kaihatsu*) (Tokyo, 1964–65), 1:297.
7. *Ta-lung*, pp. 16, 32, 35, 39; CKKY I: 606, 628.
8. *Ta-lung*, pp. 3–6. Shanghai's factories housed 98,580 cotton spindles in 1894; 525,488 in 1904; and 625,876 in 1914 (Onoe Etsuzō, *Chūgoku no sangyō ritchi ni kansuru kenkyū* [Tokyo, 1971], p. 301).
9. *Ta-lung*, p. 7; another job acquired after a British firm had declined it is described on page 10.
10. Ibid., pp. 8, 20–21.
11. Yang Ta-chin, *Hsien-tai Chung-kuo shih-yeh chih* (Shanghai and Ch'angsha, 1935–38), 1:866–96.
12. Wartime yarn prices rose much faster than the cost of cotton, creating unprecedented profits in spinning. At the same time, the base spindle price charged by the largest U.S. producer, a leading exporter to China, rose from $2.00 to $6.75. See Yen Chung-p'ing, *Chung-kuo mien-fang-chih shih-k'ao* (Peking, 1963), p. 172, and Gibb, *Saco-Lowell*, p. 470.
13. *Ta-lung*, pp. 20, 23, 32.
14. Ibid., 33–35, 51–54.
15. Ibid., 45, 52.
16. Ibid., 47, 50–52, 63–67.
17. These data, based on a factory survey of China proper (excluding Manchuria) directed by Liu Ta-chün (D. K. Lieu), are compiled in Ta-chung Liu and Kung-chia Yeh, *The Economy of the Chinese Mainland* (Princeton, 1965), pp. 426–28. The survey included firms using mechanical power and employing over five workers. Engineering consists of machinery, electrical appliances, transportation equipment, and shipbuilding, and includes repair as well as manufacturing.
18. Kung-chia Yeh, "Capital Formation in Mainland China, 1931–36 and 1952–57," (Ph.D. dissertation, Columbia University, 1964), p. 225.
19. Shang-hai she-hui-chü, *Shang-hai chih kung-yeh* (Shanghai, 1930), pp. 126–31, 137–38; Liu Ta-chün, *Chung-kuo kung-yeh tiao-ch'a pao-kao* (Shanghai, 1937), 2:1–40, and *Shang-hai kung-yeh-hua yen-chiu* (Ch'angsha, 1940), pp. 56–57.
20. For example Yang, *Shih-yeh-chih*, 1:866–96; SMR Tenshin jimusho chōsaka, *Sainan ni okeru seizō kōgyō* (Tientsin, 1936), p. 63; *Min-sheng shih-yeh kung-ssu shih-yi-chou-nien chi-nien-k'an* (Shanghai, 1937);

Ministry of Industry, Bureau of Foreign Trade, comp., *China Industrial Handbooks: Chekiang* (Shanghai, 1935), pp. 669–73.

21. Lists of Chinese machinery products appear in Ch'en Chen, ed., *Chung-kuo chin-tai kung-yeh shih tzu-liao* (Tokyo, 1966), collection IV, 2:801; Ku Yü-hsien, "Thirty Years of Machine-building," in *San-shih-nien lai chih Chung-kuo kung-ch'eng*, ed. Chou K'ai-ch'ing (Taipei, 1967), 2:8–17; and Ōtsuka Reizō, *Shina kōgyō sōkan* (Tokyo, 1942), 2:19–23.
22. Ministry of Industry, Bureau of Foreign Trade, comp., *China Industrial Handbooks: Kiangsu* (Shanghai, 1933), passim; Yang, *Shih-yeh chih* 1:866–96. See also Wang Tzu-chien and Wang Chen-chung, *Ch'i-sheng hua-shang shao-ch'ang tiao-ch'a pao-kao* (Shanghai, 1935), pp. 62–67, and Ōtsuka, *Shina kōgyō sōkan*, 2:21.
23. *Matchi kōgyō hōkokusho* (Nanking, 1940), p. 24.
24. Ministry of Industry, *Industrial Handbooks: Kiangsu*, p. 630.
25. Ibid., pp. 524, 548, 585–86, 763–67; Yang, *Shih-yeh chih*, 1:866–96; SMR Chōsabu, *Kita Shina*, pp. 489–90; SMR Sōmubu chōsaka, *Shina kōjō jijō* (Dairen, 1928), pp. 67–68, 169–70; China, Maritime Customs, *Decennial Reports, 1922–31* (Shanghai, 1933), 1:530, 588; *Chōsha no juyō kōjō chōsa* (Nanking, 1940), p. 94.
26. *Ta-lung*, pp. 17, 47; SMR Chōsabu, *Kita Shina*, p. 590.
27. Ibid., pp. 589–91, 623–28. Prices for ten types of equipment, including lathes and milling, shaping, and grinding machines, are listed on pp. 500–1.
28. Ibid., pp. 480, 489–90; *Chōsha*, p. 56; SMR Tenshin jimusho chōsaka, *Shina ni okeru san sōda oyobi chisso kōgyō* (hereafter SSCK) (Tientsin, 1937), pp. 69, 149.
29. *Ta-lung*, p. 50.
30. SMR Chōsabu, *Kita Shina*, pp. 500–1; Ministry of Industry, *Industrial Handbooks: Kiangsu*, pp. 318, 346–47, 429, 431, 438, 524; China, Maritime Customs, *Decennial Reports*, 1922–31; 1:562; Ōtsuka, *Shina kōgyō sōkan*, 2:25.
31. The problem of undercapitalization in industrial enterprises is discussed in many sources, for instance, Leonard G. Ting, "Chinese Modern Banks and the Finance of Government and Industry," *Nankai Social and Economic Quarterly* 8.3(1935):597–608.
32. Investigators found ironworks, foundries, or machine shops in 67 of 146 cities surveyed in 1933 (Liu, *Chung-kuo kung-yeh*, vol. 3).
33. This type of development sequence is analyzed by Rosenberg, "Technological Change." For illustrative material, see Gibb, *Saco-Lowell*; Strassmann, *Risk and Technological Innovation*; Thomas R. Navin, *The Whitin Machine Works Since 1831* (Cambridge, 1950); Kajinishi Mitsuhaya, *Toyota Sakichi* (Tokyo, 1962); Kozo Yamamura, "The Decade of Sowing: The Absorption of Western Technology by the Electric Machinery and Machine Tool Industries of Japan during the 1920s" (unpublished, 1976).
34. Early acid producers are mentioned in SSCK, p. 123. Various issues of

Nung-shang t'ung-chi piao indicate that annual production of sulphuric, hydrochloric, and nitric acids did not exceed 600 tons during 1912–21 (reported 1916 output of 6.2 million catties or over 3,700 tons of nitric acid [no. 5, p. 354] appears to be one of many printing errors in this unreliable source).

35. Estimated cloth output for 1919–31 from Bruce L. Reynolds, "Weft: The Technological Sanctuary of Chinese Handspun Yarn," *Ch'ing-shih wen-t'i* 3.2(1974):6; for 1931–36, from Chang, *Industrial Development*, pp. 119, 123.
36. Average annual match imports (in thousands of boxes) declined from 511 in 1911–15 to 299 in 1916–20, 94 in 1921–30, and 15 during 1931–34 (calculated from *Matchi kōgyō hōkokusho*, pp. 108–10). Use of chemicals in other industries is mentioned in Ministry of Industry, *Industrial Handbooks: Kiangsu*, p. 661, and *Industrial Handbooks: Chekiang*, p. 625; SSCK, pp. 129, 150; China, Maritime Customs, *Decennial Reports, 1922–31*, 1:329; Yang, *Shih-yeh chih*, 1:545.
37. CKKY I:513–20; SSCK, pp. 1–30. Soda exports to Japan began in 1926 (China, Maritime Customs, *Annual Trade Report and Returns: Tientsin, 1926* [Shanghai, 1927], p. 96).
38. Liu, *Chung-kuo kung-yeh*, 2:630, reports 1932 output from two plants totaling 5,220 tons. Imports in that year amounted to 2,998 tons (China, Maritime Customs, *The Trade of China, 1933* [Shanghai, 1934], 2:93–95).
39. *Chung-kuo kuo-huo*, pp. 73, 115, 175, 191, 213, 231, 237. See also SSCK, p. 30.
40. Ministry of Industry, *China Industrial Handbooks: Kiangsu*, pp. 655–56.
41. In addition to the Shanghai data shown in table 1.3, Fang Hsien-t'ing, "A Statistical Analysis of Chinese Industrialization," *Ching-chi t'ung-chi chi-k'an* 1.1(1932):80–127, shows the importance of scale economies in textile and flour mills.
42. SSCK, pp. 69, 149, 154–55.
43. SSCK, pp. 4, 30–32, 154. Li-chung's chief engineer was a former director of Nankai University's chemical research institute (p. 144).
44. SSCK, pp. 4, 129; CKKY, I:514; SMR Chōsabu, *Kita Shina*, pp. 690–91.
45. SSCK, pp. 144, 147, 155–56; SMR Chōsabu, *Kita Shina*, pp. 641, 663.
46. SSCK, pp. 17, 129, 136; SMR Chōsabu, *Kita Shina*, p. 638.
47. SSCK, pp. 114–15. However, the price differential between ICI (British) and Yung-li's soda ash was greater in T'aiyuan, Chinan, Harbin, and Kwangtung than in Tientsin or Shanghai, showing that transport rate policy was partially effective in strengthening the competitive position of domestic goods.
48. A 1938 survey showing that most of Tientsin's dyeing plants bought chemicals from both foreign and domestic sources illustrates customer balance between imports and local products. (SMR Chōsabu, *Kita Shina*, pp. 473–91). Quality problems are mentioned in the same source (p. 688) and in SSCK, pp. 113, 145.

49. SSCK, pp. 50–51, 66, 126–127, 134–35, 150; SMR Chōsabu, *Kita Shina*, p. 664.
50. However, we should note early forays into ammonia manufacture, as well as the creation of the China Agricultural Chemical Plant by two Chekiang University staff members in 1933. See SSCK, pp. 153–54, 159–62, and *Chung-kuo kuo-huo*, pp. 213–14.
51. Thomas G. Rawski, "The Growth of Producer Industries, 1900–1971," in *China's Modern Economy in Historical Perspective*, ed. Dwight H. Perkins (Stanford, 1975), p. 214.
52. For Chinese blunders, see Albert Feuerwerker, "China's Nineteenth Century Industrialization: The Case of the Hanyehping Coal and Iron Company, Limited," in *The Economic Development of China and Japan*, ed. C. D. Cowan (London, 1964), pp. 79–110. Anshan's early history is described in M. Gardner Clark, *Development of China's Steel Industry and Soviet Technical Aid* (Ithaca, 1973), pp. 1–2, and in *Manshū kaihatsu, 1:233*–35.
53. Feuerwerker, "China's Nineteenth Century Industrialization," p.90.
54. Clark, *China's Steel Industry*, p. 46, referring to blending coal.
55. Ibid., 45–48, 52–53; Manshū *kaihatsu*, 2:462.
56. Clark, *China's Steel Industry*, p. 1; *Manshū kaihatsu*, 1:297, and 2:461; Ch'en, *Chung-kuo kung-yeh*, collection IV, 1:746.
57. Anshan capital from *Manshū kaihatsu*, 2:461. Manchukuo yen were worth slightly less than Chinese yuan during 1932–37, each being equivalent to about U.S. $0.30 (*The Manchoukuo Yearbook 1942* [Hsinking, 1941], pp. 254–55, and Liang-lin Hsiao, *China's Foreign Trade Statistics, 1864–1949* [Cambridge, 1974], p. 192). Liu and Yeh, *Economy of the Chinese Mainland*, p. 504, report average exchange rates of 98.41 and 97.50 Chinese yuan per 100 Manchukuo yen for 1933 and 1934 respectively. Among 177 capital and profit figures compiled from annual reports of ninety-eight private Chinese firms during 1933–37, there were only five reports of capital in excess of 10 million yuan, and only the Shen-hsin Textile Plant had assets larger than Anshan's. Annual profits of over 1 million yuan appear in nine instances, with only one figure surpassing 2 million yuan (CKKY I:649–55).
58. Application of one test indicates that China experienced "marked improvement" in financial effectiveness during the 1930s because the ratio of bank deposits to national product rose more than five percentage points in ten years. But the terminal position (1936) barely escapes the boundary (15 percent ratio of currency plus deposits to GNP) separating financial networks that made "negligible" contribution and those that made "some" contribution to financing industry and agriculture. For the test, see Irma Adelman and Cynthia T. Morris, *Society, Politics and Economic Development* (Baltimore, 1967), pp. 120–22. Data on aggregate product, currency, and deposits are from K. C. Yeh, "Capital Formation," in *Economic Trends in Communist China*, ed. Alexander Eckstein, Walter

Galenson, and Ta-chung Liu (Chicago, 1968), p. 510; Arthur N. Young, *China's Nation-building Effort* (Cambridge, 1971), pp. 170–71, 486–89; and Ting, "Chinese Modern Banks," p. 580.

59. Ting, "Chinese Modern Banks," p. 596, provides data showing that the annual yield calculated from average monthly prices of actively traded domestic securities averaged 17.3 percent per annum between 1928 and June 1935, surpassing 20 percent in 21 of 87 months and dropping below 11 percent only once.

60. Mishina Yoritata, *Hokushi minzoku kōgyō no hattatsu* (Tokyo, 1942), pp. 79–84, gives data showing the low share of commercial bank loans offered to industry. Data for large commercial banks show over three-fourths of industrial loans going to textiles and flour milling and virtually none to producer industries (Mishina, p. 80; Ting, "Chinese Modern Banks," p. 605).

61. Feuerwerker, "China's Nineteenth Century Industrialization," pp. 106–8; Ku Yüan-t'ien, "China's Iron and Steel Industry," *Ching-chi t'ung-chi chi-k'an* 2.3(1933):705–9; Fang Hsien-t'ing and Ku Yüan-t'ien, "Bird's Eye View of China's Iron and Steel Industry," in *Chung-kuo ching-chi yen-chiu*, ed. Fang Hsien-t'ing (Ch'angsha, 1938), p. 634; Ch'en, *Chung-kuo kung-yeh*, collection IV, 2:752.

62. *Manshū kaihatsu*, 2:488, discusses Japanese reluctance to promote machinery manufacture prior to 1930. The limited role of engineering in Japanese plans for Manchuria is evident from its omission from a list of nineteen industries placed under direct or indirect state control during 1933; with the exception of motor vehicles, civilian machinery was relegated to the private sector (*Fifth Report on Progress in Manchuria to 1936* [Dairen, 1936], pp. 99–100).

63. *The Manchuria Yearbook, 1931*, (Tokyo, 1931), pp. 120–25, 180. Dye production reached its cyclical peak in 1925.

64. Employment data from *The Manchuria Yearbook, 1932–33* (Tokyo, 1932), p. 180 (excluding enterprises with fewer than six workers). Output value from Rawski, "Producer Industries," p. 217.

65. Imports of machinery and tools rose from 5.1 to 38.9 million Manchukuo yuan between 1932 and 1936 (*Sixth Report on Progress in Manchuria to 1939* [Dairen, 1939], p. 96); the highest estimate of 1936 machinery output is 50.4 million yen, only 18 percent above the 1931 figure mentioned above (Rawski, "Producer Industries," p. 219).

66. Achievements of the large plants are recounted in *Manshū kaihatsu*, 1:197; 2:136–39, 490–92. Annual exports of Chinese machinery to Manchuria were equivalent to several hundred thousand Japanese yen during 1929–31 and varied between 15,000 and 130,000 yen during 1932–37. See *The Manchuria Yearbook, 1931*, pp. 224–25; *The Manchuria Yearbook, 1932–33*, p. 375; *The Manchoukuo Yearbook, 1934* (Tokyo, 1934), pp. 430, 582; China, Maritime Customs, *The Trade of China*, various issues.

67. *The Manchoukuo Yearbook, 1934*, pp. 331, 342–43, 412; *Fifth Report on Progress*, pp. 103–4.
68. *The Manchoukuo Yearbook, 1934*, pp. 426–28; Clark, *China's Steel Industry*, p. 2.
69. Three-quarters of Manchuria's 1929–31 pig iron output was exported; during 1932–35, exports to Japan alone accounted for 84 percent of total production. See *The Manchoukuo Yearbook, 1934*, pp. 330–33; *Manshū kaihatsu*, 2:484; Kantōkyoku kambō bunshoka, *Kantōkyoku tōkei sanjū nenshi* (Dairen, 1937), p. 343.
70. Ministry of Industry, *Industrial Handbooks: Kiangsu*, pp. 657–59, lists numerous rural areas as potential mineral sources for chemical manufacture and describes the efforts of the K'ai-ch'eng Acid Works to obtain pyrites from several localities. In addition to the citations in note 50 in this chapter, we should also note Ta-lung's efforts to penetrate rural markets. These included sales of engines with attachments for pumping, milling, and other farm operations to "new style rich peasants" in Kiangsu during the early 1920s and an abortive effort to establish a branch plant to produce engines and farm tools for local markets at the end of the same decade (*Ta-lung*, pp. 20, 33). Charles J. Ferguson, ed., *Andersen, Meyer & Company Limited of China* (Shanghai, 1931) describes the widespread activities of a particularly energetic foreign firm in introducing pumps, engines, and even tractors to rural buyers. Bruce Reynolds directed me to this source.
71. Impressively detailed plans for public investments by the Nanking government in steel, machinery, chemicals, power, and cement appear in Shih-yeh-pu, kung-yeh-ssu, *Shih-yeh-pu kung-yeh shih-cheng kai-k'uang* (Nanking, 1934).
72. Albert O. Hirschman, *The Strategy of Economic Development* (New Haven, 1958), p. 121.

Chapter 2

1. *First Five-Year Plan for Development of the National Economy of the People's Republic of China in 1953–1957* (Peking, 1956), p. 39.
2. Ibid., p. 51. Lin I-fu, "Actively Take Steps to Fully Utilize the Productive Capacity of Existing Industries," *Chi-hua ching-chi* 3(1958):7, reports that the share of 1952–57 output from existing units may have surpassed 70 percent. Pai Ou, "Brief Discussion of the Direction and Tasks of the Machinery Industry During the First and Second Five-Year Plans," CHKY 12(1957):5, states that new plants accounted for only 19 percent of machinery output in 1957.
3. The unreliability of available data can be illustrated by the following widely varying estimates (in thousands of annual tons) of capacity at six

Manchurian cement plants: Fushun, 25–80; Anshan, 0–100; Hsiaotun, 120–50; Liaoyang, 75–90; Pench'i, 90–100; Antung, 0–50. Data from Economic Encyclopedia of the Northeast, vol. 12, *The Cement Industry* (Washington, 1947), p. 103, and Pauley, *Japanese Assets*, p. 211.

4. The importance of each of these factors can be seen from detailed plant studies contained in Naikaku sōri daijin kambō chōsa shitsu, *Chūkyō tekkōgyō chōsa hōkokusho (kigyō hen)*, vol. 1 (Tokyo, 1956). Clark, *China's Steel Industry*, p. 4, mistakenly asserts that no Japanese technicians remained at Anshan after 1949. In fact, 100 Japanese, many of them technicians, worked there until 1953 (Naikaku sōri daijin, *Chūkyō tekkōgyō*, 1:179); Japanese technicians at other plants are mentioned in the same source, pp. 254, 262, 298–99.
5. Ibid., 1:165, 180. Earlier Japanese methods had required higher technical skills among ordinary workers (1:245).
6. Recruitment of villagers to work at Anshan and Pench'i is mentioned in Naikaku sōri daijin, *Chūkyō tekkōgyō*, 1:177, 196. Output and productivity data from Clark, *China's Steel Industry*, pp. 3, 12; Pauley, *Japanese Assets*, chapter 5 and appendix 5; Onoe, *Chūgoku no sangyō ritchi*, p. 301; Chang Hsü-sheng, *Wo-kuo she-hui chu-i kung-yeh-chung t'i-kao lao-tung sheng-ch'an-lü ti t'u-ching* (Peking, 1956), p. 26.
7. *Jen-min jih-pao* (hereafter JMJP), April 19, 1953; the gap was 22 percent in 1950 and 21 percent in 1951.
8. Clark, *China's Steel Industry*, pp. 11–15; Naikaku sōri daijin, *Chūkyō tekkōgyō*, 1:195–232; JPRS 5744(1960):1.
9. Criticisms of smaller firms appeared in *Hsin-hua jih-pao* (Chungking), August 23, 1952, and June 4, 1953; JMJP, February 6, March 14, and September 29, 1953, and February 2, 1954; *Kung-jen jih-pao*, May 17, 1953, and *Chung-kuo ch'ing-nien pao*, August 28, 1954. Enterprise performance data from Chen, *Statistics*, p. 263.
10. JMJP, January 16 and December 6, 1954.
11. SCMP 610(1953):9; JMJP, April 4 and September 8, 1954. The former source presents a bleak view of the machinery industry in 1953, commenting that "utter confusion reigns over the allocation of production tasks, arrangement of production procedures, organization and distribution of labor power, inspection and care of equipment, supply of materials and tools" in many state factories.
12. Ch'eng Ch'i-hsing, "Opinions on Reforming Material and Technical Supply Work," CHKY 24(1956):4; U.S. Consulate General, Hong Kong, *Extracts from China Mainland Magazines* (hereafter ECMM) 90(1957):22. Annual directives for machinery and metallurgy did not appear until April and June 1957; see "FMMB Directive for 1957," CHKY 9(1957):2–8, and "Ministry of Metallurgy Production Plans for 1957," *Yeh-chin pao* 45(1957):34.
13. *Chieh-fang jih-pao*, January 7, 1952, and JMJP, June 19, 1957.
14. A September report stated that "the ministries of the central government

and governments of the provinces, municipalities and regions are now drawing up plans for 1958 on the basis of control figures (draft) laid down at the recent national planning conference" (SCMP 1612[1957]:13).

15. "FMMB Directive for 1957;" Chiang Li, "Several Problems as Seen from Four Chinan Plants," CHKY 1(1957):31; "Technical Reform Work in the Past Year," CHKY 6(1957):7–13; Chiang Cheng, "Shortcomings and Problems in Technical Work," CHKY 12(1957):25–26, 35; "Opinions and Demands of Factory Directors," CHKY 10(1957):7–9, and 11(1957):7–10.
16. ECMM 100(1957):34–39; Pai, "Bricf Discussion," p. 5.
17. Rawski, "Producer Industries," p. 223.
18. Liu and Yeh, *Economy of the Chinese Mainland*, pp. 141, 157, find that with 1933=100, gross value added for 1952 in mining, utilities, and producer manufacturing becomes 282.4 or 331.7 depending on the choice of 1933 or 1952 prices. Chang, *Industrial Development*, p. 67, finds that wartime industrial output reached a peak of 76 percent above the 1933 base during 1942. Comparisons of post–1949 commodity output with wartime peak levels appear in Hsüeh Mu-chiao, Su Hsing, and Lin Tse-li, *The Socialist Transformation of the National Economy in China* (Peking, 1960), p. 69.
19. Estimates for 1936–41 calculated from tables 6 and 7 of Alexander Eckstein, Kang Chao, and John Chang, "The Economic Development of Manchuria: The Rise of a Frontier Economy," *Journal of Economic History* 34.1(1974):254–55; commodity output data for later years appear in Onoe, *Chūgoku no sangyō ritchi*, p. 221. Chang Chen, *Ti-i-ko wu-nien chi-hua-chung ti hua-hsüeh kung-yeh* (Peking, 1956), p. 13, states that most Japanese-built chemical plants produced nothing before Japan's surrender. Japanese plans to produce up to fifty thousand machine tools annually also were never realized; Liaoning's 1949 output of less than five hundred machine tools surpassed the 1943 peak by 11 percent (Onoe, *Chūgoku no sangyō ritchi*, pp. 247, 250, 253).
20. Shanghai's industrial employment fell from a prewar level of over 300,000 to only 27,000 at the end of 1937, but climbed to 237,000 by the end of 1938; in 1939, industrial output reportedly surpassed the 1936 level (Ching Sheng, *Chan-shih Chung-kuo ching-chi lun-k'uo*[n.p., 1944], p. 70). Wang Chi-shen et al., *Chan-shih Shang-hai ching-chi* (Shanghai, 1945), pp. 192–94, shows that while 1943 textile output plunged to under 6 percent of the 1936 level, the city's stock of textile machinery rose by about 5 percent between 1936 and 1944. Output estimate for North China by Wang Foh-shen cited in Chang, *Industrial Development*, p. 74.
21. Szechwan's 1949 output of electric power, for example, accounted for only 3.4 percent of the national total despite a thirteen-fold increase over the 1936 figure (Chen, *Statistics*, pp. 186, 206, and Chu Ta-ching, "The Power Sector in the Past Ten Years," in *Shih-nien-lai chih Chung-kuo ching-chi*, comp. T'an Hsi-hung (Shanghai, 1948), 1:J–15). Data on Chungking metal processing from Liu, *Chung-kuo kung-yeh*, 3:170–93; Ou-yang Lun, "The

Machinery Sector in the Past Ten Years," in *Shih-nien-lai chih Chung-kuo ching-chi*, 1:F–22; *Chung-hua nien-chien 1948* (Nanking, 1948), 2:1500.

22. Clark, *China's Steel Industry,* chap. 2; Naikaku sōri daijin, *Chūkyō tekkōgyō*, vol. 1, chap. 6–10.
23. Harbin Electric Motor Plant was one firm whose customers returned many defective items (*Hei-lung-chiang jih-pao*, September 14, 1954). The army returned a shipment of 140 cranes to the Canton General Machinery Works, complaining that the cranes could lift only half the designed load and were dangerous to operate (*Kuang-chou jih-pao*, April 3, 1954). Typical complaints from commercial officials appear in Su Lin, *T'an-t'an wo-kuo kuo-tu shih-ch'i ti chia-ko cheng-ts'e* (Shanghai, 1956), p. 47.
24. Advances in output and technique are described in *Chūgoku no tekkōgyō to kikai kōgyō* (hereafter WKKT)(Tokyo, 1964), pp. 21–32, and by Clark, *China's Steel Industry*, who concludes (p. 6) that "the Chinese received the best technical aid and equipment available anywhere" from the Soviet Union.
25. WKKT, p. 92; SCMP 549(1953):24–25, 581(1953):27, 643(1953):25, 662(1953):45.
26. Liu and Yeh, *Economy of the Chinese Mainland*, pp. 209, 428, 575; *Chung-hua nien-chien 1948*, 2:1501; WKKT, p. 83.
27. Instances of weather damage are chronicled in "Chichihar #1 Machine Tool Plant Has Neglected Care of Equipment for a Long Time," CHKY 18(1953):6–7; JMJP, March 2, 1950, and March 15, 1953; *Hsin Hu-nan pao*, August 21, 1954. Targets of newspaper attacks for failure to lubricate equipment included Harbin Machinery Works (*Ha-erh-pin jih-pao*, July 8, 1954) and Wusih Machine Tool Plant (*Kung-jen jih-pao*, August 1, 1956).
28. Full details of the Nanking plant's failings appear in JMJP, March 15, 1953, and in "Nanking Machine Tool Plant Damages 22 of 28 New Machine Tools in Less Than Half a Year," CHKY 18(1953):8–9. Information on Anshan from Clark, *China's Steel Industry*, p. 5. The frequency of these problems is evident from the contents of industrial journals in these years. One issue of CHKY contained the following items, in addition to the two cited above: "Chungking Machine Tool Plant Installs 9 Lathes, Uses 7 and Wrecks 7," "Shenyang Heating Equipment Plant Wrecks 5 Planing Machines in 8 Days," and "Shenyang Mining Machinery Plant Ignores Inspection, Maintenance and Repair from Top to Bottom," (18[1953]:9–12).
29. Inflexibility of older workers is described in "Better Training for Basic Level Production Leaders Is an Important Task," *Chung kung-yeh t'ung-hsün* (hereafter CKYTH) 29(1954):17–23, and illustrated by William Hinton, *Iron Oxen* (New York, 1970), chap. 6. Resistance to new standards and techniques appears in *Liao-ning jih-pao*, December 29, 1954, and Ching Nan, "How Li Feng-en Organizes the Workers to Implement the Expert's Suggestions," CKYTH 11(1956):19–21.
30. JMJP, June 3, 1953.

31. *Ta-kung pao* (Hong Kong), November 19, 1952, and March 23, 1953; *Liao-ning jih-pao*, November 20, 1954; Naikaku sōri daijin, *Chūkyō tekkōgyō*, 1:303–4; SCMP 1524(1957):8; JMJP, January 21 and October 30, 1955.
32. The number of technical personnel per thousand workers in state and joint (state-private) enterprises rose from forty-one to seventy-three between 1952 and 1955 (Chao I-wen, *Hsin Chung-kuo ti kung-yeh* [Peking, 1957], p. 30). For a typical report involving employment of new graduates at the Harbin Measuring and Cutting Tool Plant, see *Chung-kuo ch'ing-nien pao*, January 15, 1955.
33. "Better Training for Production Leaders," p. 17.
34. Planned and realized industrial investment from *First Five-Year Plan*, p. 39, and *Ten Great Years* (Peking, 1960), p. 61.
35. Reports of idle capacity include "FMMB Directive for 1957," pp. 2–4; Pai, "Brief Discussion," p. 5; Ching Lin, "On the Proportional Relation between Steel and Machine-building," *Chi-hua ching-chi* 9(1957):14; *An-hui jih-pao*, June 2, 1957; *Hei-lung-chiang jih-pao*, January 16, 1957; "A Rational Method of Assignment to Save Labor Power," *Lao-tung* 5(1957):9–10. For excessive stockpiles, see "Why Does the Demand for Double-wheel and Double-blade Plows Drop and Why Is Their Production Suspended?" translated in ECMM 56(1956):24–28; Men Chin-ju, "Begin a Production and Economy Campaign on the Production Front," *Chi-hua ching-chi* 1(1957):3; Hsieh Pei-i, "Judiciously Plan This Year's Production of Machinery and Electrical Equipment," *Chi-hua ching-chi* 3(1957):8; and Ch'en Wang-ch'i, "Begin a Production and Economy Campaign and Strengthen Fiscal Control over Basic Construction," *Ts'ai-cheng* 4(1957):11.
36. Productive capacity of FMMB enterprises (3 billion yuan) from Ching Lin, "Proportional Relation," p. 14; 1957 output of 2.4 billion yuan from Chang Kuang-en, "Big Character Poster," *Chi-hua ching-chi* 4(1958):25.
37. Lin I-fu, "Actively Take Steps," p. 7, reports excess capacity at the Ch'angch'un #1 Motor Vehicle Plant, Shenyang Pneumatic Tool Plant, Harbin Electric Meter Plant, and Anshan Seamless Steel Tube Works, all built with Soviet aid. Investment policy and sectoral balancing are discussed in Ching Lin, "Proportional Relation," and Yü Chien-t'ing, "The Problem of Proportional Relation between Our Steel and Machinery Industries," *Ching-chi yen-chiu* 6(1957):20–26.
38. *First Five-Year Plan*, p. 75.
39. For reports of low utilization rates, see Chang Hsü-sheng, *Wo-kuo lao-tung*, p. 55; ECMM 64(1957):19–20; Sha Ying, "On the Relation between Coastal and Interior Industry," *Hsin-hua pan-yüeh-k'an* 24(1956):52. Mao Tse-tung's 1956 assertion that "we have not laid enough stress on industry in the coastal regions" ("On Ten Major Relationships," translated in *Mao Tse-tung Unrehearsed*, ed. Stuart Schram [Harmondsworth, England, 1974], p. 65) was followed by widespread advocacy of increased priority for

coastal industry. Representative sources include ECMM 50(1956):20–23, and 60(1956):24–26; also SCMP 1335(1956):5–11.

40. Between 1950 and March 1956, Shanghai sent 210,000 workers and cadres to other regions, including 63,000 technically skilled workers and 5,400 engineers and technicians (Sha, "Coastal and Interior Industry," p. 52).
41. Estimated Shanghai machinery output of 0.639 billion yuan (1952) and 1.700 billion yuan (1957) from Thomas G. Rawski, "China's Industrial Performance, 1949–73," in *Quantitative Measures of China's Economic Output*, ed. Alexander Eckstein (Ann Arbor, 1980), table 4. If chemicals accounted for 7.3 percent of Shanghai's 1957 industrial output (this is the 1958 figure given in Chen, *Statistics*, p. 228) and for 5 percent of Shanghai's 1952 output (assumed), then the three components mentioned in the text would account for 25.7 percent of 1952 producer output and for 41.1 percent of incremental output during 1952–57.
42. Charles Kennedy and A. P. Thirlwall, "Surveys in Applied Economics: Technical Progress," *Economic Journal* 82.1(1972):39, discuss the case of the Horndal ironworks in Sweden that "experienced no new investment for fifteen years yet output per man hour rose steadily by 2 percent per annum."
43. Typical instances of these problems appear in *Yün-nan jih-pao*, September 3, 1954; *Kung-jen jih-pao*, November 20, 1954; JMJP, March 13, 1955; *Shan-hsi jih-pao*, November 22, 1956; "Poor Product Quality Is an Important Cause of Failure to Complete State Plans," CHKY 13(1956):14–15; Meng Chin-hua, "A Problem in Determining Plan Fulfillment for Local Machinery Industry on the Basis of Gross Output Value," *T'ung-chi kung-tso* 4(1957):5–6.
44. Hsü Tu-t'an, "Anshan Steel Works Should Reverse the Phenomenon of Low Product Quality," CKYTH 11(1956):29; "FMMB and Ministry of Construction Hold a Joint Meeting of Factory Directors and Managers to Arrange Basic Construction Plans for 1956," CHKY 2(1956):31.
45. Individual initiative reversed this tendency in some cases: Chang Yu, "How We Reached and Surpassed Designed Capacity Ahead of Schedule," CHKY 10(1956):16–17; Liu Chien-nan, "Chou Tsung: An Engineer Who Energetically Adds New Products," CKYTH 15(1956):25–27.
46. SCMP 610(1953):9, 1022(1955):8, 1061(1955):31.
47. "FMMB Directive for 1957," pp. 4–5, and Hsieh, "Judiciously Plan," p. 10. Similar statements appeared in JMJP, September 20, 1953.
48. SCMP 1534(1957):10; "Poor Product Quality," pp. 14–15.
49. "Directive on Expanding Output of Top-grade Steel," CKYTH 21(1954):2–3; *Ajia keizai jumpō* 220(1954):10–11, 304(1956):29.
50. Tang Shih, "What the Soviet Experts Have Contributed to China's Power Industry in the Past Eight Years," translated in ECMM 116(1958):34.
51. Cheng, *Machine-building*, pp. 248–49; SCMP 1564(1957):22.
52. In 1957, imports of machinery (including complete plants) were 193 percent higher than in 1952, but domestic machinery production rose by

340 percent in the same interval. Output data from table 2.1; imports from U.S. Central Intelligence Agency, *Foreign Trade in Machinery and Equipment Since 1952* (Washington, D.C., 1975), pp. 1, 4. On the low cost of import substitutes, see Hsü Pao-min, "Economic Significance of Using General Technical Equipment," *Yeh-chin pao* 19(1957):28; JMJP, June 7, 1957; Kang Chao, *Capital Formation in Mainland China, 1952–1965* (Berkeley, 1974), pp. 36–37, 160–63.

53. As late as 1956, a meeting concerned with conflict between construction companies and their industrial customers was informed by a Soviet expert that in the USSR the two sides cooperate "like brothers" ("FMMB and Ministry of Construction," p. 31). In China, as in Eastern Europe, "there is little evidence that the Russian economic administrators helped the satellites to develop their planning systems or gave them any warning of the difficulties and problems they were likely to meet" (Ely Devons, *Papers on Planning and Economic Management*, ed. Sir Alec Cairncross [Manchester, 1970], p. 92).

54. Substantial FFYP investment in chemical fertilizer plants, for example, was undertaken without detailed study of what mix of nitrogenous, phosphate, and potassium fertilizers would be desirable for China (P'an Kuang-chi, "Opinions on How to Develop the Basic Chemical Industry," *Hua-hsüeh kung-yeh* [hereafter HHKY] 8[1957]:33). I have found only one indication of systematic effort to forecast demand in this period: "Problems We Consider in Drawing Up Proposed Long-Term Standards for the Machine Tool Industry," CHKY 11(1956):25–27. Anshan's Seamless Tube Mill, Shenyang #1 and #2 Machine Tool plants, Ch'angch'un #1 Motor Vehicle Plant, Loyang Bearing Works, and Harbin Electric Meter Plant were among the new plants that had difficulty producing or marketing planned outputs.

55. Absence of demand projections is discussed in "Opinions and Demands of Factory Directors," CHKY 10(1957):7–8, and 11(1957):7–9; Li Li-jen, "Discussion on Developing Research Work in the Machine Tool Industry," CHKY 14(1957):7; "Present Tasks of the Heavy Machinery Industry," CHKY 5(1958):3. Officials at the Loyang Bearing Works complained that steel producers were not only unable to supply appropriate materials, but in some cases were unaware of the new plant's existence! See Wang Te-yüan, "Perceive the Conditions of Steel Supply, Dig Up Latent Sources of Domestic Supply," CHKY 9(1957):29, 13.

56. Little is known about the development of technical standards in China. However, by 1960 there was a multiple structure including first- and second-rank national as well as provincial guidelines. See the reports translated in JPRS 8124(1961):51–52, 8581(1961):83–85, and 8826(1961):15–17.

57. The low initial level of quality control personnel is reported in *Kung-jen jih-pao*, March 22, 1953, and August 10, 1955. Examples of conflict between inspectors and output-conscious managers appear in *T'ien-chin*

jih-pao, June 6, 1953: JMJP, September 20, 1953, and March 15, 1955; *Tung-pei jih-pao*, April 8, 1954.

58. By 1958, the industry and communications sectors included a total of 415 research institutes with 59,200 employees (*Ten Great Years*, p. 203).
59. Chiang, "Several Problems"; Ti Yün-ch'ing, "Discussion of Several Current Problems in Enterprise Technical Work," CHKY 16(1957):21, 23; Li Li-jen, "Discussion on Research," p.8.
60. Clark, *China's Steel Industry*, pp. 33–38.
61. "How to Carry Out Technical Preparations at a Plant with Unit Production," CHKY 3(1957):10–11. For similar reports, see *Liao-ning jih-pao*, December 29, 1954; "Technical Reform Work," p. 12; "FMMB Directive for 1957," p. 5; Pai, "Brief Discussion," p. 4; Chiang, "Shortcomings and Problems," p. 25.
62. Hsia Na, "Technical Policy at Heavy Machinery Plants," CHKY 1(1957):11, reports that 90 percent of defectives in heavy machinery resulted from problems in casting, forging, and other "rough processing." Problems at individual units are described in Meng Chih-chien, "On Mechanization of Casting," CHKY 13(1957):5–8. Data on annual output of casting workshops from Cheng, *Machine-building*, p. 145.
63. Data on waste rates are reported in Chen, *Statistics*, p. 275.
64. For lists of new products, see *Ten Great Years*, chap. 4.
65. P'eng T'ao, "Fully Implement the Principle of Frugal National Construction," HHKY 1(1958):3. P'eng's deputy Chang Chen expressed similar views in "For Better Fulfillment of the Second Five-Year Plan Tasks for Chemical Construction," HHKY 11(1957):13–14.

Chapter 3

1. Mao Tse-tung, "Talks at the Chengtu Conference," translated in *Mao Tse-tung Unrehearsed*, ed. Schram, pp. 98–99.
2. Jan S. Prybyla, *The Political Economy of Communist China* (Scranton, 1970), pp. 224–55, describes the 1957 interlude.
3. These decrees are discussed in Audrey Donnithorne, *China's Economic System* (London, 1967), pp. 151–57, 165–68.
4. Janos Kornai, *Rush versus Harmonic Growth* (Amsterdam, 1972). The essence of rushing is that "quality is lagging behind quantity . . . there are not sufficient reserves: adaptation is not sufficiently flexible or quick . . . there are shortages in material, energy, spare parts, capacity, labour" (p. 90). In applying Kornai's terminology to China, I emphasize what he calls the physical as opposed to the human aspects of harmony and rush (p. 42).
5. *Lü-ta jih-pao*, September 28 and October 12, 1958.
6. Plant data from JMJP, November 6, 1958; *Liao-ning jih-pao*, January 17, 1959; *Wen-hui pao* (Shanghai), February 27, 1959; *Yün-nan jih-pao*,

January 15, 1959. Report on simplified machine tools from *Ta-kung pao* (Peking), September 27, 1959. Output of machine tools for 1959 and 1960 from Cheng, *Machine-building*, p. 248.

7. See *Communist China 1955–1959* (Cambridge, 1962), documents 10 and 11.
8. JMJP, August 19, 1957; SCMP 1696(1958):26, 1702(1958):29, 1703 (1958):3.
9. SCMP 1970(1959):11–12; JPRS 8728(1961):10–11.
10. JPRS 1048-D(1960):1–12.
11. Mao Tse-tung, "Speech At the Lushan Conference," in *Mao Tse-tung Unrehearsed*, ed. Schram, p. 142.
12. Labor force estimates from Emerson, *Nonagricultural Employment*, p. 143.
13. On this period, see Byung-joon Ahn, "Adjustments in the Great Leap Forward and Their Ideological Legacy, 1959–62," in *Ideology and Politics in Contemporary China*, ed. Chalmers Johnson (Seattle, 1973), especially pp. 275–76; U.S. Consulate General, Hong Kong, *Current Background* (hereafter CB), 824 (1967):4, and 905(1970). A summary of the contents of the unpublished "Seventy Articles" appears in *Documents of Chinese Communist Party Central Committee, September 1956–April 1959* (Hong Kong, 1971), 1:689–93.
14. On Shih-ching-shan, see Clark, *China's Steel Industry*, p. 17, and "Fifteen Years of Great Results," *Lao-tung* 10(1964):14. Shansi data from Li Yü-heng and Ch'ang Pao-yü, "T'aiyüan Saves Labor to Aid Agriculture," *Lao-tung* 9(1962):15. Shanghai reports from Lu Yün-ho and Ch'en Kuo-t'ai, "Find Ways to Save Labor," *Lao-tung* 4(1962):19, and "Display Revolutionary Spirit, Struggle for a New High Tide in Shanghai's Chemical Output for 1965," HHKY 2(1965):2. Similar reports are scattered throughout the 1961–65 issues of *Chi-hsieh kung-yeh, Hua-hsüeh kung-yeh*, and *Lao-tung* held by the Library of Congress.
15. Item 34 of the "Seventy Articles" (*Documents*, 1:691), and Han Kuang, "Several Problems Concerning Technical Work in Industry," translated in ECMM 295(1962):4.
16. JPRS 29161(1965):55.
17. JPRS 29104(1965):40; Hu Pu-chou, "Establish Revolutionary Ambitions, Progress, and Advance," CHKY 15(1964):21; Liu Yao-ming, "With Politics Leading, Results Are Great," CHKY 7(1966):17.
18. Han, "Several Problems," p. 4; Jacques Charrière, "Planification et gestion des unités de production," in Charles Bettelheim, Jacques Charrière, and Hélène Marchisio, *La construction du socialisme en Chine* (Paris, 1968), p. 58; SCMP 3608(1966):3–6.
19. Hu Pu-chou, "Establish Revolutionary Ambitions," p. 20.
20. Profitability requirement from item 9 of the "Seventy Articles" (*Documents*, 1:689). Enterprise reports from Kung Shih, "Study the Advanced, Uncover Idle Capacity," *Lao-tung* 8(1963):17; Liang Ta,

"Enforce Economy, Reform Management, Advance Production," CHKY 9(1963):11; Wang Shu-hui, "Management of Circulating Capital," CHKY 6(1963):14; "The Experience of Wan Hsien Ironworks in Reducing Casting Costs," CHKY 23(1963):14–16; HHKY 9(1964):26–27; "Strengthen Economic Control, Lower Product Costs," CHKY 19(1963):14–16.

21. Chu Hsi-ken, et al., "Further Develop Specialized Production of Hardware," CHKY 8(1963):29–32; Teng Chan-ming, "Problems of Developing Economic Cooperation among Industries and Firms," *Ching-chi yen-chiu* 3(1965):19–23. Further references are cited in Thomas G. Rawski, "The Economics of Chinese Machine-building, 1931–1967" (Ph.D. diss., Harvard University, 1972), pp. 187–93.
22. Quotation from JPRS 11719(1961):43–44. A vice-minister of metallurgy commented that "many enterprises have paid special attention to exert the function of the technical workers, the old workers, and the scientific departments" (JPRS 12691[1962]:14).
23. "Persist in Revolutionary Thought, Force Yourself to the Highest Attainable Level," HHKY 9(1964):6; "How We Test and Accept Technical Management Reorganization Work," CHKY 8(1963):14; JPRS 28891(1965):57–59.
24. Empirical studies of several countries show that "natural disasters are typically followed by an increase in charity. . . . Cooperation and generally selfless behavior by the victims and others near the disaster zone is strikingly evident." Perhaps a similar phenomenon occurred in post-Leap China. See Christopher M. Douty, "Disasters and Charity: Some Aspects of Cooperative Economic Behavior," *American Economic Review* 62.4(1972):580–81.
25. Carl Riskin, "China's Rural Industries: Self-Reliant Systems or Independent Kingdoms?" *China Quarterly* 73(1978): pp. 83–86.
26. Richard P. Suttmeier, *Research and Revolution* (Lexington, Mass., 1974), p. 98; JPRS 31671(1965):15–24.
27. Barry M. Richman, *Industrial Society in Communist China* (New York, 1969), chap. 8; Bruce L. Reynolds, "Central Planning in China: The Significance of Material Allocation Conferences," Association for Comparative Economic Studies *Bulletin* 17.1(1975):3–14.
28. CB 852(1968):29, 61, 91, 197; 818(1967):25.
29. CB 819(1967):18.
30. Field, Lardy, and Emerson, *Reconstruction*, p. 19.
31. SCMP 4921(1971):9, 12. The same points were made a decade earlier in "Bringing the Strength of Technical Personnel into Full Play," translated in ECMM 314(1962):47–50. Examples of reinstated specialists appear in CB 849(1968):24–26, and 854(1968):34–35; in SCMP 4840(1971):94–97, and 4870(1971):173–80; and in Stephen Andors, *China's Industrial Revolution* (New York, 1977), p. 231.
32. SCMP 5320(1973):133; 4999(1971):180–85.
33. Andors, *China's Industrial Revolution*, p. 229.

34. Christopher Howe, "Labour Organization and Incentives in Industry, Before and After the Cultural Revolution," in *Authority, Participation and Cultural Change in China*, ed. Stuart R. Schram (Cambridge, 1973), p. 252; FBIS, December 2, 1977, E13–16, and December 20, 1977, E3–6.
35. Ching Lin, *Ti-i-ko wu-nien chi-hua*, p. 8, and ECMM 64(1957):17.
36. *Ajia keizai jumpō* 310–11(1957):20, and *Jen-min shou-ts'e 1958* (Peking, 1958), p. 469.
37. *Wen-hui pao* (Shanghai), January 16 and May 26, 1958; K. C. Yeh, *Communist China's Petroleum Situation* (Santa Monica, 1962), pp. 13–19.
38. U.S. Central Intelligence Agency, *China: Economic Indicators* (Washington, D.C., 1977), pp. 20, 26, 41.
39. Equipment imports for the petroleum industry are listed in Hans Heymann, Jr., "Acquisition and Diffusion of Technology in China," in *China: A Reassessment of the Economy* (Washington, D.C., 1975), pp. 718–25.
40. "Several Facts about Organizing Plans for Completing Construction Projects," CHKY 19(1963):17–18; *Shen-chou chü-pien* (Hong Kong, 1976), p. 209.
41. Quotation from JPRS 28642(1965):18. Other references to the activities of Shanghai producers appear in *Kuang-ming jih-pao*, September 24, 1957; *Chung-kuo hsin-wen*, December 25, 1963; JPRS 29020(1965):7; and BBC W956(1977):A11. Activity at Paochi is mentioned in *Chūgoku kōgyō kōjō sōran* (Tokyo, 1965), p. 844, and BBC W803(1974):A13.
42. JPRS 28642(1965):19, and Hu Kuang, "The Developing Petroleum Equipment Industry," CHKY 20(1964):15.
43. "Shengli Journal," *The China Business Review* 5.1(1978):34.
44. Pien Po-heng, "Control Excess Consumption of Materials," HHKY 6(1957):7–8; P'an, "Opinions on the Basic Chemical Industry"; "Strengthen Economic Calculation within Enterprises," HHKY 12(1957):8–11.
45. Jung-chao Liu, "Fertiliser Application in Communist China," *China Quarterly* 24(1965):31–34, 49–50, and *China's Fertilizer Economy* (Chicago, 1970), pp. 16–17; Chao, *Capital Formation*, p. 88.
46. For fertilizer plant imports, see Heymann, "Acquisition of Technology," pp. 726–27.
47. Small-plant shares in fertilizer output calculated from U.S. Central Intelligence Agency, *China: Economic Indicators*, p. 22.
48. *Yang-ch'eng wan-pao*, January 9, 1964, and Ching Lin, *Ti-i-ko wu-nien chi-hua*, p. 8.
49. For Shanghai, see SCMP 3422(1965):24–25, and 5317(1973):29–30. For other areas, see JMJP, November 7, 1964; BBC W758(1974):A4, A13, and W804(1974):A14; Dwight H. Perkins et al., *Rural Small-Scale Industry in the People's Republic of China* (Berkeley, 1977), pp. 66, 96; and New China News Agency, *Daily News Release*, June 1, 1965.

50. JPRS 35070(1966):25.
51. Carl Djerassi, "Some Observations on Current Fertility Control in China," *China Quarterly* 57(1974):46–49; Masumi Sato, "The Realities and Technological Trends of China's Heavy and Chemical Industries," *Chinese Economic Studies* 4.3(1971):184–88.
52. For machine tools, see "The Technical Level of China's Machine Tool Industry," translated in JPRS 31644(1965):1–32; Kojima Reiitsu, "China's Machine Tool Industry," in *Chūgoku keizai no chōki tembō II*, ed. Ishikawa Shigeru (Tokyo, 1966), pp. 339–42; and Sato, "Realities," pp. 173–75. For metallurgical equipment, see SCMP 3480(1965):18; 5449(1973):95, and 5453(1973):76. JMJP, September 27, 1965, and SCMP 4812(1971):59, provide examples of model changes at leading plants. On machinery prices, see U.S. Central Intelligence Agency, *Prices of Machinery and Equipment in the People's Republic of China* (Washington, D.C., 1975), p. 2, and Thomas G. Rawski, "Industrial Performance," in *Quantitative Measures*, tables H–1 and H–2.
53. "NMTBA Metalworking Technology Symposium and Trade Mission to the People's Republic of China" (McLean, Va., 1975), pp. 5, 9, 13, 18.
54. For further detail, see Perkins et al., *Rural Industry*, and Jon Sigurdson, *Rural Industrialization in China* (Cambridge, 1977).
55. Perkins et al., *Rural Industry*, pp. 69–71; Thomas G. Rawski, "Choice of Technology and Technical Innovation in China's Economic Development" in *The Relevance of China's Experience for the Other Developing Countries*, ed. Robert F. Dernberger (forthcoming), table 6.
56. *Chūgoku shiryō geppō* 109(1957):39; FBIS, January 31, 1978, E12; Hsiao Han, "Developing Coal Industry at High Speed," *Peking Review* 8(1978):6; SCMP 4992(1971):28; author's trip notes as a member of the Rural Small-Scale Industry Delegation, June 13, 1975.
57. FBIS, January 6, 1978, E17–19.
58. Nicholas R. Lardy, "Centralization and Decentralization in China's Fiscal Management," *China Quarterly* 61(1975):31, 40, 56; Rawski, "Industrial Performance" in *Quantitative Measures*, table 4.
59. Projects that received Soviet aid are listed in *1967 Fei-ch'ing nien-pao* (Taipei, 1967), pp. 850–55.
60. Ibid., and *T'ien-chin jih-pao*, October 4, 1957.
61. Lardy, "Centralization and Decentralization," p. 40.
62. *SCMP Supplement* 101(1962):6–7, and 150(1966):8.
63. Robert M. Field, Nicholas R. Lardy, and John P. Emerson, *Provincial Industrial Output in the People's Republic of China: 1949–75* (Washington, D.C., 1976) pp. 11, 17; FBIS, December 8, 1977, E5.
64. ECMM 314(1962):47.
65. Yuan-li Wu and Robert B. Sheeks, *The Organization and Support of Scientific Research and Development in Mainland China* (New York, 1970), p. 149, identify 651 research and development institutions, of which 53 or 8.1 percent were located in Shanghai. Only Peking, with 234 units, could claim a larger research establishment. However, one report describes

some Shanghai researchers as "personnel of low attainment and skill level" (JPRS 29104[1965]:27).

66. Hu Kuang, "Petroleum Equipment," p. 15; *Eastern Horizon* 15.5(1976):40; table 1.2 in this book. Technical articles written by Ta-lung personnel appear in the following issues of the engineering journal *Shanghai chi-hsieh*: 10(1964):6 9; 11(1965):18; 12(1965):34–35; 1(1966):36–37, 43.
67. For Tientsin, see FBIS, January 5, 1978, K4. For Shanghai, see *SCMP Supplement* 131(1965):26, and FBIS, December 8, 1977, E5.
68. JPRS 33603(1966):11.
69. *SCMP Supplement* 131(1965):17; JPRS 29626(1965):32–33, and 30743(1965):23; Ross Terrill, *Flowers on an Iron Tree* (Boston, 1975), p. 15.
70. BBC W801(1974):A11.
71. Hu Kuang, "Petroleum Equipment," p. 15.
72. BBC W804(1974): A11; JPRS 31658(1965):19; CHKY 7(1962):11; Joan Robinson, *Economic Management in China* (London, 1973), pp. 22–23; JPRS 29021(1965):58–59.
73. JPRS 28876(1965):2; 29937(1965):26–32; 33835(1966):8–9; *New China's First Quarter-Century* (Peking, 1975), pp. 119–29; BBC W804(1974): A12; W762(1974):A12.
74. JPRS 30743(1965):24.
75. BBC W800(1974):A16.
76. SCMP 3492(1965):3. Alexander Eckstein first drew my attention to this issue.
77. JPRS 31671(1965):2. Recent reports indicate major improvement in this plant's performance (*Shen-chou chü-pien*, p. 62).
78. JPRS 31671(1965):23; SCMP 3492(1965):3.
79. SCMP 3275(1964):4–5.
80. FBIS, December 8, 1977, E11.
81. Raymond Vernon, *Metropolis 1985* (New York, 1963). Arthur L. Stinchcombe suggested this parallel between Shanghai and New York.
82. Compare the following U.S. example: "Indeed, one of the compensations of slack business for the engineer-entrepreneur . . . was the chance of devoting more time to innovations. It is not surprising . . . that the automatics, the universals, the gear shapers, and the grinding machines were developed most rapidly during the depressions of the 1870's and the 1890's. The relatively prosperous 1880's were years of quantitative rather than qualitative progress. Depressions tended to shift the attention of businessmen to ways of cutting costs" (Strassmann, *Risk and Technological Innovation*, p. 154).
83. Hsiang Jung, "Big Drama on a Small Stage," *Peking Review* 22(1975):19—20.
84. BBC W871(1976): A11; author's trip notes as a member of the Rural Small-Scale Industry Delegation, July 1, 1975.
85. BBC W871(1976):A11.

86. FBIS, January 9, 1978, E1–11; BBC W879(1976):A7; W881(1976):A5 and W883(1976):A7.
87. BBC W871(1976):A11, A13; W881(1976):A6.
88. BBC W878(1976):A6.
89. BBC W866(1976):A3–4; W871(1976):A10; W887(1976):A12; W888 (1976):A5; W890(1976):A5–6.
90. BBC W883(1976):A10.
91. *Miscellany of Mao Tse-tung Thought* (*1949–1968*) (Arlington, 1974), 2:307, 446; Hsiang, "Big Drama," p. 21.
92. *Peking Review* 4(1975):23.

Chapter 4

1. Chinese industrial data are discussed in Thomas G. Rawski, "Chinese Industrial Production, 1952–1971," *Review of Economics and Statistics* 55.2(1973):169–81, and "Industrial Performance," in *Quantitative Measures*; also see Field, Lardy, and Emerson, *Reconstruction*.
2. The Chinese concept of industry includes the extractive industries, electric power, and manufacturing; treatment of other utilities is uncertain. For elaboration, see Chen, *Statistics*, pp. 28–29, and Liu and Yeh, *Economy of the Chinese Mainland*, pp. 489–92. The relation between gross value and value added measures of Chinese industrial output is discussed in the sources cited in the previous note.
3. Field, Lardy, and Emerson, *Reconstruction*, pp. 5–7.
4. See Rawski, "Industrial Performance," in *Quantitative Measures*. Use of gross rather than net values tends to diminish the estimated growth rate because of a positive correlation between sectoral output growth and rates of value added. In addition, the gross value approach overlooks the impact of cost reductions clustered in rapidly growing industrial branches, thus creating additional reason to expect value added to outgrow gross output value.
5. Field, "Civilian Industrial Production," p. 170, and U.S. Central Intelligence Agency, *China: Economic Indicators*, p.14, suggest lower shares of producer goods in industrial output for recent years than those shown in table 4.4.
6. Chinese statements that output of "heavy industry" in 1970 and 1973 was thirty-eight and sixty times the 1949 level (Field, "Civilian Industrial Production," p. 170, and *Cheng-chih ching-chi-hsüeh chi-ch'u chih-shih* [Shanghai, 1975], p. 307) indicate that recent output totals resemble those in the second column of table 4.4. However, Field, Lardy, and Emerson have shown that statements of this type may be based on chain-index calculations that cannot be attempted for the producer sector without further study of price changes (see *Reconstruction*, p. 17, and *Provincial*

Output, p. 9). As a result, it is not yet possible to say whether these statements coincide with the estimates shown in table 4.4.

7. Data for 1933 (in terms of 1933 prices) calculated from Liu and Yeh, *Economy of the Chinese Mainland*, pp. 142–43; figures for 1952 and 1973 (in terms of 1952 prices) calculated from Rawski, "Industrial Performance," in *Quantitative Measures*, table 33 and from table 4.1 of this book.
8. Rawski, "Industrial Performance," in *Quantitative Measures*, tables 16, 27, and 34. This statement applies equally to calculations based on 1952 and 1975 prices. Alternative indices of machinery output are shown in table 4.11.
9. K. C. Yeh, "China's National Income, 1931–36" (unpublished, 1977) contains tentative estimates showing that modern industry accounted for about one-fifth of the 20 percent increment in China's gross domestic product between 1914–18 and 1931–36.
10. Refinement of this calculation to account for differences in concept and price base between Perkins's estimates and my own would not significantly alter these results.
11. Rawski, "Producer Industries," pp. 224–25.
12. Gross agricultural output per worker for 1975 is estimated at 242–64 yuan (1957 prices) or, using the price deflator calculated from Ishikawa, *National Income*, p. 50, 260–89 yuan in terms of 1952 prices. See Rawski, *Industrialization, Technology and Employment*, p. 97.
13. Ibid., p. 30.
14. Perkins et al., *Rural Industry*, p. 8.
15. Examples of innovations appear in ibid.; *New China's First Quarter-Century*, p. 22; JPRS 33403(1965):114; SCMP 4851(1971):183–88; Hsiao, "Coal Industry," pp. 6–7.
16. Table 3.4 in this book; Perkins et al., *Rural Industry*, p. 99; Rawski, *Industrialization, Technology and Employment*, p. 47.
17. Sigurdson, *Rural Industrialization*, pp. 141, 143, 160; Perkins et al., *Rural Industry*, pp. 176, 186–87.
18. Heymann, "Acquisition of Technology," pp. 708–29, supplemented by recent developments reported in such sources as *The China Business Review*.
19. Quotation from "Some Problems in Speeding Up Industrial Development," translated in *Issues and Studies* 13.7(1977):103. I am indebted to Dorothy J. Solinger for calling my attention to this important source. In 1957, the coal industry reported labor productivity as 0.978 tons per man-day for all personnel (Chen, *Statistics*, p. 263). In 1975, labor productivity at the K'ai-lan coal complex, a model unit described as "among China's most heavily mechanized," was approximately 0.85 tons per man-day, and visitors to another important mining area near Ta-t'ung (Shansi) report productivity figures of less than 0.8 tons per man-day for all employees. See Rawski, *Industrialization, Technology and Employment*, p. 119; U.S.

Central Intelligence Agency, *China: The Coal Industry* (Washington, D.C., 1976), p.13; "Australian Coal Mission to the People's Republic of China," (unpublished, 1976) sec. 4.1–4.2.

20. "Some Problems in Speeding Up Industrial Development," pp. 103–4; FBIS, December 13, 1977, E15; Hsiao, "Coal Industry."
21. In 1957, the yuan price of a typical Chinese-made lathe was about 1.8 times the dollar price of a comparable U.S. product. At that time, a factory worker's salary of approximately 600 yuan per year was no more than one-tenth of the dollar earnings of a comparable American worker. These figures suggest that relative factor costs in the two countries could easily differ by a ratio of 18 to 1! Lathe prices from U.S. Central Intelligence Agency, *People's Republic of China: Estimated Yuan Value of Foreign Trade in Machinery and Equipment, 1951–73* (Washington, D.C., 1976), p. 9.
22. John C. H. Fei and Gustav Ranis, *Development of the Labor Surplus Economy* (Homewood, Ill., 1964), p. 66.
23. See also Perkins et al., *Rural Industry*, pp. 13–18, 71–81, 117–53.
24. Information on Loyang Tractor Works provided by Doris Dohrenwend. Report on the spread of farm machinery plants is from FBIS, November 30, 1977, E15.
25. Perkins et al., *Rural Industry*, p. 74.
26. "Report of SMMT Trade Mission to the People's Republic of China, 2–17 November 1973," (unpublished, 1974), p. 32.
27. "Shengli Journal," p. 34.
28. "Report of SMMT Trade Mission," p. 20.
29. David Scott, "China Opens Doors for Rare View of Auto Production," *Automotive Engineering* 82.8(1974):30.
30. Heymann, "Acquisition of Technology," pp. 691–92.
31. Bohdan O. Szuprowicz, "Electronics in China: A Prerequisite to Superpower Status," (unpublished, North Bergen, N.J., 1976), p.2; "NMTBA Symposium," p. 13.
32. U.S. Central Intelligence Agency, *China's Cement Industry* (Washington, D.C., 1977), pp. 4–5; Perkins et al., *Rural Industry*, pp. 177–87.
33. H. F. Mark, "China Visit—June 1972," (unpublished), p. 27.
34. Perkins et al., *Rural Industry*, pp. 238–41; Sigurdson, *Rural Industrialization*, chap. 3; James B. Stepanek, "Planning of Urban Small-Scale Industry in China," (unpublished [1978]).
35. Perkins et al., *Rural Industry*, p. 240.
36. Ibid., pp. 66, 99, 287–88.
37. U. S. Central Intelligence Agency, *China: Economic Indicators*, p. 26.
38. Chinese statements concerning 1957 import dependence appear in Cheng, *Machine-building*, p. 66, and SCMP 3392(1965):21.
39. Calculations based on official exchange rates result in shares of imports in apparent machinery consumption of 24 percent for 1952, 18 percent for 1957, and a maximum of 3 percent for all years after 1960 for which estimates of both imports and domestic production are available.

40. U.S. Central Intelligence Agency, *People's Republic of China: Yuan Value of Trade*; and Robert M. Field, "Real Capital Formation," in *Quantitative Measures*, table 19.
41. Rawski, *Industrialization, Technology and Employment*, chap. 4.
42. Ibid., p. 58; U.S. Central Intelligence Agency, *China: Economic Indicators*, p. 22; tables 3.2 and 4.13, in this book.
43. Perkins et al., *Rural Industry*, p. 200.
44. Rawski, *Industrialization, Technology and Employment*, p. 85.
45. "Farm Mechanization: Targets for 1980," *Peking Review* 8(1978):10. Japanese figures calculated from Keizō Tsuchiya, "Economics of Mechanization in Small-Scale Agriculture," in *Agriculture and Economic Growth: Japan's Experience*, ed. Kazushi Ohkawa, Bruce F. Johnston, and Hiromitsu Kaneda (Princeton, 1969), p. 158, and Yujiro Hayami and Vernon W. Ruttan, *Agricultural Development* (Baltimore, 1971), p. 340.
46. Ch'eng Chin-chieh, "The Way Liuchi Commune Wins Its Higher Grain and Cotton Yields," translated in ECMM 473(1965):4.
47. Rawski, *Industrialization, Technology and Employment*, pp. 93–97.
48. Perkins et al., *Rural Industry*, pp. 72–73.
49. Alex Inkeles and David H. Smith, *Becoming Modern* (Cambridge, 1974), chap. 11–13.
50. Application of Indian weights to Chinese sectoral output indices raises the overall index because of the sharply increased weight attached to petroleum, China's fastest growing industry.
51. Index of manufacturing output compiled from *Yearbook of National Accounts Statistics*, 1971 edition (New York, 1973), 1:105, and the 1975 edition (New York, 1976), 1:144, and from Joel Bergsman and Arthur Candal, "Industrialization," in *The Economy of Brazil*, ed. Howard S. Ellis (Berkeley, 1969), p. 42. Shares of textiles (including clothing and footwear), food, and beverages for 1939 and 1949 are from Bergsman and Candal's article; for 1965, from the *Yearbook of National Accounts Statistics*, 1971 edition, 1:106. The latter source also shows a 1969 share for these sectors of 29.1 percent; for 1973, a figure of 25 percent is assumed. Inclusion of the small mining and utility sectors would not alter the conclusions reached in the text.
52. Joel Bergsman, *Brazil: Industrialization and Trade Policies* (London, 1970), pp. 157–58, 166–68.
53. Mark Frankena, "The Industrial and Trade Control Regime and Product Designs in India," *Economic Development and Cultural Change* 22.2(1974):253–56.
54. John W. Mellor, *The New Economics of Growth* (Ithaca, 1976). The long list of recommendations that parallel actual Chinese policies and programs includes rural infrastructure investments in health, education, electrification, communication, transport, water control, and agricultural research; increased supplies of chemical fertilizer, water, credit, and risk-sharing arrangements for farm households; diversification of agriculture into labor-intensive activities; expansion of rural industry centered on light

engineering; indirect taxation of rising farm incomes; and administrative decentralization aimed at fostering local resource mobilization. Mellor's principal deviations from Chinese methods are his advocacy of lower food grain prices and his suggestion that investment in capital-intensive urban industries should be curtailed, at least in the short run, to free resources for rural investments.

55. Bela Balassa, "Growth Strategies in Semi-Industrial Countries," *Quarterly Journal of Economics* 84.1(1970):45.
56. Japanese data compiled from *Estimates of Long-term Economic Statistics of Japan Since 1868*, ed. Kazushi Ohkawa et al., vol. 3, *Capital Stock*, (Tokyo, 1966), pp. 198–201, and vol. 10, *Mining and Manufacturing* (Tokyo, 1972), pp. 235–37.
57. On the weakness of Japan's prewar producer establishments see, among others, John E. Orchard, *Japan's Economic Position* (New York, 1930), p. 144, and chap. 14; G.C. Allen, *A Short Economic History of Modern Japan* (London, 1962), pp. 150–51, and "The Heavy Industries" in *The Industrialization of Japan and Manchukuo, 1930–1940*, ed. E. B. Schumpeter (New York, 1940), pp. 596–624.

Chapter 5

1. This and the following section draw on my earlier essay "China's Industrial System," in *China: A Reassessment of the Economy* (Washington, D.C., 1975), 175–98.
2. Donnithorne, *China's Economic System*, pp. 25–26.
3. Paraphrase based on author's notes as a member of the Rural Small-Scale Industry Delegation, June 14, 1975.
4. For example, Kuo-chün Chao, *Economic Planning and Organization in Mainland China* (Cambridge, 1963), 1: 66–68; Richman, *Industrial Society*, pp. 709–10, 747–50; Mitch Meisner, "The Shenyang Transformer Factory—A Profile," *China Quarterly* 52(1972):721; "Collective Notes of the First Friendship Delegation of American Radical Political Economists to the People's Republic of China" (Ann Arbor, 1972), p. 18; Alexander Eckstein, *China's Economic Development* (Ann Arbor, 1975), p. 360.
5. Hsieh, "Judiciously Plan," p. 9.
6. The rationality of paying heavily for promptness is a major theme of Robert C. Repetto, *Time in India's Development Programmes* (Cambridge, 1971). U.S. defense procurement uses systems "in which the control of time is often achieved at large costs in performance and money" (Carl Kaysen, "Improving the Efficiency of Military Research and Development," *Public Policy* 12 [1963]:254).
7. SCMP 1446(1957):15, with emphasis added.
8. *Kung-jen jih-pao*, July 19, 1955. Similar accounts are cited in Rawski, "Chinese Machine-building," p. 264.

9. "We Must Fulfill This Year's Plan for Trial Manufacture of New Products," CKYTH 14(1956):14.
10. David Granick, *Management of the Industrial Firm in the USSR* (New York, 1954), and Joseph S. Berliner, *Factory and Manager in the USSR* (Cambridge, 1957) investigate the Soviet scene.
11. In 1966, Richman found that fifty-eight of seventy-four persons at or above the level of shop chief had held their posts for at least four years (*Industrial Society*, p. 299). In contrast to this, David Granick, *The Red Executive* (Garden City, 1961), p. 112, cites studies of the 1930s showing that under 15 percent of Soviet managers held their posts for as long as five years. The size and significance of premiums in Soviet industry is stressed by Berliner, *Factory and Manager*, chap. 3 and 4, and by many others. In China, however, even the extent to which managers and engineers were eligible for premiums is not clear; see Christopher Howe, *Wage Patterns and Wage Policy in Modern China, 1919–1972* (Cambridge, 1973), pp. 121–27; Dwight H. Perkins, *Market Control and Planning in Communist China* (Cambridge, 1966), p. 121; Donnithorne, *China's Economic System*, pp. 208–10. However, Bruce L. Reynolds, "The Adaptation of Russian Planning Practices in China's First Five-Year Plan" (unpublished [1976]), pp. 36–39 presents evidence that bonuses may have been quite significant in Chinese industry during the 1950s.
12. David Granick, *Soviet Metal-fabricating and Economic Development* (Madison, 1967), especially chap. 7.
13. Richman, *Industrial Society*, p. 719.
14. Eckstein, *China's Economic Development*, pp. 360–61. See also SCMP 4815(1971):206–11, and Charles Bettelheim's observation that "Given the conditions under which the plan is elaborated . . . plans are in most cases not only fulfilled, but over-fulfilled" (*Cultural Revolution and Industrial Organization in China* [New York, 1974], pp. 59–60).
15. SCMP 1446(1957):16.
16. Morris Bornstein, "Economic Reform in Eastern Europe," in *East European Economies Post-Helsinki* (Washington, D.C., 1977), p. 128.
17. The Kirin situation is described by the Corporation's Vice-Director Yang Ling, "Study the Experience of Ta-ch'ing, Persist in Maintaining High Standards of Equipment Management," HHKY 9(1964):28–32.
18. On the revival of piece rates in the early 1960s, see items 25–28 of the "Seventy Articles" (*Documents*, 1:691); Howe, *Wage Patterns*, pp. 122–23; and *Lao-tung*, which published several discussions of wage and bonus policy during 1962 and 1964. For 1977, see FBIS, December 2, 1977, E13–18, and December 20, 1977, E3–6. Earlier discussions that describe the adverse effect of piece rates on product quality include Ch'u Hsüeh "Inquiry into the Problem of Piece-work Wages," *Ts'ai-cheng yen-chiu* 6(1958): 49–52, and Chu Wen-wu et al., "Why Does Shanghai Diesel Engine Plant Eliminate Piece Rates During the Great Leap Forward?" *Ts'ai-cheng yen-chiu* 7(1958):22–24.

19. Li Tso-wen, "From the Principle of Return of Loans to the Supervisory Role of the Bank," translated in ECMM 309(1962):12.
20. Typical statements relating profits to investment grants appear in JPRS 32281(1965):14; SCMP 4941(1971):141; *Peking Review* 22(1975):18; BBC W874(1976):A2, W880(1976):A6, and W910(1977):A8; and FBIS, January 8, 1976, K1.
21. "Some Problems in Speeding Up Industrial Development," p. 99, and *Peking Review* 3(1977):14.
22. See Audrey Donnithorne, "China's Cellular Economy: Some Economic Trends since the Cultural Revolution," *China Quarterly* 52(1972):605–19; Lardy, "Centralization and Decentralization," *China Quarterly* 61(1975):25–60, followed by Donnithorne's "Comment," *China Quarterly* 66(1976):328–40, and Lardy's "Reply," *China Quarterly* 66(1976):340–54.
23. Richman, *Industrial Society*, pp. 712–20; Reynolds, "Central Planning," and Perkins et al., *Rural Industry*, chap. 2, all discuss the participation of subnational administrative levels in industrial planning and supply work. Vice-Premier Yü Ch'iu-li speaks of localities meeting their "iron and steel requirements . . . with locally-available foreign exchange" ("Yu Chiu-li Summation Report on Agricultural Mechanization," FBIS, January 31, 1978, E20).
24. "Some Problems in Speeding Up Industrial Development," pp. 99–100, and Yü Ch'iu-li, "Mobilize the Whole Party and the Nation's Working Class and Strive to Build Taching-Type Enterprises Throughout the Country," *Peking Review* 22(1977):21.
25. A. Doak Barnett, *Uncertain Passage* (Washington, D.C., 1974), p. 139.
26. Perkins et al., *Rural Industry*, p. 276.
27. Ibid., 276–77; "Some Problems in Speeding Up Industrial Development," p. 100–101.
28. Meisner, "Shenyang Transformer Factory," p. 721.
29. Author's notes as a member of the Rural Small-Scale Industry Delegation, July 6, 1975.
30. Robinson, *Economic Management in China*, pp. 20, 24–25, 33.
31. The following examples illustrate the scale of transfers: "From 1958 the State allocated 2,950 million yuan for capital construction in Ninghsia up to 1974 and financial subsidies equivalent to 110% of the region's revenue in this period" (BBC W870[1976]:A3); "From 1950 to 1976, investments by the state in Shanghai's capital construction amounted only to 7.5 per cent of its revenue delivered to the state, while the accumulation funds it provided for the country amounted to 41.9 per cent of the nation's total investments in capital construction" ("Shanghai: A Coastal Industrial Base," *Peking Review* 4[1978]:11). Lardy, "Centralization and Decentralization" and "Reply" analyzes these fiscal transfers in detail.
32. Paraphrase based on author's notes as a member of the Rural Small-Scale Industry Delegation, July 7, 1975.

33. Pierre-Henri Cassou, "The Chinese Monetary System," *China Quarterly* 59(1974):561, 564.
34. FBIS, December 22, 1977, E7.
35. SCMP 4839(1971):56–57. In 1965, Shanghai's machine tool producers responded to pressure for large output increases by planning to concentrate on familiar "bread and butter items" (New China News Agency, *Daily News Release*, March 17, 1965).
36. FBIS, January 11, 1978, E15.
37. *The China Business Review* 4.5(1977):8.
38. SCMP 1551(1957):3.
39. Pai, "Brief Discussion," p. 6; Hsiang Lin, "How to Implement the Principle of Frugal National Construction," CHKY 11(1957):19–20.
40. Liu Pao-tung, "We Hope 444 Plant Can Turn Around and Save Metal Materials," CHKY 20(1956):25.
41. JMJP, May 26, 1953; April 2, 1954; December 16, 1955; and "Several Measures for Strengthening Production and Technical Preparation at Shenyang Heavy Machinery Plant," CHKY 23(1954):4.
42. Absence of interest charges on fixed capital is asserted by Donnithorne, *China's Economic System*, p. 437, and seems implicit in descriptions offered to visitors ("Collective Notes," p. 118). Hsü I, "On Several Problems of Economic Accounting," *Ching-chi yen-chiu* 4(1958):64, 72–73, shows how integration made Anshan's steel costs deceptively low.
43. Donnithorne, *China's Economic System*, p. 169.
44. SCMP 3416(1965):405; 3453(1965):7; 3492(1965):6–7 and *Ta-kung pao* (Peking), February 13, 1965.
45. SCMP 3473(1965):3.
46. JPRS 31708(1965):11–20; 32103(1965):93–96; 32281(1965):13–18; 32420 (1965):66; 33043(1965):53–54, 63–68; 33403(1965):94–108; and Teng, "Economic Cooperation," pp. 19–23.
47. Stepanek, "Urban Small-Scale Industry."
48. Scott, "Auto Production," p. 32.
49. "Some Problems in Speeding Up Industrial Development," p. 104.
50. Labor hoarding is mentioned in SCMP 3427(1965): 7; 4831(1971): 127–34; 5004(1971):2. For illicit use of circulating funds to finance investment projects, see Donnithorne, *China's Economic System*, pp. 421–23, 429, and "Some Problems in Speeding Up Industrial Development," p. 106. Product stockpiles are mentioned in JMJP, November 27, 1956, and in many recent visitor accounts.
51. JMJP, February 17, 1953. T'angshan Steelworks tried a similar gambit in the following year ("Why Issue Quotas for Consumption of Raw Materials per Unit of Product?" CKYTH 21[1954]:38).
52. SCMP 1519(1957):9. The 2 to 6 percent range is from "Why Issue Quotas," p. 39; 3 to 5 percent was the customary figure for machinery plants (Ch'eng, "Material and Technical Supply Work," p.4).

53. Glimpses into the shadowy world of expediters, teahouse exchange networks, black markets, and semilegal barter among firms can be found in the following sources: JMJP, August 30, 1956; *Liao-ning jih-pao*, November 9, 1956; Donnithorne, *China's Economic System*, pp. 175, 289–91, 478; John Burns, "Racketeers Prey on China Systems," *New York Times*, January 28, 1974, p. 5; Bruce L. Reynolds, "Territorial Decentralization in Chinese and Russian Economic Planning" (unpublished, 1976), and "Procurement Pressure in China: The Manager as Entrepreneur" (unpublished, 1977); and the 1975 reports cited by Stepanek, "Urban Small-Scale Industry," p. 10.
54. SCMP 1481(1957):11.
55. Donnithorne, *China's Economic System*, pp. 526–27; Reynolds, "Central Planning"; Eckstein, *China's Economic Development*, p. 362.
56. SCMP 5034(1971):107.
57. SCMP 5064(1972):182–83, and "Some Problems in Speeding Up Industrial Development," p. 106.
58. As Ely Devons put it, "When one reads about the behaviour and problems of the firm in Russia, what is striking is the similarity, not the contrast, with the problems and behaviour of firms in England or the United States" (*Papers on Planning and Economic Management*, p. 85).
59. Bernard M. Baruch, *American Industry in the War* (New York, 1941), p. 71.
60. Balassa, "Growth Strategies," and Jagdish N. Bhagwati and Padma Desai, *India, Planning for Industrialization* (London, 1970), provide numerous examples.
61. Harvey Leibenstein, "X-Efficiency versus Allocative Efficiency," reprinted in *Beyond Economic Man* (Cambridge, 1976), p. 46, with emphasis as in the original.
62. Paul Harper, "The Party and the Unions in Communist China," *China Quarterly* 37(1969):84–119, describes the dual trade union objective of representing and manipulating the membership.
63. FBIS, January 3, 1978, E17. A 1957 report that Anshan workers on rotating piece-rate jobs called in sick when assigned to low-paying tasks suggests the mentality that leads to goldbricking ("Improving the Form of Piece Rates for Steelworkers," *Lao-tung* 7[1957]:13).
64. Stanley B. Mathewson et al., *Restriction of Output Among Unorganized Workers* (New York, 1931), p. 146.
65. On the origins of cadre labor, see Andors, *China's Industrial Revolution*, pp. 70–73, 83, 103–4. Recent praise for this policy appears in "Some Problems in Speeding Up Industrial Development," p. 97; "Chairman Hua Kuo-feng's Speech at the National Conference on Learning from Taching in Industry," *Peking Review* 21(1977):11, and Yü, "Mobilize the Whole Party," pp. 13, 20.
66. Michael J. Piore, "The Impact of the Labor Market upon the Design and Selection of Productive Technique within the Manufacturing Plant,"

Quarterly Journal of Economics 82.4(1968):605–6; Leibenstein, "Allocative Efficiency," pp. 34–44; James R. Bright, *Automation and Management* (Boston, 1958), pp. 90–92.

67. SCMP 4847(1971):3.
68. A management consultant asserts that European firms incur excessive wage costs of 20 to 30 percent and that efficiency varies inversely with the degree of industrial concentration; oil, computer, tobacco, beer, and cosmetic firms show the worst performance, while textile producers who "have to be pretty hardnosed to survive" do best in economizing on labor (*New York Times*, February 1, 1974, p. 40).
69. Richman, *Industrial Society*, p. 719; Perkins et al., *Rural Industry*, p. 278.
70. Richard P. Suttmeier, "Science Policy Shifts, Organizational Change and China's Development," *China Quarterly* 62(1975):215, traces the emphasis on close links between research and production back to the 1950s. On the Soviet situation, see Joseph S. Berliner, "Prospects for Technological Progress," in *Soviet Economy in a New Perspective* (Washington, D.C., 1976), pp. 440–41.
71. Donald B. Keesing, "Economic Lessons from China," *Journal of Development Economics* 2 (1975):14.
72. "Some Problems in Speeding Up Industrial Development," p. 94.
73. BBC W957(1977):A1.
74. FBIS, January 3, 1978, E17.

Chapter 6

1. Achievement of specific world technical standards is claimed in BBC W866(1976):A4; W870(1976):A4; W871(1976):A13; and W890(1976):A5.
2. Author's notes as a member of the Rural Small-Scale Industry Delegation, June 13, 1975.
3. Perkins et al., *Rural Industry*, pp. 13–18, 71–81; Yü, "Agricultural Mechanization," pp. E12–14.
4. Albert O. Hirschman, *A Bias for Hope* (New Haven, 1971), pp. 25–26.
5. S. B. Saul, "The Nature and Diffusion of Technology," in A. J. Youngson ed., *Economic Development in the Long Run* (New York, 1972), p. 47.
6. H. J. Habakkuk, *American and British Technology in the Nineteenth Century* (Cambridge, 1967), p. 52.
7. Harless D. Wagoner, *The U.S. Machine Tool Industry From 1900–1950* (Cambridge, 1968), p. 29; Strassmann, *Risk and Technological Innovation*, p. 154.
8. G.C. Allen, *Japan's Economic Expansion* (London, 1965), p. 134.
9. Kazushi Ohkawa and Henry Rosovsky, *Japanese Economic Growth* (Stanford, 1973), pp. 91–95, 218–28.
10. This is based on published sources such as Piore, "Impact of the Labor Market," and Ronald Dore, *British Factory–Japanese Factory* (London, 1973), and also on a series of visits to Japanese factories during 1969–70.

11. Derek T. Healey, "Development Policy: New Thinking about an Interpretation," *Journal of Economic Literature* 10.3(1972):757–97, offers a typically pessimistic view of both planning and import substitution.
12. Perkins et al., *Rural Industry*, chap. 5–7.
13. L. Nabseth and G. F. Ray, eds., *The Diffusion of New Industrial Processes* (Cambridge, 1974), p. 302, conclude their international study with the observation that profitability calculations "are very subjective" and "very much linked with management attitudes, especially when experience of the technology is scarce and perhaps contradictory." Navin, *The Whitin Machine Works*, p. 423, cites *esprit de corps*, patriotism, and "close-knit camaraderie" in explaining the success of an inexperienced wartime work force in surpassing earlier standards of precision and technique.

Bibliography

Titles of Chinese- and Japanese-language articles are given in translation only. Chinese-language materials written by corporate authors are identified by their titles only.

Adelman, Irma, and Morris, Cynthia T. *Society, Politics and Economic Development*. Baltimore: Johns Hopkins University Press, 1967.

Ahn, Byung-joon. "Adjustments in the Great Leap Forward and Their Ideological Legacy, 1959–62." In *Ideology and Politics in Contemporary China*, edited by Chalmers Johnson, pp. 257–300. Seattle: University of Washington Press, 1973.

Ajia keizai jumpō [Asian economic tri-monthly]. Tokyo.

Allen, G. C. "The Heavy Industries." In *The Industrialization of Japan and Manchukuo, 1930–1940*, edited by E. B. Schumpeter, pp. 596–624. New York: Macmillan, 1940.

———. *Japan's Economic Expansion*. London: Oxford University Press, 1965.

———. *A Short Economic History of Modern Japan*. 2d ed. London: Allen & Unwin, 1962.

American Iron and Steel Institute. *Annual Statistical Report*. New York: American Iron and Steel Institute, annual.

An-hui jih-pao [Anhwei daily]. Hofei.

Andors, Stephen. *China's Industrial Revolution*. New York: Pantheon, 1977.

"Australian Coal Mission to the People's Republic of China." Unpublished, 1976.

Balassa, Bela. "Growth Strategies in Semi-Industrial Countries." *Quarterly Journal of Economics* 84.1(1970):24–47.

Barnett, A. Doak. *Uncertain Passage*. Washington, D.C.: Brookings, 1974.

Baruch, Bernard M. *American Industry in the War*. New York: Prentice-Hall, 1941.

Bergsman, Joel. *Brazil: Industrialization and Trade Policies*. London: Oxford University Press, 1970.

Bergsman, Joel, and Candal, Arthur. "Industrialization: Past Success and Future Problems." In *The Economy of Brazil*, edited by Howard S. Ellis, pp. 29–73. Berkeley: University of California Press, 1969.

Berliner, Joseph S. *Factory and Manager in the USSR*. Cambridge, Mass.: Harvard University Press, 1957.

———. "Prospects for Technological Progress." In *Soviet Economy in a New Perspective*, pp. 431–46. Washington, D.C.: Government Printing Office, 1976.

Bettelheim, Charles. *Cultural Revolution and Industrial Organization in China*. New York: Monthly Review Press, 1974.

"Better Training for Basic Level Production Leaders Is an Important Task." CKYTH 29(1954):17–23.

Bhagwati, Jagdish N., and Desai, Padma. *India, Planning for Industrialization*. London: Oxford University Press, 1970.

Bornstein, Morris. "Economic Reform in Eastern Europe." In *East European Economies Post-Helsinki*, pp. 102–134. Washington, D.C.: Government Printing Office, 1977.

Bright, James R. *Automation and Management*. Boston: Harvard University Graduate School of Business Administration, 1958.

"Bringing the Strength of Technical Personnel into Full Play." Translated in ECMM 314(1962):47–50.

British Broadcasting Corporation. *Summary of World Broadcasts: Pt. 3, The Far East, Weekly Economic Report*.

Burns, John. "Racketeers Prey on China Systems." *New York Times*, January 28, 1974, p. 5.

Cassou, Pierre-Henri. "The Chinese Monetary System." *China Quarterly* 59(1974):559–66.

"Chairman Hua Kuo-feng's Speech at the National Conference on Learning from Taching in Industry." *Peking Review* 21(1977):7–14.

Chang Chen. "For Better Fulfillment of the Second Five-Year Plan Tasks for Chemical Construction." HHKY 11(1957):12–16.

———. *Ti-i-ko wu-nien chi-hua-chung ti hua-hsüeh kung-yeh* [The chemical industry in the First Five Year Plan]. Peking: Chung-hua ch'üan-kuo k'o-hsüeh chi-shu p'u-chi hsieh-hui, 1956.

Chang, Ch'un-ch'iao. "On Exercising All-Round Dictatorship Over the Bourgeoisie." *Peking Review* 14(1975):5–11.

Chang Hsü-sheng. *Wo-kuo she-hui-chu-i kung-yeh-chung t'i-kao lao-tung sheng-ch'an-lü ti t'u-ching* [The path to raising labor productivity in China's socialist industry]. Peking: Ts'ai-cheng ching-chi ch'u-pan she, 1956.

Chang, John K. *Industrial Development in Pre-Communist China*. Chicago: Aldine, 1969.

Chang Kuang-en. "Big Character Poster." *Chi-hua ching-chi* 4(1958):25.

Chang Yu. "How We Reached and Surpassed Designed Capacity Ahead of Schedule." CHKY 10 (1956): 16–17.

Chao I-wen. *Hsin Chung-kuo ti kung-yeh* [Industry of new China]. Peking: T'ung-chi-ch'u-pan she, 1957.

Chao, Kang. *Capital Formation in Mainland China, 1952–1965*. Berkeley: University of California Press, 1974.

———. *The Rate and Pattern of Industrial Growth in Communist China*. Ann Arbor: The University of Michigan Press, 1965.

Chao, Kuo-chün *Economic Planning and Organization in Mainland China*. 2 vols. Cambridge, Mass.: Harvard University Press, 1963.

Charrière, Jacques. "Planification et gestion des unités de production." In Charles Bettelheim, Jacques Charrière, and Hélène Marchisio, *La construction du socialisme en Chine*, pp. 47–77. Paris: Maspero, 1968.

Ch'en Chen, ed. *Chung-kuo chin-tai kung-yeh-shih tzu-liao* [Materials on China's modern industrial history], collection IV. 2 vols. 1961. Reprint. Tokyo: Daian, 1966.

Ch'en Chen and Yao Lo, eds. *Chung-kuo chin-tai kung-yeh-shih tzu-liao*[Materials on China's modern industrial history], collection I. 1957. Reprint. Tokyo: Daian, 1966.

Chen, Nai-ruenn. *Chinese Economic Statistics*. Chicago: Aldine, 1967.

Ch'en Wang-ch'i. "Begin a Production and Economy Campaign and Strengthen Fiscal Control over Basic Construction." *Ts'ai-cheng* 4(1957):11–13.

Ch'eng Ch'i-hsing. "Opinions on Reforming Material and Technical Supply Work." CHKY 24(1956):4–6.

Cheng-chih ching-chi-hsüeh chi-ch'u chih-shih [Basic knowledge on political economy]. Shanghai: Shang-hai jen-min ch'u-pan she, 1975.

Ch'eng Chin-chieh. "The Way Liu-chi Commune Wins Its Higher Grain and Cotton Yields." Translated in ECMM 473(1965):1–7.

Cheng, Chu-yuan. *The Machine-building Industry in Communist China*. Chicago: Aldine, 1971.

Chi-hsieh kung-yeh [Machinery industry]. Peking.

Chi-lin jih-pao [Kirin daily]. Ch'angch'un.

Chiang Cheng. "Shortcomings and Problems in Technical Work." CHKY 12(1957):25-26, 35.

Chiang Li. "Several Problems as Seen from Four Chinan Plants." CHKY 1(1957):30–31.

"Chichihar #1 Machine Tool Plant Has Neglected Care of Equipment for a Long Time." CHKY 18(1953):6–7.

Chieh-fang jih-pao [Liberation daily]. Shanghai.

The China Business Review. Washington, D.C. (Bimonthly).

China, Maritime Customs. *Annual Trade Report and Returns*.

———. *Decennial Reports, 1922–31*. Shanghai: Inspectorate General of Customs, 1933.

———. *The Trade of China* (annual).

Ching Lin. "On the Proportional Relation between Steel and Machine-building." *Chi-hua ching-chi* 9(1957):11–15.

———. *Ti-i-ko wu-nien chi-hua-chung ti chi-ch'i chih-tsao-yeh* [The machine-building industry in the First Five-Year Plan]. Peking: Chung-kuo ch'üan-kuo k'o-hsüeh chi-shu p'u-chi hsieh-hui, 1955.

Ching Nan. "How Li Feng-en Organizes the Workers to Implement the Expert's Suggestions," CKYTH 11(1956):19–21.

Ching Sheng. *Chan-shih Chung-kuo ching-chi lun-k'uo* [Records of China's wartime economy]. N.p., 1944.

Chōsha no juyō kōjō chōsa [Survey of Ch'angsha's main factories]. Nanking: Chūshi kensetsu shiryō seibi iinkai, 1940.

Chu Hsi-ken et al. "Further Develop Specialized Production of Hardware." CHKY 8(1963):29–32.

Ch'u Hsüeh. "Inquiry into the Problem of Piece-work Wages." *Ts'ai-cheng yen-chiu* 6(1958):49–52.

Chu Ta-ching. "The Power Sector in the Past Ten Years." In *Shih-nien-lai chih Chung-kuo ching-chi* [China's economy in the past ten years], compiled by T'an Hsi-hung. 3 vols. Shanghai: Chung-hua shu-chü, 1948.

Chu Wen-wu et al. "Why Does Shanghai Diesel Engine Plant Eliminate Piece Rates during the Great Leap Forward?" *Ts'ai-cheng yen-chiu* 7(1958):22–24.

Chūgoku kōgyō kōjō sōran [Handbook of China's industries and plants]. Tokyo: Ajia kenkyūjo, 1965.

Chūgoku no tekkōgyō to kikai kōgyō [China's steel and machinery industries]. Tokyo: Ajia keizai kenkyūjo, 1964. Includes partial translation of *Wo-kuo kang-t'ieh, tien-li, mei-t'an, chi-hsieh, fang-chih, tsao-chih kung-yeh ti chin-hsi* [Past and present of China's steel, power, coal, machinery, textile, and paper industries]. Peking: T'ung-chi ch'u-pan she, 1958.

Chūgoku sangyō bōeki sōran [Handbook of China's industry and trade]. Tokyo: Ajia tsūshinsha, 1963.

Chūgoku shiryō geppō [China materials monthly]. Tokyo.

Chung-hua nien-chien 1948 [China yearbook, 1948]. 2 vols. Nanking: Chung-hua nien-chien she, 1948.

Chung-kuo ch'ing-nien pao [China youth news]. Peking.

Chung-kuo hsin-wen [China news]. Canton.

Chung-kuo kuo-huo kung-ch'ang shih-lüeh [Capsule histories of Chinese factories]. Shanghai: Kuo-huo shih-yeh ch'u-pan she, 1935.

"Chungking Machine Tool Plant Installs 9 Lathes, Uses 7, and Wrecks 7." CHKY 18(1953):9–10.

Clark, M. Gardner. *Development of China's Steel Industry and Soviet Technical Aid.* Ithaca: New York State School of Industrial and Labor Relations, 1973.

"Collective Notes of the First Friendship Delegation of American Radical Political Economists to the People's Republic of China." Mimeographed. Ann Arbor, 1972.

Communist China 1955–1959. Cambridge, Mass.: Harvard University Press, 1962.

"Concentrating Production of Standard Parts Is Economically Rational." CHKY 22(1957):18.

Crook, Frederick W. "The Commune System in the People's Republic of China, 1963–74." In *China: A Reassessment of the Economy*, pp. 366–410. Washington, D.C.: Government Printing Office, 1975.

Devons, Ely. *Papers on Planning and Economic Management*. Edited by Sir Alec Cairncross. Manchester, England: Manchester University Press, 1970.

"Directive on Expanding Output of Top-grade Steel." CKYTH 21(1954):2–3.

"Display Revolutionary Spirit, Struggle for a New High Tide in Shanghai's Chemical Output for 1965." HHKY 2(1965):1–4.

Djerassi, Carl. "Some Observations on Current Fertility Control in China." *China Quarterly* 57(1974):40 62.

Documents of Chinese Communist Party Central Committee, September 1956–April 1959. Vol. 1. Hong Kong: Union Research Institute, 1971.

Donnithorne, Audrey. "Centralization and Decentralization in China's Fiscal Management, Comment." *China Quarterly* 66(1976):328–40.

______. "China's Cellular Economy: Some Economic Trends since the Cultural Revolution." *China Quarterly* 52(1972):605–19.

______. *China's Economic System*. London: Allen and Unwin, 1967.

Dore, Ronald. *British Factory–Japanese Factory*. London: Allen & Unwin, 1973.

Douty, Christopher M. "Disasters and Charity: Some Aspects of Cooperative Economic Behavior." *American Economic Review* 62.4(1972):580–90.

Eastern Horizon. Hong Kong.

Eckstein, Alexander. *China's Economic Development*. Ann Arbor: The University of Michigan Press, 1975.

Eckstein, Alexander; Chao, Kang; and Chang, John. "The Economic Development of Manchuria: The Rise of a Frontier Economy." *Journal of Economic History* 34.1(1974):239–64.

Economic Encyclopedia of the Northeast, vol. 12. *The Cement Industry*. English translation of *Tung-pei ching-chi hsiao ts'ung-shu*. Mukden: Northeast China Resources Investigation Committee, 1947. Mimeographed. Washington, D.C., 1947.

Emerson, John P. *Nonagricultural Employment in Mainland China: 1949–1958*. Washington, D.C.: U.S. Department of Commerce, 1965.

Estimates of Long-Term Economic Statistics of Japan Since 1868. Edited by Kazushi Ohkawa et al. 13 vols. Tokyo: Toyo keizai shinpo sha, 1965– .

"The Experience of Wan Hsien Ironworks in Reducing Casting Costs." CHKY 23(1963):14–16.

Fang Hsien-t'ing. "A Statistical Analysis of Chinese Industrialization." *Ching-chi t'ung-chi chi-k'an* 1.1(1932):80–127.

Fang Hsien-t'ing and Ku Yüan-t'ien. "Bird's Eye View of China's Iron and Steel Industry." In *Chung-kuo ching-chi yen-chiu* [Studies of China's economy], edited by Fang Hsien-t'ing, pp. 633–63. Ch'angsha: Shang-wu yin-shu-kuan, 1938.

"Farm Mechanization: Targets for 1980." *Peking Review* 8(1978):10–14.

1967 Fei-ch'ing nien-pao [1967 yearbook of Chinese Communism]. Taipei: Fei-ch'ing yen-chiu tsa-chih-she, 1967.

Fei, John C. H., and Ranis, Gustav. *Development of the Labor Surplus Economy*. Homewood, Ill.: Irwin, 1964.

Ferguson, Charles J., ed. *Andersen, Meyer & Company Limited of China*. Shanghai: Kelly & Walsh, 1931.

Feuerwerker, Albert. "China's Nineteenth Century Industrialization: The Case of the Hanyehping Coal and Iron Company, Limited." In *The Economic Development of China and Japan*, edited by C. D. Cowan, pp. 79–110. London: Allen & Unwin, 1964.

Field, Robert M. "Civilian Industrial Production in the People's Republic of China: 1949–74." In *China: A Reassessment of the Economy*, pp. 146–74. Washington, D.C.: Government Printing Office, 1975.

———. "Real Capital Formation in the People's Republic of China, 1952–73." *In Quantitative Measures of China's Economic Output*, edited by Alexander Eckstein. Ann Arbor: The University of Michigan Press, 1980.

Field, Robert M.; Lardy, Nicholas R.; and Emerson, John P. *Provincial Industrial Output in the People's Republic of China: 1949–75*. Washington, D.C.: U.S. Department of Commerce, 1976.

———. *A Reconstruction of the Gross Value of Industrial Output by Province in the People's Republic of China, 1949–73*. Washington, D.C: U.S Department of Commerce, 1975.

"Fifteen Years of Great Results." *Lao-tung* 19(1964):13–17.

Fifth Report on Progress in Manchuria to 1936. Dairen: South Manchurian Railroad Company, 1936.

First Five-Year Plan for Development of the National Economy of the People's Republic of China in 1953–1957. Peking: Foreign Languages Press, 1956.

"First Ministry of Machine-building Directive for 1957." CHKY 9(1957):2–8.

"First Ministry of Machine-building and Ministry of Construction Hold a Joint Meeting of Factory Directors and Managers to Arrange Basic Construction Plans for 1956." CHKY 2(1956):30–31.

Frankena, Mark. "The Industrial and Trade Control Regime and Product Designs in India." *Economic Development and Cultural Change* 22.2(1974): 249–64.

Gibb, George S. *The Saco-Lowell Shops*. Cambridge, Mass.: Harvard University Press, 1950.

Granick, David. *Management of the Industrial Firm in the USSR*. New York: Columbia University Press, 1954.

———. *The Red Executive*. Garden City, N.Y.: Doubleday, 1961.

———. *Soviet Metal-fabricating and Economic Development*. Madison: University of Wisconsin Press, 1967.

Ha-erh-pin jih-pao [Harbin daily]. Harbin.

Habakkuk, H. J. *American and British Technology in the Nineteenth Century*. Cambridge: Cambridge University Press, 1967.

Han Kuang. "Several Problems Concerning Technical Work in Industry." Translated in ECMM 295(1962):1–8.

Harper, Paul. "The Party and the Unions in Communist China." *China Quarterly* 37(1969):84–119.

Hayami, Yujiro, and Ruttan, Vernon W. *Agricultural Development*. Baltimore: Johns Hopkins Press, 1971.

Healy, Derek T. "Development Policy: New Thinking about an Interpretation." *Journal of Economic Literature* 10.3(1972):757–97.

Hei-lung-chiang jih-pao [Heilungkiang daily]. Harbin.

Heyman, Hans, Jr. "Acquisition and Diffusion of Technology in China." In *China: A Reassessment of the Economy*, pp. 678–729. Washington, D.C.: Government Printing Office, 1975.

Hinton, William. *Iron Oxen*. New York: Random House, 1970.

Hirschman, Albert O. *A Bias for Hope*. New Haven: Yale University Press, 1971.

———. *The Strategy of Economic Development*. New Haven: Yale University Press, 1958.

"How to Carry Out Technical Preparations at a Plant with Unit Production." CHKY 3(1957):10–12, 24.

"How We Test and Accept Technical Management Reorganization Work." CHKY 8(1963):13–15.

Howe, Christopher. "Labour Organization and Incentives in Industry, Before and After the Cultural Revolution." In *Authority, Participation and Cultural Change in China*, edited by Stuart Schram, pp. 233–56. Cambridge: Cambridge University Press, 1973.

———. *Wage Patterns and Wage Policy in Modern China, 1919–1972*. Cambridge: Cambridge University Press, 1973.

Hsia Na. "Technical Policy at Heavy Machinery Plants." CHKY 1(1957):10–13.

Hsiang Jung. "Big Drama on a Small Stage." *Peking Review* 22(1975):18–21.

Hsiang Lin. "How to Implement the Principle of Frugal National Construction." CHKY 11(1957):18–21, 23.

Hsiang Wen. "Changes at Ta-lung Show the Value of Old Plants." CHKY 20(1964):18–20.

Hsiao, Han. "Developing Coal Industry at High Speed." *Peking Review* 8(1978):5–7.

Hsiao, Liang-lin. *China's Foreign Trade Statistics, 1864–1949*. Cambridge, Mass.: Harvard University East Asian Research Center, 1974.

Hsieh Lan. "Study the Advanced, Catch the Advanced." CKYTH 16(1956):12–15.

Hsieh Pei-i. "Judiciously Plan This Year's Production of Machinery and Electrical Equipment." *Chi-hua ching-chi* 3(1957):8–10.

Hsin Hu-nan pao [New Hunan news]. Ch'angsha.

Hsin-hua jih-pao [New China Daily]. Chungking.

Hsü I. "On Several Problems of Economic Accounting." *Ching-chi yen-chiu* 4(1958):62–74.

Hsü Pao-min. "Economic Significance of Using General Technical Equipment." *Yeh-chin pao* 19(1957):27–28.

Hsü Tu-t'an. "Anshan Steel Works Should Reverse the Phenomenon of Low Product Quality." CKYTH 11(1956):28–30.

Hsüeh Mu-chiao; Su Hsing; and Lin Tse-li. *The Socialist Transformation of the Economy in China*. Peking: Foreign Languages Press, 1960.

Hu Kuang. "The Developing Petroleum Equipment Industry." CHKY 20(1964):14–15.

Hu-pei jih-pao [Hupei daily]. Hankow.

Hu Pu-chou. "Establish Revolutionary Ambitions, Progress, and Advance." CHKY 15(1964):20–24.

Hua-hsüeh kung-yeh [Chemical industry]. Peking.

"Improving the Form of Piece Rates for Steelworkers." *Lao-tung* 7(1957):13–14.

Inkeles, Alex, and Smith, David H. *Becoming Modern*. Cambridge, Mass.: Harvard University Press, 1974.

Ishikawa, Shigeru. *National Income and Capital Formation in Mainland China*. Tokyo: Institute of Asian Economic Affairs, 1965.

Jen-min jih-pao [People's daily]. Peking.

Jen-min shou-ts'e 1958 [People's handbook for 1958]. Peking: Ta-kung pao, 1958.

Kajinishi Mitsuhaya. *Toyota Sakichi*. Tokyo: Yoshikawa Hirobunkan, 1962.

Kantōkyoku kambō bunsho ka. *Kantōkyoku tōkei sanjū nenshi* [Thirty years of Kantōkyoku statistics]. Dairen: Kantōkyoku kambō bunsho ka, 1937.

Kaysen, Carl. "Improving the Efficiency of Military Research and Development." *Public Policy* 12(1963):219–73.

Keesing, Donald B. "Economic Lessons from China." *Journal of Development Economics* 2(1975):1–32.

Kennedy, Charles, and Thirlwall, A. P. "Surveys in Applied Economics: Technical Progress." *Economic Journal* 82.1(1972):11–72.

Kojima Reiitsu. "China's Machine Tool Industry." In *Chūgoku keizai no chōki tembō II* (Long-term prospects for China's economy—II), edited by Ishikawa Shigeru, pp. 323–65. Tokyo: Ajia keizai kenkyūjo, 1966.

———. "Industrial Production and the Chemical Industry." In *Chūgoku no kagaku kōgyō* [China's chemical industry], edited by Kambara Shū, pp. 26–39. Tokyo: Ajia keizai kenkyūjo, 1970.

———. "Iron and Steel Industry." In *Chūgoku keizai no chōki tembō IV* [Long-term prospects for China's economy—IV], edited by Ishikawa Shigeru, 2:71–100. Tokyo: Ajia keizai kenkyūjo, 1971.

Kornai, Janos. *Rush versus Harmonic Growth*. Amsterdam: North Holland, 1972.

Ku Min. "Experiences of Shanghai Machine Tool Plant in Developing a Production and Economy Campaign." CHKY 9(1963):6–8.

Ku Yü-hsien. "Thirty Years of Machine-building." In *San-shih-nien-lai chih Chung-kuo kung-ch'eng* [Thirty years of Chinese engineering], edited by Chou K'ai-ch'ing, vol. 2, pp. 1–42. Reprint. Taipei: Hua-wen shu-chü, 1967.

Ku Yüan-t'ien. "China's Iron and Steel Industry." *Ching-chi t'ung-chi chi-k'an* 2.3(1933):693–728.

Kuang-chou jih-pao [Canton daily]. Canton.

Kuang-ming jih-pao [Kuang-ming daily]. Peking.

Kung-jen jih-pao [Daily worker]. Peking.

Kung Shih. "Study the Advanced, Uncover Idle Capacity." *Lao-tung* 8(1963):16–19.

Lardy, Nicholas R. "Centralization and Decentralization in China's Fiscal Management." *China Quarterly* 61(1975):25–60.

______. "Centralization and Decentralization in China's Fiscal Management—Reply." *China Quarterly* 66(1976):340–54.

Lao-tung [Labor]. Peking.

Leibenstein, Harvey. "X-Efficiency versus Allocative Efficiency." In *Beyond Economic Man*, pp. 29–47. Cambridge, Mass.: Harvard University Press, 1976.

Li Li-jen. "Discussion on Developing Research Work in the Machine Tool Industry." CHKY 14(1957):6–8, 35.

Li Tso-wen. "From the Principle of Return of Loans to the Supervisory Role of the Bank." Translated in ECMM 309(1962):11–14.

Li Yü-heng and Ch'ang Pao-yü. "T'ai-yüan Saves Labor to Aid Agriculture." *Lao-tung* 9(1962):15–16.

Liang Ta. "Enforce Economy, Reform Management, Advance Production." CHKY 9(1963):9–11.

Liao-ning jih-pao [Liaoning daily]. Shenyang.

Lin I-fu. "Actively Take Steps to Fully Utilize the Productive Capacity of Existing Industries." *Chi-hua ching-chi* 3(1958):7–10.

Liu Chien-nan. "Chou Tsung: An Engineer Who Energetically Adds New Products." CKYTH 15(1956):25–27.

Liu, Jung-chao. *China's Fertilizer Economy*. Chicago: Aldine, 1970.

______. "Fertiliser Application in Communist China." *China Quarterly* 24(1965):28–52.

Liu Pao-tung. "We Hope 444 Plant Can Turn Around and Save Metal Materials." CHKY 20(1956):25.

Liu Ta-chün. *Chung-kuo kung-yeh tiao-ch'a pao-kao* [Report on a survey of China's industries]. 3 vols. Shanghai: Ching-chi t'ung-chi yen-chiu-so, 1937.

______. *Shang-hai kung-yeh-hua yen-chiu* [Studies of Shanghai's industrialization]. Ch'angsha: Commercial Press, 1940.

Liu, Ta-chung, and Kung-chia Yeh. *The Economy of the Chinese Mainland*. Princeton: Princeton University Press, 1965.

Liu Yao-ming. "With Politics Leading, Results Are Great." CHKY 7(1966):17.

Lü-ta jih-pao [Lü-shun and Ta-lien daily]. Lü-ta.

Lü Yün-ho and Ch'en Kuo-t'ai. "Find Ways to Save Labor." *Lao-tung* 4(1962):19.

"Main Technical and Economic Indicators of Advanced Small-Scale Synthetic Ammonia Plants." HHKY 14(1964):27.

The Manchoukuo Yearbook 1934. Tokyo: Tōa keizai chōsakyoku, 1934.

The Manchoukuo Yearbook 1942. Hsinking: Manchoukuo Yearbook Company, 1941.

The Manchuria Yearbook, 1931. Tokyo: Tōa keizai chōsakyoku, 1931.

The Manchuria Yearbook, 1932–33. Tokyo: Tōa keizai chōsakyoku, 1932.

Manshū kaihatsu yonjū nenshi [Forty-year history of Manchuria's development]. 3 vols. Tokyo: Manshū kaihatsu yonjū nenshi kankō kai, 1964–65.

Mao Tse-tung Unrehearsed, edited by Stuart Schram. Harmondsworth, England: Penguin, 1974.

Mark, H. F. "China Visit—June 1972." Unpublished.

Matchi kōgyō hōkokusho [Report on the match industry]. Nanking: Chūshi kensetsu shiryō seibi iinkai, 1940.

Matheson, JeNelle. *Construction Equipment: A Market Assessment for the People's Republic of China*. Washington, D.C.: U.S. Department of Commerce, 1976.

Mathewson, Stanley B., et al. *Restriction of Output Among Unorganized Workers*. New York: Viking Press, 1931.

McFarlane, Ian H. "Construction Trends in China, 1949–74." In *China: A Reassessment of the Economy*, pp. 311–22. Washington, D.C.: Government Printing Office, 1975.

Meisner, Mitch. "The Shenyang Transformer Factory—A Profile." *China Quarterly* 52(1972):717–37.

Mellor, John W. *The New Economics of Growth*. Ithaca: Cornell University Press, 1976.

Men Chin-ju. "Begin a Production and Economy Campaign on the Production Front." *Chi-hua ching-chi* 1(1957):1–4.

Meng Chih-chien. "On Mechanization of Casting." CHKY 13(1957):5–8.

Meng Chin-hua. "A Problem in Determining Plan Fulfillment for Local Machinery Industry on the Basis of Gross Output Value." *T'ung-chi kung-tso* 4(1957):5–8.

Min-sheng shih-yeh kung-ssu shih-yi-chou-nien chi-nien k'an [Commemorative of the eleventh anniversary of the Min-sheng Industrial Company]. Shanghai: Chung-hua shu-chü, 1937.

Ministry of Industry, Bureau of Foreign Trade, comp. *China Industrial Handbooks: Chekiang*. Shanghai: Ministry of Industry, Bureau of Foreign Trade, 1935.

———. *China Industrial Handbooks: Kiangsu*. Shanghai: Ministry of Industry, Bureau of Foreign Trade, 1933.

"Ministry of Metallurgy Production Plans for 1957." *Yeh-chin pao* 45(1957):34.

Miscellany of Mao Tse-tung Thought (1949–1968). 2 vols. (JPRS 61269-1 and 61269-2). Arlington, Va.: JPRS, 1974.

Mishina Yoritata. *Hokushi minzoku kōgyō no hattatsu* [Development of native industry in north China]. Tokyo: Chūō kōronsha, 1942.

Miyashita Haruo. "Insecticide Industry." In *Chūgoku no kagaku kōgyō* [*China's chemical industry*], edited by Kambara Shū, pp. 178–206. Tokyo: Ajia keizai kenkyūjo, 1970.

Nabseth, L., and Ray, G.F., eds. *The Diffusion of New Industrial Processes*. Cambridge: Cambridge University Press, 1974.

Naikaku sōri daijin kambō chōsa shitsu. *Chūkyō tekkōgyō chōsa hōkokusho* (kigyō hen) [Survey report on Communist China's iron and steel industry, enterprise edition]. 2 vols. Tokyo: Finance Ministry Printing Office, 1956.

Nan-ching jih-pao [Nanking daily]. Nanking.

"Nanking Machine Tool Plant Damages 22 of 28 New Machine Tools in Less Than Half a Year." CHKY 18(1953):8–9.

Navin, Thomas R. *The Whitin Machine Works Since 1831*. Cambridge, Mass.: Harvard University Press, 1950.

New China News Agency. *Daily News Release*. Hong Kong.

New China's First Quarter-Century. Peking: Foreign Languages Press, 1975.

"NMBTA Metalworking Technology Symposium and Trade Mission to the People's Republic of China, November 17–27, 1975." Unpublished report by the National Machine Tool Builders' Association, McLean, Va.

Nung-shang pu. *Nung-shang t'ung-chi piao* [Statistical tables of agriculture and commerce]. No. 1 (1912) and no. 5 (1916). Shanghai: Chung-hua shu-chü, annual.

Ohkawa, Kazushi, and Rosovsky, Henry. *Japanese Economic Growth*. Stanford: Stanford University Press, 1973.

Onoe Etsuzō. *Chūgoku no sangyō ritchi ni kansuru kenkyū* [Studies in the location of Chinese industry]. Tokyo: Ajia keizai kenkyūjo, 1971.

"Opinions and Demands of Factory Directors." CHKY 10(1957):7–9, and 11(1957):7–10.

Orchard, John E. *Japan's Economic Position*. New York: McGraw-Hill, 1930.

Ōtsuka Reizō. *Shina kōgyō sōkan* [General survey of China's industries]. 2 vols. Tokyo: Seikatsu sha, 1942.

Ou-yang Lun. "The Machinery Sector in the Past Ten Years." In *Shih-nien-lai chih Chung-kuo ching-chi* [China's economy in the past ten years], compiled by T'an Hsi-hung. 3 vols. Shanghai: Chung-hua shu-chü, 1948.

Pai Ou. "Brief Discussion of the Direction and Tasks of the Machinery Industry During the First and Second Five-Year Plans." CHKY 12(1957):2–8.

P'an Kuang-chi. "Opinions on How to Develop the Basic Chemical Industry." HHKY 8(1957):33–35.

Pauley, Edwin W. *Report on Japanese Assets in Manchuria*. Washington, D.C.: n.p., 1946.

Peking Review.

P'eng T'ao. "Fully Implement the Principle of Frugal National Construction." HHKY 1(1958):1–3.

Perkins, Dwight H. "Constraints Influencing China's Agricultural Performance." In *China: A Reassessment of the Economy*, pp. 350–65. Washington, D.C.: Government Printing Office, 1975.

———. "Growth and Changing Structure of China's Twentieth-Century Economy." In *China's Modern Economy in Historical Perspective*, edited by Dwight H. Perkins, pp. 115–65. Stanford: Stanford University Press, 1975.

———. *Market Control and Planning in Communist China*. Cambridge, Mass.: Harvard University Press, 1966.

———, et al. *Rural Small-Scale Industry in the People's Republic of China.* Berkeley: University of California Press, 1977.

"Persist in Revolutionary Thought, Force Yourself to the Highest Attainable Level." HHKY 9(1964):6–13.

Pien Po-heng. "Control Excess Consumption of Materials." HHKY 6(1957):7–8.

Piore, Michael J. "The Impact of the Labor Market upon the Design and Selection of Productive Technique within the Manufacturing Plant." *Quarterly Journal of Economics* 82.4(1968):602–20.

"Poor Product Quality Is an Important Cause of Failure to Complete State Plans." CHKY 13(1956):14–15.

"Present Tasks of the Heavy Machinery Industry." CHKY 5(1958):2–4.

"Problems We Consider in Drawing Up Proposed Long-Term Standards for the Machine Tool Industry." CHKY 11(1956):25–27.

Prybyla, Jan S. *The Political Economy of Communist China.* Scranton: International Textbook Company, 1970.

"A Rational Method To Save Labor Power." *Lao-tung* 5(1957):9–10.

Rawski, Thomas G. "China's Industrial Performance, 1949–73." In *Quantitative Measures of China's Economic Output*, edited by Alexander Eckstein. Ann Arbor. The University of Michigan Press, 1980.

———. "China's Industrial System." In *China: A Reassessment of the Economy*, pp. 175–98. Washington, D.C.: Government Printing Office, 1975.

———. "Chinese Industrial Production, 1952–1971." *Review of Economics and Statistics* 55.2(1973):169–81.

———. "Choice of Technology and Technical Innovation in China's Economic Development." In *The Relevance of China's Experiences for the Other Developing Countries.* Edited by Robert F. Dernberger. Forthcoming.

———. "The Economics of Chinese Machine-building, 1931–1967." Ph. D. dissertation, Harvard University, 1972.

———. "The Growth of Producer Industries, 1900–1971." In *China's Modern Economy in Historical Perspective*, edited by Dwight H. Perkins, pp. 203–34. Stanford: Stanford University Press, 1975.

———. *Industrialization, Technology and Employment in the People's Republic of China.* World Bank Staff Working Paper, no. 291. Washington, D.C.: World Bank, 1978.

———. "The Role of China in the World Energy Situation." Unpublished report prepared for the Brookings Institution, 1973.

Repetto, Robert C. *Time in India's Developmet Programmes.* Cambridge, Mass.: Harvard University Press, 1971.

"Report of SMMT Trade Mission to the People's Republic of China, 2–17 November 1973." Unpublished report by the Society of Motor Manufacturers and Traders Limited, London, 1974.

Reynolds, Bruce L. "The Adaptation of Russian Planning Practices in China's First Five-Year Plan." Unpublished, 1976.

______. "Central Planning in China: The Significance of Material Allocation Conferences." Association for Comparative Economic Studies, *Bulletin* 17.1(1975):3–14.

______. "Procurement Pressure in China: The Manager as Entrepreneur." Unpublished, 1977.

______. "Territorial Decentralization in Chinese and Russian Economic Planning." Unpublished, 1976.

______. "Weft: The Technological Sanctuary of Chinese Handspun Yarn." *Ch'ing-shih wen-t'i* 3.2(1974):1–19.

Richman, Barry M. *Industrial Society in Communist China.* New York: Random House, 1969.

Riskin, Carl. "China's Rural Industries: Self-Reliant Systems or Independent Kingdoms?" *China Quarterly* 73(1978):77–98.

______. "Small Industry and the Chinese Model of Development." *China Quarterly* 46(1971):245–73.

Robinson, Joan. *Economic Management in China.* London: Anglo-Chinese Educational Institute, 1973.

Rosenberg, Nathan. "Technological Change in the Machine Tool Industry, 1840–1910." *Journal of Economic History* 23.4(1963):414–43.

Sato, Masumi. "The Realities and Technological Trends of China's Heavy and Chemical Industries." *Chinese Economic Studies* 4.3(1971):161–93.

Saul, S.B. "The Nature and Diffusion of Technology." In *Economic Development in the Long Run*, edited by A. J. Youngson, pp. 36–61. New York: St. Martins, 1972.

Scott, David. "China Opens Doors for Rare View of Auto Production." *Automotive Engineering* 82.8(1974):30–33.

"Several Facts about Organizing Plans for Completing Construction Projects." CHKY 19(1963):17–18.

"Several Measures for Strengthening Production and Technical Preparation at Shenyang Heavy Machinery Plant." CHKY 23(1954):3–7.

Sha Ying. "On the Relation between Coastal and Interior Industry." *Hsin-hua pan-yüeh-k'an* 24(1956):50–53.

Shan-hsi jih-pao [Shansi daily]. T'aiyüan.

Shang-hai chi-hsieh [Shanghai machinery]. Shanghai.

Shang-hai she-hui-chü. *Shang-hai chih-kung-yeh* [Shanghai's industry]. Shanghai: Chung-hua shu chü, 1930.

"Shanghai: A Coastal Industrial Base." *Peking Review* 4(1978):11–13.

Shen-chou chü-pien [Great Changes in China]. Hong Kong: Ching-chi tao-pao she, 1976.

"Shengli Journal." *The China Business Review* 5.1(1978):31–35.

"Shenyang Heating Equipment Plant Wrecks 5 Planing Machines in 8 Days." CHKY 18(1953):10.

"Shenyang Mining Machinery Plant Ignores Inspection, Maintenance, and Repair from Top to Bottom." CHKY 18(1953):11–12.

Shih-yeh pu, kung-yeh ssu. *Shih-yeh-pu shih-cheng kai-k'uang* [Industrial projects under the Ministry of Industry] Nanking: Shih-yeh pu, kung-yeh ssu, 1934.

Shin Chūgoku no kikai kōgyō [New China's machinery industry]. Tokyo: Tōa keizai kenkyūkai, 1960.

Sigurdson, Jon. *Rural Industrialization in China.* Cambridge, Mass.: Harvard University Press, 1977.

Sixth Report on Progress in Manchuria to 1939. Dairen: SMR, 1939.

Smil, Vaclav, and Woodard, Kim. "Perspectives on Energy in the People's Republic of China," *Annual Review of Energy 1977* 2:307–42.

SMR. Chōsabu. *Kita Shina kōjō jittai chōsa hōkokusho—Tenshin no bu* [Survey report on North China's factories—Tientsin]. Dairen: SMR, 1939.

———. Sōmubu chōsaka. *Shina kōjō jijō* [Conditions in Chinese factories]. Dairen: SMR, 1928.

———. Tenshin jimusho chōsaka. *Sainan ni okeru seizō kōgyō* [Chinan's manufacturing industries]. Tientsin: SMR, 1936.

———. Tenshin jimusho chōsaka. *Shina ni okeru san sōda oyobi chisso kōgyō* [China's acid, soda, and nitrogen industries]. Tientsin: SMR, 1937.

"Some Problems in Speeding Up Industrial Development." Translated in *Issues and Studies* 13.7(1977):90–113.

Stepanek, James B. "Planning of Urban Small-Scale Industry in China." Unpublished, 1978.

Strassmann, W. Paul. *Risk and Technological Innovation.* Ithaca: Cornell University Press, 1959.

"Strengthen Economic Calculation within Enterprises." HHKY 12(1957):8–11.

"Strengthen Economic Control, Lower Product Costs." CHKY 19(1963):4–6.

Su Lin. *T'an-t'an wo-kuo kuo-tu shih-ch'i ti chia-ko cheng-ts'e*[On China's price policy in the transition period.]. Shanghai: Jen-min ch'u-pan she, 1956.

Su Tai-yün. *Wo-kuo kuo-tu shih-ch'i-chung kung-yeh fa-chan su-tu ti chi-ko wen-t'i* [Several problems concerning the pace of China's industrial development during the transition period]. Shanghai: Shang-hai jen-min ch'u-pan she, 1956.

Sun Ching-chih, ed. *Economic Geography of the East China Region.* Translated in JPRS 11438(1961).

Suttmeier, Richard P. *Research and Revolution.* Lexington, Mass.: D.C. Heath, 1974.

———. "Science Policy Shifts, Organizational Change, and China's Development." *China Quarterly* 62(1975):207–41.

Swamy, Subraminian. "Economic Growth in China and India, 1952–1970: A Comparative Appraisal." *Economic Development and Cultural Change* 21.4, pt. 2(1973):1–83.

Szuprowicz, Bohdan O. "Electronics in China: A Prerequisite to Superpower Status." Unpublished report, 21st Century Research, North Bergen, N. J., 1976.

Ta-chung jih-pao [Mass daily]. Chinan.

Ta-kung pao (formerly *Ta-kung jih-pao*) [Impartial daily]. Hong Kong.

Ta-kung pao [Impartial daily]. Peking.

Ta-lung chi-ch'i-ch'ang ti fa-sheng fa-chan yü kai-tsao [Birth, development, and reform of Ta-lung Machinery Works]. Shanghai: Shang-hai jen-min ch'u-pan she, 1959.

Tang Shih. "What the Soviet Experts Have Contributed to China's Power Industry in the Past Eight Years." Translated in ECMM 116(1957):34–38.

"The Technical Level of China's Machine Tool Industry." Translated in JPRS 31644(1965):1–32.

"Technical Reform Work in the Past Year." CHKY 6(1957):7–13.

Teece, D.J. "Technology Transfer by Multinational Firms: The Resource Cost of Transferring Technological Know-How." *Economic Journal* 87(1977): 242–61.

Ten Great Years. Peking: Foreign Languages Press, 1960.

Teng Chan-ming. "Problems of Developing Economic Cooperation among Industries and Firms." *Ching-chi yen chiu* 3(1965):19–23.

Terrill, Ross. *Flowers on an Iron Tree: Five Cities of China*. Boston: Little, Brown, 1975.

Ti Yün-ch'ing. "Discussion of Several Current Problems in Enterprise Technical Work." CHKY 16(1957):21–23.

T'ien-chin jih-pao [Tientsin daily]. Tientsin.

Ting, Leonard G. "Chinese Modern Banks and the Finance of Government and Industry." *Nankai Social and Economic Quarterly* 8.3(1935):578–616.

Tsuchiya, Keizō. "Economics of Mechanization in Small-Scale Agriculture." In *Agriculture and Economic Growth: Japan's Experience*, edited by Kazushi Ohkawa, Bruce F. Johnston, and Hiromitsu Kaneda, pp. 155–72. Princeton: Princeton University Press, 1969.

Tung-pei jih-pao [Northeast daily]. Shenyang.

United Nations Economic and Social Council for Asia and the Pacific. *Statistical Yearbook for Asia and the Pacific, 1975*. Bangkok, Thailand: United Nations, 1976.

United States Central Intelligence Agency. *China: The Coal Industry*. Research Aid ER76-10691. Washington, D.C.: CIA, 1976.

———. *China: Economic Indicators 1977*. Reference Aid ER77-10508. Washington, D.C.: CIA, 1977.

———. *China: International Trade, 1976–77*. ER77-10674. Washington, D.C.: CIA, 1977.

———. *China's Cement Industry*. ER77-10704. Washington, D.C.:CIA, 1977.

———. *Foreign Trade in Machinery and Equipment since 1952*. Research Aid A(ER) 75-60. Washington, D.C.: CIA, 1975.

———. *People's Republic of China: Estimated Yuan Value of Foreign Trade in Machinery and Equipment, 1951–73*. Research Aid ER76-10250. Washington, D.C.: CIA, 1976.

———. *Prices of Machinery and Equipment in the People's Republic of China*. Research Aid A(ER) 75-64. Washington D.C.: CIA, 1975.

———. *Weekly Report on Communist China*. Washington, D.C.

United States Consulate General, Hong Kong. *Current Background*.

———. *Extracts from China Mainland Magazines*.

———. *Survey of China Mainland Press*.

———. *Survey of China Mainland Press, Supplement*.

United States Foreign Broadcast Information Service. *Daily Report, People's Republic of China*.

Usack, Alfred H., Jr., and Egan, James D. "China's Iron and Steel Industry." In *China: A Reassessment of the Economy*, pp. 264–88. Washington D.C.: Government Printing Office, 1975.

Vernon, Raymond. *Metropolis 1985*. New York: Doubleday, 1963.

Wagoner, Harless D. *The U.S. Machine Tool Industry from 1900–1950*. Cambridge, Mass.: MIT Press, 1968.

Wang Chi-shen et al. *Chan-shih Shang-hai ching-chi* [Shanghai's wartime economy]. Shanghai: Shang-hai ching-chi yen-chiu so. 1945.

Wang Hsin-min. "Opinions on Developing Our Diesel and Coal-gas Engine Industry." CHKY 5(1957):5–7.

Wang Hu-sheng. "Several Problems of Classifying Heavy and Light Industry." *Ching-chi yen-chiu* 4(1963):16–26.

Wang Shu-hui. "Management of Circulating Capital." CHKY 6(1963):14–15.

Wang Te-yüan. "Perceive the Conditions of Steel Supply, Dig Up Latent Sources of Domestic Supply." CHKY 9(1957):29, 13.

Wang Tzu-chien and Wang Chen-chung. *Ch'i-sheng hua-shang shao-ch'ang tiao-ch'a pao-kao* [Survey report on Chinese-owned spinning plants in seven provinces]. Shanghai: Commercial Press, 1935.

"We Must Fulfill This Year's Plan for Trial Manufacture of New Products." CKYTH 14(1956):13–15.

Wen-hui pao [Wen-hui daily]. Hong Kong.

Wen-hui pao [Wen-hui daily]. Shanghai.

"Why Does the Demand for Double-wheel and Double-blade Plows Drop and Why Is Their Production Suspended?" Translated in ECMM 56(1956):24–28.

"Why Issue Quotas for Consumption of Raw Materials per Unit of Product?" CKYTH 21(1954):38–39.

Wu, Yuan-li, and Sheeks, Robert B. *The Organization and Support of Scientific Research and Development in Mainland China*. New York: Praeger, 1970.

Yamamura, Kozo. "The Decade of Sowing: The Absorption of Western Technology by the Electric Machinery and Machine Tool Industries of Japan During the 1920s." Unpublished, 1976.

Yang-ch'eng wan-pao [Canton evening news]. Canton.

Yang Ling. "Study the Experience of Tach'ing, Persist in Maintaining High Standards of Equipment Management," HHKY 9(1964):28–32.

Yang Ta-chin. *Hsien-tai Chung-kuo shih-yeh chih* [Gazetteer of China's industries]. Shanghai and Ch'angsha: Commercial Press, 1935–38.

Yearbook of National Accounts Statistics. New York: U.N. Statistical Office, annual.

Yeh, K.C. "Capital Formation." In *Economic Trends in Communist China*, edited by Alexander Eckstein, Walter Galenson, and Ta-chung Liu, pp. 509–47. Chicago: Aldine, 1968.

______. "Capital Formation in Mainland China, 1931–36 and 1952–57." Ph.D. dissertation, Columbia University, 1964.

______. "China's National Income, 1931–36." Unpublished, 1977.

______. *Communist China's Petroleum Situation*. Santa Monica: Rand Corp., 1962.

Yen Chung-p'ing. *Chung-kuo mien-fang-chih shih-k'ao* [Draft history of China's cotton textile industry]. Peking: K'o-hsüeh ch'u-pan she, 1963.

Young, Arthur N. *China's Nation-building Effort*. Cambridge, Mass.: Harvard University Press, 1971.

Yü Chien-t'ing. "The Problem of Proportional Relation between Our Steel and Machinery Industries." *Ching-chi yen-chiu* 6(1957):20–26.

Yü Ch'iu-li [Yu Chiu-li]. "Mobilize the Whole Party and the Nation's Working Class and Strive to Build Taching-type Enterprises throughout the Country." *Peking Review* 22(1977):5–23.

______. "Yu Chiu-li Summation Report on Agricultural Mechanization." FBIS, January 31, 1978, E6–25.

Yün-nun jih-pao [Yunnan daily]. K'unming.

Index